ROUGH
GUIDES

POCKET **ROUGH GUIDE**

SAN FRANCISCO

written and researched by
CHARLES HODGKINS AND STEPHEN KEELING

CONTENTS

SAN FRANCISCO

As inspiring and charismatic as its singular setting, San Francisco stands apart from other US destinations; in fact, you'll struggle to find many places like it anywhere in the world. The famed city is surrounded on three sides by churning water and threaded with a grid of streets that courageously tackles thirty-degree gradients, elements that transcend geography to infuse San Francisco with the boldly independent spirit for which it's known. This impression is evident not only in the city's clanging cable cars and charming pastel-hued Victorian architecture, but also in its reputation for championing progressive ideals and LGBTQ rights. Even the weather patterns here are idiosyncratic: summer sometimes doesn't arrive until mid-September.

Dolores Park

When to visit

San Francisco is notorious for its absence of the usual four seasons – the city enjoys one of the most stable climates you'll encounter anywhere – with rain generally confined between November and April, and the only snowfall being rare dustings atop the Bay Area's peaks. Summer in San Francisco proper is often marked (or marred, depending on your perspective) by the city's signature thick fog, while the rest of the Bay Area sees temperatures soar above 27°C (80°F) and beyond. Early to mid-autumn finds San Francisco enjoying its sunniest weather, when daytime temperatures regularly crest 20°C (70°F). Regardless of when you visit, it's smart to arm yourself with an extra layer in case fog sweeps in unannounced.

San Francisco may be distinctly West Coast in the relaxed perspective and lifestyle it perpetuates, but its laidback atmosphere certainly doesn't breed complacency. This is a city that was built around dynamism – a quality that continues to shape it today and helps make it such a compelling destination. In the late 1840s, this once somnolent bay-side hamlet (originally named Yerba Buena) rose almost overnight from its fishing village origins via its crucial role in the Gold Rush of 1849 to become the first great metropolis of the American west. This mass migration of fortune-seekers to the nascent territory of California initiated a turbulent history that has also seen the city endure silver and dotcom booms and busts, a paralysing longshoremen strike, the bulldozing of neighbourhoods in the name of urban renewal, assassinations of political leaders, an AIDS epidemic, and, most infamously, a pair of cataclysmic earthquakes: the first flattened almost the entire city in 1906, the second fatally pancaked a double-decker Oakland freeway and dislodged a section of the Bay Bridge in 1989. In every instance, San Francisco's unflappable character emerged intact.

You'll quickly discover that San Francisco is also unique among western US cities for its compactness and wealth of transport options, to say nothing of its walkability (provided you're not put off by a few hills). For all its major sights, vaunted culinary culture, vibrant arts scene and other visitor-luring credentials, the city can be surprisingly understated – a place where you can enjoy a memorable stay by simply wandering the heroic hills and bay-side paths, exploring its discrete neighbourhoods and broad range of cafés and bars, lazily whiling away an

Point Bonita Lighthouse

Ice cream heaven

San Francisco has been a sweet-tooth paradise since **Ghirardelli** (see page 64) started making chocolate here during the Gold Rush, but its ice-cream makers have also blossomed. Stalwarts such as **Swensen's** (see page 52) and **Fentons Creamery** (see page 128) are still around, while **Mitchell's** (see page 93) and **Smitten** (see page 113) offer contemporary flavours.

afternoon at Dolores Park or Baker Beach and, above all, just doing what happens. Like any truly captivating city, San Francisco suitably rewards visitors' impulsiveness.

Complementing densely built San Francisco is the greater Bay Area, an ever-growing region that's the fifth most populous metropolitan area in the US. While its suburban communities have expanded up mountainsides and even onto landfill sites on San Francisco Bay's shores through the decades, the Bay Area remains home to an uncommonly ample acreage of protected open spaces –

particularly in Marin County, the Peninsula and the East Bay.

The estimable cities of Oakland and Berkeley are within easy reach of San Francisco via public transport, but to absorb the full scope of the region's allure and explore anywhere of note beyond these communities, you'll certainly want your own wheels. Expect to spend most of your days outdoors, whether along the sublime Marin and San Mateo coastlines, in the humbling redwood groves of Muir Woods, cycling or picnicking on Angel Island in the middle of the bay, or trundling between wineries in the oenophile magnets of Sonoma and Napa.

Swan Oyster Depot

Where to...

Shop

Rather than relying on indoor malls – although a few smaller, stylish ones do exist here – San Francisco thrives on personable street-level **shopping**. **Union Square** is the place to go for big-name brands, but it's in its distinctive neighbourhoods that the city's retail charm comes into its own. Visit **Upper Haight** for **vintage and secondhand apparel**, or **Hayes Valley** if you've got money to burn on impossibly trendy clothing and homeware in boutiques such as *Metier* (see page 111). North Beach and the Mission are best for handmade accessories and locally designed couture, while **Cow Hollow** is full of less edgy, but still charming, women's clothiers.

Eat

For scope, adventure and quality, San Francisco and the Bay Area may be unmatched for exceptional **eating** opportunities. It's all here: haute cuisine legends such as *Gary Danko* (see page 65) and, further afield, Berkeley's *Chez Panisse* (see page 128) and Yountville's *French Laundry* (see page 138), on down the budget ladder to outstanding *taquerias* and dim sum joints. The city's **dining scene** is more innovative than ever, and while you can still, for example, head to **North Beach** for reliably delicious Italian food, intrepid diners can unearth phenomenal pizza all over the city. Whether you crave Japanese, Indian, a smashing deli sandwich or a burger, you're never far from something fantastic to bite into here.

Drink

A hard-**drinking** town going back to the Gold Rush and subsequent Barbary Coast era, San Francisco has never met a shot, pint or cocktail it wouldn't swig. The city is awash with watering holes: point yourself towards **Downtown** and **South of Market** for classy hotel lounges and destinations popular with the after-work crowd; **North Beach** for evocative neighbourhood bars; the **Mission** and **Lower Haight** for cool dives like *Noc Noc* (see page 115); the **Castro** for LGBTQ nightspots; and the **Richmond** and **Sunset** for Irish pubs aplenty. Bring ID to prove you're 21 or over and expect last call by 2am.

Party

San Francisco's renowned **live music and performing arts scenes** are stronger than ever, with the **SFJAZZ Center** (see page 115) hitting the ground running, a number of rock clubs and theatres packed nightly, and the acclaimed **San Francisco Symphony** (see page 81) at the top of its game. As for the city's late-night dance culture, if you can take it at face value – don't come expecting Ibiza – you're bound to enjoy its relatively low-key style. Several choice clubs are concentrated in South of Market and haven't lost a step over the years in the face of competition from less inviting mega-clubs elsewhere in the neighbourhood and Downtown.

San Francisco at a glance

North Beach and the hills p.44.
San Francisco's captivating "Piccola Italia" sits between three of the city's most desirable slanted neighbourhoods; food is a major attraction here, but the area is also celebrated for its connection with the Beats.

The northern waterfront p.56.
With Alcatraz, Fisherman's Wharf, the Presidio and the Golden Gate Bridge in its midst, this is the San Francisco of world renown.

Civic Center and around p.78.
Discover big government, major cultural institutions and rough living, all in the shadow of City Hall.

Golden Gate Park and beyond p.116.
One of the grandest greenspaces anywhere, with myriad gardens, windmills and meadows, plus a clutch of fabulous museums, from Renzo Piano's massive California Academy of Sciences to the art-filled de Young Museum and Legion of Honor.

West of Civic Center p.106.
Choose between Hayes Valley boutiques, the "Painted Ladies" of Alamo Square, peaceful Japantown and Lower Haight hipsters in this sprawling area.

The Castro and around p.98.
In a city known for its tolerance and celebratory spirit, this pole star of LGBTQ culture leads the way. Pink Triangle Park, the GLBT History Museum and other monuments to Harvey Milk chronicle the community's long history of activism.

Chinatown and Jackson Square p.36.
America's original Chinese quarter features thronged markets, colourful streets and contemplative temples, while Jackson Square is rich in nineteenth-century architecture.

Downtown and the Embarcadero p.24.
From Union Square and the skyscraper-lined Financial District to bay-side Embarcadero and its historic Ferry Building, the city's commercial and transit hub hums with activity.

Around the Bay Area p.132. ▷
Island parks, landmark peaks, world-class wine and the rugged Pacific coastline all beckon.

South of Market p.68.
This former industrial district of warehouses and decaying factories has been revitalized with absorbing museums, hip bars and new restaurants.

The Mission and around p.86.
This kaleidoscopic neighbourhood – and its imaginative restaurants, Latino murals and animated street life – engages all the senses.

Oakland and Berkeley p.124. ▷
These complementary East Bay cities hold great cultural and natural appeal – not to mention sunnier weather than San Francisco.

15

Things not to miss

It's not possible to see everything that San Francisco has to offer in one trip – and we don't suggest you try. What follows is a selective taste of the city's highlights, from clattering cable cars to world-class art museums.

> Lombard Street
See page 47
Check your brakes, then twist your way down the succession of hairpin turns on the "crookedest street in the world".

< Cable cars
See page 25
These glorious old trolleys have rattled their way up and down San Francisco's steepest grades since 1873.

∨ San Francisco Pride
See page 157
Queer culture exuberantly takes over much of the city on a late June weekend, with boisterous parades, outlandish costumes and the colours of the rainbow flag all taking centre stage.

< Asian Art Museum
See page 79
The first stop on any art admirer's itinerary should be this world-class collection.

∨ UC Berkeley
See page 124
Tour the leafy hillside campus of one of America's most celebrated universities.

< **Coit Tower**
See page 45
This distinctive Art Deco pillar is the city's ultimate promontory.

∨ **Caffe Trieste**
See page 51
This local institution and Beat poet hangout is where espresso made its West Coast debut in 1956.

THINGS NOT TO MISS

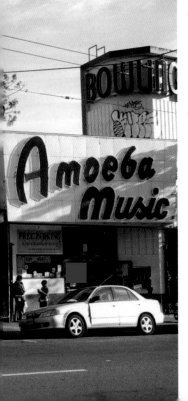

∧ Castro Theatre
See page 98
This Mediterranean Revival beauty is the city's grande dame of cinema.

‹ Amoeba Music
See page 111
A real record store, one of America's best remaining, set in a former Upper Haight bowling alley.

∧ de Young Museum
See page 117
Fine art exhibitions, site-specific installations and singular architecture unite at this Golden Gate Park mainstay.

∨ Mission District
See page 86
Bustling *taquerias*, iconic Mission Dolores and a mix of Latino and Anglo cultures make for one of the city's liveliest neighbourhoods.

∧ Golden Gate Bridge

See page 62

It's nearly impossible to imagine San Francisco without the orange towers of this famously graceful crossing – experiencing it first-hand (driving, cycling or walking) is a singular thrill.

< Heinold's First and Last Chance Saloon

See page 130

Jack London really did drink at this authentic nineteenth-century pub, built in 1880 from the remains of a whaling ship.

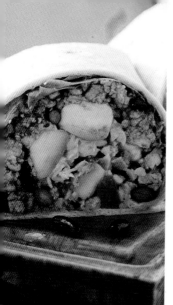

< Papalote
See page 113
Home to over two hundred
taquerias, San Francisco invented
the super burrito in 1961; try
these giant meals-in-one at
Cal-Mex powerhouse *Papalote*.

**∨ Muir Woods
National Monument**
See page 133
Cross the Golden Gate to
commune with California's
giant redwoods and soak up
mesmerizing views of the city.

Day One in San Francisco

 Ferry Building and the Embarcadero. See page 28. Visit the Ferry Building's gourmet marketplace for a light breakfast before setting out along the bay-front walkway.

Filbert Steps and Coit Tower. See page 45. Take your time ascending these garden-flanked steps en route to a prized panorama from the emblematic 210-ft column atop Telegraph Hill.

North Beach. See page 44. Meander through the city's snug Italian-American neighbourhood, where shops, cafés and Washington Square Park all beckon.

Coit Tower

 Tony's Pizza Napoletana. See page 53. The pizza at this bustling spot is always impeccable, thanks to the skills of twelve-time (and counting) World Pizza Champion Tony Gemignani.

Chinatown. See page 36. Adjacent to North Beach, Chinatown seems a world all of its own, with chaotic commerce along Stockton and Grant streets and serene temples on nearby Waverly Place.

Ride a cable car. See page 25. Make the short walk to the Cable Car Museum and Powerhouse, then hop aboard a nineteenth-century trolley for a rattling ride back to Market Street.

Ride a cable car

San Francisco Giants game. See page 72. Catch a night-time contest at bay-side AT&T Park, where the garlic fries and sausages are as great as the views.

 21st Amendment Brewery or North Beach bars. See page 75. Linger in South of Market for a post-game pint at the ballpark-adjacent brewpub, or head back up to buzzing North Beach, where late-night drinking options abound.

San Francisco Giants game at AT&T Park

Day Two in San Francisco

Boudin Bakery, Bakers Hall. See page 65. Head to Fisherman's Wharf for breakfast at this iconic bakery; sample the classic sourdough French toast or feast on fresh crab cakes. It's a short walk from here to the Alcatraz ferry.

Alcatraz. See page 56. Book your morning tickets to this stark island in advance; catching the first ferry allows you to have the creepy old stockade seemingly all to yourself – if you can take the desolation.

Blue Barn Gourmet. See page 64. Out of prison and back on the mainland, grab lunch-to-go from this excellent sandwich and salad shop on Chestnut Street.

Palace of Fine Arts. See page 60. Enjoy your lunch as you admire the swans and the Palace of Fine Arts' majestic open rotunda from a bench flanking its lovely lagoon.

Crissy Field. See page 61. Stroll the paths or sit on the beach and watch the passing ships at this popular greenspace in the shadow of the great orange bridge.

Golden Gate Bridge. See page 62. The ambitious can make the 4.5-mile round-trip walk over this instantly recognizable span; everyone, however, will want to ogle its imposing beauty regardless.

The Slanted Door. See page 34. Reserve ahead of time, then settle in at this highly regarded waterfront restaurant for peerless French-Vietnamese cuisine.

Great American Music Hall or Beach Blanket Babylon. See pages 86 or 55. Check to see what's on at the Great American Music Hall, the city's finest music venue; if it's a Saturday, aim to catch a 9pm performance of Beach Blanket Babylon in North Beach.

Alcatraz

Palace of Fine Arts

The Slanted Door

Foodie San Francisco

San Francisco flaunts a wealth of culinary marvels, from long-established fine dining stalwarts to a more recent wave of *taquerias*, mobile food trucks and farm-to-table haunts.

Dottie's True Blue Café. See page 74. Start your day right at this breakfast specialist, which has been knocking together inexpensive plates for over twenty years; expect cornbread and chipotle jelly, tasty frittatas, zucchini cakes, pulled pork, and at least five kinds of hot sauce on every table.

Papalote. See page 113. Don't leave San Francisco without sampling the local burritos. *Papalote* serves up some of the best; sumptuous blends of rice, beans, *pico de gallo* (salsa) and *carne asada* (grilled steak) or roast chicken.

Dottie's True Blue Café

Blue Bottle Coffee. See page 73. Grab an exquisite afternoon espresso or cappuccino at San Francisco's hip coffee chain, established in Oakland in the early 2000s. Roasted locally, beans are sourced from Colombia, El Salvador, Ethiopia, Guatemala and Kenya.

SoMa StrEat Food Park. See page 74. Trawl the rotating lineup of mobile food trucks – from Bacon Bacon to Cheese Gone Wild – at this converted car park, which is also home to TV screens, carnival games, free wi-fi and a beer garden with heaters.

SoMa StrEat Food Park

State Bird Provisions. See page 114. End the day with a spectacular dinner at Stuart Brioza and Nicole Krasinski's Michelin-starred restaurant, which specializes in Californian fusion small plates, from guinea hen dumplings to cumin lamb stir-fry with dates.

Bob's Donuts. See page 51. Still hungry in the middle of the night? This celebrated donut shop has been open 24 hours a day since 1960, supplying a late-night crowd with a steady stream of freshly glazed treats.

State Bird Provisions

San Francisco for Kids

Attractions like Fisherman's Wharf and the Zoo will certainly thrill kids, but the city's simpler pleasures are just as enticing, from watching street entertainers to rattling cable-car rides.

Aquarium of the Bay. See page 57. The extraordinary touch pools – with juvenile bat rays, leopard sharks and skates – make this a big favourite with kids, as well as the river otter exhibit and two lengthy viewing tunnels beneath the main tanks.

Fisherman's Wharf and Hyde Street Pier. See page 56. Touristy but fun, with crab shacks, barking sea lions and plenty of family-friendly, if kitsch, attractions. Aim for the Musée Méchanique (see page 57), an amusing collection of vintage arcade machines, and the historic boats on Hyde Street Pier (free for children aged 15 years and under).

Ghirardelli Original Chocolate Manufactory. See page 64. Ghirardelli Square became the master chocolatier's headquarters in 1893, and still retains a factory-themed Ghirardelli café today, with a real ice-cream fountain.

Cable car rides. See page 25. Riding San Francisco's famous clattering old cable cars up and down seemingly impossible gradients is always a thrill – as much for adults as for children.

San Francisco Zoo. See page 121. The Children's Zoo is particularly good here, with a meerkat and prairie dog exhibit, red pandas and an insect area full of creepy crawlies. There's also a restored carousel and the "Little Puffer" miniature steam train.

Exploratorium. See page 46. Conveniently close to Fisherman's Wharf, this hands-on science museum is a great option on a rainy day; it's packed with interactive exhibits, displays and games to entertain youngsters.

Aquarium of the Bay

Ghirardelli Original Chocolate Manufactory

San Francisco Zoo

PLACES

San Francisco at night

Downtown and the Embarcadero

The commercial heart of San Francisco, densely built Downtown comprises animated Union Square and the more serious, skyscraper-lined Financial District – the Bay Area's traditional retail and business hubs, respectively – as well as inviting bay-front boulevard the Embarcadero. One of San Francisco's most-visited areas, this is the city's original nerve centre, and the Gold Rush's early prosperity transformed the districts (much of which sit on landfill) into the financial heart of the western US. Today, a major portion of the Bay Area workforce streams in every weekday, while locals and visitors alike board cable cars along Market Street, enjoy Union Square's retail hubbub and indulge in culinary treats at the Embarcadero's imposing yet lovely Ferry Building.

Union Square

MAP P.26, POCKET MAP A12
Bordered by Post, Stockton, Geary and Powell sts Ⓜ #8, #30, #45, F, J, K, L, M, N, T; Ⓒ Powell.

The retail powerhouse of San Francisco, the area around **Union Square** is home to scores of high-end shops, hotels and restaurants that absorb hordes of visitors (and their dollars) daily. The area pulses with life during the winter holidays, when an ice rink and towering Christmas tree take over the square, a granite-lined open space fringed by palm trees and sprinkled with potted foliage and plenty of seating.

Built on the former site of an enormous sand dune that was shipped over to the northern waterfront to help create the strand at Aquatic Park (see page 57), the plaza takes its name from its role as a gathering place for Unionist supporters on the eve of the US Civil War (somewhat confusingly, the 97ft column rising from the centre commemorates

an 1898 victory in the Spanish–American War). Directly beneath Union Square sits the world's first underground parking garage, which doubled as an air-raid shelter when it was opened.

Maiden Lane

MAP P.26, POCKET MAP B12
Immediately east of Union Square, between Kearny and Stockton sts Ⓜ #8, #30, #45, F, J, K, L, M, N, T; Ⓒ Powell.

Home to San Francisco's greatest concentration of bordellos in the late 1800s – when, ironically, it had yet to take on its current name – **Maiden Lane** is now lined with pavement cafés, designer shops, prohibitively expensive wedding dress boutiques and the only Frank Lloyd Wright-designed building in San Francisco.

Known as Morton Street in its earlier, more debauched, era, today's version is usually closed to traffic, making it all the more pleasant to stroll its two-block length and wander into Wright's creation at no. 140 (now a high-end retailer). Featuring an inviting arched portal carved into a wall of tan brick, the low-slung structure opened in 1949 – more than a decade before Wright's Guggenheim Museum in New York (the design of which borrows the sweeping interior ramp from this building).

Lotta's Fountain

Lotta's Fountain

MAP P.26, POCKET MAP B12
Intersection of Market and Kearny sts
Ⓜ #2, #3, #8, #9, #10, #12, F, J, K, L, M, N, T; Ⓑ Montgomery.

Amid a busy Market Street intersection sits beautifully restored **Lotta's Fountain**, a caramel-coloured mini-tower best known as an impromptu message centre in the wake of San Francisco's 1906 earthquake and fire; four years later, famed opera coloratura soprano Luisa Tetrazzini sang a free Christmas Eve performance from the top of the fountain that drew thousands. Today's metallic gold-brown version is a reconstruction of the original, which was an 1875 gift from superstar actress Lotta Crabtree to her adoptive city. For decades the fountain provided water to residents and their horses, but the troughs were long ago removed, making it a waterless, if attractive, relic.

1 Montgomery Terrace

MAP P.26, POCKET MAP B12
Montgomery St at Post St Ⓜ #2, #3,

San Francisco's cable cars

The brainchild of enterprising engineer **Andrew Hallidie**, San Francisco's **cable cars** began negotiating the city's tortuous hills in 1873 after Hallidie witnessed a team of horses become badly injured while trying to pull a dray up a steep, muddy slope. Today, riding one of San Francisco's cable cars is a singular experience, but there's a certain strategy to skirting the lengthy waits that often accompany a ride on one of these popular nineteenth-century vehicles, all of which terminate Downtown along **Market Street**. Arriving by 10am should ensure speedy boarding, but if the wait at the highest-profile boarding area at the foot of **Powell Street** is already too long, try the **California Street** queue at the intersection of California and Market streets, which rattles over Nob Hill and is the oldest and least-ridden (all things relative) of the city's three lines. If you're set on experiencing hair-raising thrills, hold out for the **Powell-Hyde line**, which tackles a 21-degree incline between Fisherman's Wharf (see page 56) and Russian Hill. To learn more, visit the **Cable Car Museum and Powerhouse** (see page 40) and see Essentials for practical information (see page 151).

Transamerica Pyramid

#8, #9, #10, #12, F, J, K, L, M, N, T; Ⓜ Montgomery. Mon–Fri 9am–5pm. Free. One of a number of slightly obscure public open spaces sprinkled throughout Downtown and South of Market, **1**

Montgomery Terrace was created when the top of the building was beheaded in the early 1980s. This lofty hideaway – a fine and uncrowded spot for an alfresco lunch on a pleasant day – overlooks one of Downtown's most humming intersections and is home to a charming fountain, attractive seasonal foliage and a unique astrolabe. To reach it, enter through the lobby of the Wells Fargo building directly below and take the lift to the top; you can also find it via the third floor of Crocker Galleria at 50 Post St – look for the sign on the east side of the mall that reads "Roof Garden".

Allegory of California mural

MAP P.26, POCKET MAP B12
155 Sansome St at Pine St Ⓜ #1, #2, #3, #8, #9, #10, #12; Ⓜ Montgomery. Tour first and third Mon of month, 3pm; book through Ⓦ sfcityguides.org. Free.

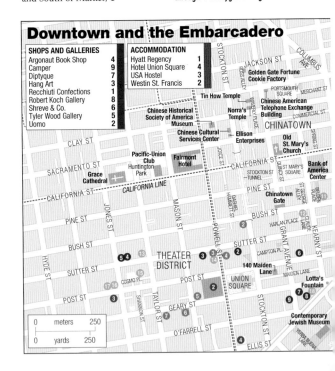

Downtown and the Embarcadero

SHOPS AND GALLERIES
Argonaut Book Shop 4
Camper 9
Diptyque 7
Hang Art 3
Recchiuti Confections 1
Robert Koch Gallery 8
Shreve & Co. 6
Tyler Wood Gallery 5
Uomo 2

ACCOMMODATION
Hyatt Regency 1
Hotel Union Square 4
USA Hostel 3
Westin St. Francis 2

One of San Francisco's finest Art Deco structures, the City Club is home to a private organization made up of San Francisco business leaders. Twice monthly, however, the building's tenth floor is made available to tour groups wishing to view Diego Rivera's striking **Allegory of California mural**. Rivera made the staircase ceiling here his canvas in the early 1930s, using agriculture and industry as major elements in this, his first mural in the US. Considering that the Pacific Stock Exchange Lunch Club met regularly in the City Club during the Great Depression, the selection of such an anti-capitalist artist baffled many when the work was commissioned.

Transamerica Pyramid

MAP P.26, POCKET MAP B11
600 Montgomery St at Washington St Ⓜ #1, #8, #10, #12; Ⓑ Montgomery.

The **Transamerica Pyramid** is the second tallest building in San Francisco, and certainly the most recognizable. Upon opening to business tenants in 1972, the 853ft tower and its four triangular sides became a flashpoint of architectural controversy in a city that, until the previous decade, had a relatively humble skyline. To this day, it remains the Financial District's definitive skyscraper and is far less scorned by locals than the broad-shouldered hulk of 555 California St (formerly the **Bank of America Center**) a few blocks southwest. Due to heightened security, the 27th-floor observation deck is no longer publicly accessible.

The Embarcadero

MAP P.26, POCKET MAP J1–M4
Ⓜ #2, #6, #14, #21, #31, F, J, K, L, M, N, T; Ⓑ Embarcadero.

Perhaps no other area of San Francisco has experienced such

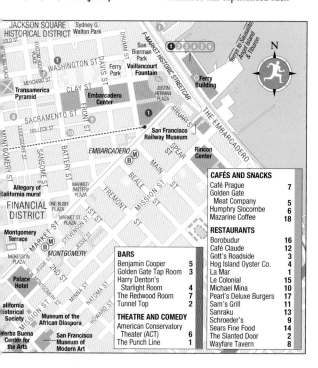

CAFÉS AND SNACKS

Café Prague	7
Golden Gate Meat Company	5
Humphry Slocombe	6
Mazarine Coffee	18

RESTAURANTS

Borobudur	16
Café Claude	12
Gott's Roadside	3
Hog Island Oyster Co.	4
La Mar	1
Le Colonial	15
Michael Mina	10
Pearl's Deluxe Burgers	17
Sam's Grill	11
Sanraku	13
Schroeder's	9
Sears Fine Food	14
The Slanted Door	2
Wayfare Tavern	8

BARS

Benjamin Cooper	5
Golden Gate Tap Room	3
Harry Denton's Starlight Room	4
The Redwood Room	7
Tunnel Top	2

THEATRE AND COMEDY

American Conservatory Theater (ACT)	6
The Punch Line	1

Ferry Plaza Farmers Market

a riches-to-rags-to-riches-again saga as the **Embarcadero**, the bay-side boulevard that borders the northeast edge of the Financial District. Following its original heyday in the first half of the twentieth century as a thriving port and ferry commuter centre, the Embarcadero was gruesomely covered for over three decades by the ill-fated Embarcadero Skyway, an elevated freeway that ran directly overhead before being demolished a few years after 1989's Loma Prieta Earthquake, which rendered it unfit to carry traffic. A cavalcade of improvements has ensued, including an immensely popular pedestrian promenade, the San Francisco Giants' AT&T Park (see page 72) at the Embarcadero's southern end, and the arrival of the vintage streetcars that clatter along Muni's F-Market line – to say nothing of the Ferry Building's remarkable revival.

Ferry Building

MAP P.26, POCKET MAP C11
1 Embarcadero Ⓜ #2,# 6, #14, #21, #31, F, J, K, L, M, N, T; Ⓑ Embarcadero. ☎ 415 983 8030, Ⓦ ferrybuildingmarketplace.com.

Much like the waterfront corridor it anchors, the circa-1892 **Ferry Building** has recovered from a lengthy period of neglect, misguided modification and the shadowy presence of the Embarcadero Skyway, to become one of San Francisco's finest Beaux Arts showpieces; it's also a National Historic Landmark, with its signature Moorish clock tower modelled after that of Seville's famed Giralda.

In the mid-1930s, just before the opening of San Francisco's pair of bridges, 50,000 daily commuters used the Ferry Building. The era's growing fascination with the automobile, however, caused ferry traffic to diminish greatly, and in 1955 the building's dignified nave was unceremoniously turned into offices, a few years before the double-decker Embarcadero Skyway rudely cut off the Ferry Building from Market Street entirely.

Today, the stoutly constructed building is now known as much (if not more) for its gourmet culinary marketplace as for being a terminus for the Bay Area's revitalized commuter ferry service. Three times weekly, locals flock here for the **Ferry Plaza Farmers Market** (Tues & Thurs 10am–2pm, Sat 8am–2pm; ☎ 415 291 3276, ⓦ cuesa.org), when a cornucopia of fresh California-grown produce – as well as prepared foods from several Bay Area restaurants – is sold from numerous stalls that flank the building.

Vaillancourt Fountain

MAP P.26, POCKET MAP C11

Justin Herman Plaza Ⓜ #2, #6, #14, #21, #31, F, J, K, L, M, N, T; Ⓑ Embarcadero.

Officially named *Québec Libre!*, but known locally as the **Vaillancourt Fountain** after its creator, French-Canadian Armand Vaillancourt, this jumble of square-tubed concrete has few rivals as San Francisco's most infamous piece of modernist art. The jumbo sculpture initially aimed to complement, however awkwardly, the now long-gone Embarcadero Skyway when it was unveiled in 1971, while its visual connection to eastern Canada and the concept of provincial sovereignty has always been mysterious at best. In its lifetime, it's been described as "inspired by air-conditioning ducts" and "the product of a giant dog with square bowels".

The distinctive fountain featured prominently in one scene of U2's 1988 film *Rattle and Hum*, during which Bono decided to spray-paint the words "rock and roll stops the traffic" onto the tangled slab – a stunt that earned the singer no friends among San Francisco's political powers and police force.

San Francisco Railway Museum

MAP P.26, POCKET MAP C11

77 Steuart St at Mission St Ⓜ #2, #6, #14, #21, #31, F, J, K, L, M, N, T; Ⓑ Embarcadero. ☎ 415 974 1948, ⓦ streetcar.org/museum. Tues–Sun 10am–5pm. Free.

The compact **San Francisco Railway Museum** merits a short stop not only for its collection of artefacts relating to the history of San Francisco's railways, but also for its wealth of information on the several splendid historic railcars that now clatter along the city's F-Market line, which stops directly in front of the museum and continues along the Embarcadero up to Fisherman's Wharf.

Vaillancourt Fountain

Shops and galleries

Argonaut Book Shop

MAP P.26, POCKET MAP A12
786 Sutter St at Jones St Ⓜ #2, #3,
#27, #38; ⓑ Powell. ☎ 415 474 9067,
Ⓦ argonautbookshop.com. Mon–Fri
10am–5pm, Sat 10.30am–4pm.

A local institution specializing in
volumes on California and the
American West, Argonaut's best
feature is the authoritative staff,
who can point you towards books,
maps and prints.

Camper

MAP P.26, POCKET MAP B13
39 Grant Ave at O'Farrell St Ⓜ #8, #30,
#45, F, J, K, L, M, N, T; ⓑ Powell. ☎ 415 296
1005, Ⓦ camper.com. Mon–Sat 10am–7pm,
Sun 11am–6pm.

You may not stumble upon a
wealth of bargains at this stylish,
Spain-based footwear specialist, but
its retro-inspired shoes, bags and
accessories are complemented by
top salespeople who won't mind if
you simply drop by to browse.

Diptyque

MAP P.26, POCKET MAP B12
73 Geary St, between Grant and
Kearny Sts Ⓜ #8, #30, #45, F, J, K, L,
M, N, T; ⓑ Powell. ☎ 415 402 0600,
Ⓦ diptyqueparis.com. Mon–Sat 10am–6pm,
Sun noon–5pm.

Duck into this aromatic boutique
for a whiff of *Diptyque*'s high-end
perfumes and candles. Courteous
sales assistants are happy to spray
samples of the Paris-based company's
host of fragrances, including their
delightful tuberose scent.

Hang Art

MAP P.26, POCKET MAP A12
567 Sutter St at Mason St Ⓜ #8, #30,
#38, #45; ⓑ Powell. ☎ 415 434 4264,
Ⓦ hangart.com. Mon–Sat 10am–6pm,
Sun noon–5pm.

Although this mid-size gallery's
location one floor above street level
makes it easy to miss, it's worth
seeking out for its fine paintings,
sculptures and mixed-media pieces
by emerging Bay Area artists.

Recchiuti Confections

MAP P.26, POCKET MAP C11
Ferry Building Marketplace, 1 Embarcadero
Ⓜ #2, #6, #14, #21, #31, F, J, K, L, M,
N, T; ⓑ Embarcadero. ☎ 415 834 9494,
Ⓦ recchiuti.com. Mon–Fri 10am–7pm, Sat
8am–6pm, Sun 10am–5pm.

Pause at celebrated local chocolatier
Michael Recchiuti's stall inside the
Ferry Building to choose from a
wide range of handmade chocolates
and other confections (including
nibs, sauces and bars).

Robert Koch Gallery

MAP P.26, POCKET MAP B12
49 Geary St at Kearny St Ⓜ #2, #3, #8, #9,
F, J, K, L, M, N, T; ⓑ Montgomery. ☎ 415
421 0122, Ⓦ kochgallery.com. Tues–Sat
10.30am–5.30pm.

Ascend to the fifth floor at this
gallery-rich address, where the walls
of the spacious *Robert Koch Gallery*
cater to deep-pocketed buyers (and
interested visitors) and feature
photography exhibitions from new
artists and established masters alike.

Shreve & Co.

MAP P.26, POCKET MAP B12
150 Post St, between Kearny and Grant
Sts Ⓜ #2, #3, #8, #30, #38, #45, F, J, K, L,
M, N, T; ⓑ Montgomery. ☎ 415 421 2600,
Ⓦ shreve.com. Mon–Sat 10am–6pm,
Sun noon–5pm.

Founded in the days of the Gold
Rush, *Shreve & Co.* claims to be San
Francisco's oldest jeweller, and it
remains highly regarded today for its
selection of shimmering diamonds
and sophisticated timepieces.

Tyler Wood Gallery

MAP P.26, POCKET MAP A12
794 Sutter St at Jones St Ⓜ #2, #3,
#27, #38; ⓑ Powell. ☎ 415 345 1946,
Ⓦ tylerwoodgallery.com. Wed–Sat 1–5pm.

Hosting single-artist shows that
generally last two months, this
humbly sized gallery deals in avant-

garde works that span a variety of media – anything from *papier mâché* sculpture to adventurous paintings.

Uomo

MAP P.26, POCKET MAP A12
475 Sutter St at Powell St Ⓜ #8, #30, #38, #45; Ⓑ Powell. ☏ 415 989 8666, Ⓦ uomosf.com. Mon–Sat 9.30am–6.30pm.

Its Italian name translating to "man" in English, this European clothier boasts a stunning collection of suits, jackets and casual wear. True clothes hounds will want to visit during one of the shop's occasional trunk shows by the likes of *Pal Zileri* and *Canali*.

Cafés and snacks

Café Prague

MAP P.26, POCKET MAP B11
424 Merchant St at Battery St Ⓜ #1, #8, #10, #12; Ⓑ Embarcadero. ☏ 415 627 7464, Ⓦ cafepraguesf.com. Mon–Fri 11.30am–midnight, Sat 4pm–midnight.

With an inviting interior, a few outdoor tables and a number of Eastern European specialities (including Hungarian beef goulash and strudel), this affordable Czech bistro exudes a great deal of warmth.

Golden Gate Meat Company

MAP P.26, POCKET MAP C11
Ferry Building Marketplace, 1 Embarcadero Ⓜ #2, #6, #14, #21, #31, F, J, K, L, M, N, T; Ⓑ Embarcadero. ☏ 415 983 7800, Ⓦ goldengatemeatcompany.com. Mon–Fri 6.30am–7pm, Sat 7am–5.30pm, Sun 11am–5pm.

This family-operated charcuterie and butcher's shop is the best place to go in the Ferry Building for simple sandwiches (including pulled pork and barbecue beef), pot pies and small rotisserie chickens – all for under $10.

Humphry Slocombe

MAP P.26, POCKET MAP C11
Ferry Building Marketplace, 1 Embarcadero Ⓜ #2, #6, #14, #21, #31, F, J, K, L, M, N,

Mazarine Coffee

T; Ⓑ Embarcadero. Ⓦ humphryslocombe. com. Mon–Fri & Sun 11am–9.30pm, Sat 8am–9.30pm.

A dozen or so of their 125 flavours are featured daily at this frozen treats retailer in the Ferry Building (another branch sits in the Mission district). Unique choices – sour cream, toast and jam, tequila – lie alongside more traditional varieties – banana pecan, Tahitian vanilla.

Mazarine Coffee

MAP P.26, POCKET MAP B12
720 Market St Ⓜ #2, #3, #8, #9, F, J, K, L, M, N, T; Ⓑ Montgomery. ☏ 415 398 7700, Ⓦ mazarinecoffee.com. Mon–Fri 7am–5pm, Sat & Sun 8am–5pm.

Stylish, contemporary café that takes its inspiration from the Mazarine library in Paris, with authentic French pastries complemented by a range of sandwiches and gourmet coffee that's squarely West Coast.

Restaurants

Borobudur

MAP P.26, POCKET MAP A12
700 Post St at Jones St Ⓜ #2, #3, #27, #38; Ⓑ Powell. ☏ 415 775

1512,  borobudursf.com. Mon–Thurs 11.30am–10pm, Fri & Sat 11.30am–11pm, Sun 1–10pm.

Borobudur's *roti prata* (flaky fried bread) and curry dipping sauce may be San Francisco's most unheralded appetizer, while much of the rest of the menu is equally enticing. Mains cost around $10–18.

Café Claude

MAP P.26, POCKET MAP B12

7 Claude Lane at Bush St #2, #3, #8, #30, #45; Montgomery. 415 392 3505, cafeclaude.com. Mon–Sat 11.30am–10.30pm, Sun 5.30–10.30pm.

The achingly Parisian *Café Claude* is set in a narrow Downtown alley, where thickly accented waiters deliver plates of *coq au vin* ($24), and trout *amandine* ($25). Jazz bands hold court Thurs–Sat evenings.

Gott's Roadside

MAP P.26, POCKET MAP C11

Ferry Building Marketplace, 1 Embarcadero #2, #6, #14, #21, #31, F, J, K, L, M, N, T; Embarcadero. 415 318 3423, gotts.com. Daily 10am–10pm.

A large outdoor dining patio fronts the Embarcadero at this glorified diner, making it one of the best alfresco places in San Francisco to enjoy an overstuffed burger, sizeable salad or bowl of wonderfully spicy chilli con carne ($8–$13).

Hog Island Oyster Co.

MAP P.26, POCKET MAP C11

Ferry Building Marketplace, 1 Embarcadero #2, #6, #14, #21, #31, F, J, K, L, M, N, T; Embarcadero. 415 391 7117, hogislandoysters.com. Daily 11am–9pm.

Settle into a seat inside *Hog Island*'s popular bay-side dining room and choose from an extensive selection of wines, beers and oysters from the Bay Area and elsewhere. It's tough to go wrong with anything here, and you can expect to pay $18–20 for six oysters, or up to $38 for a dozen. Reservations aren't accepted, so expect a wait.

Le Colonial

MAP P.26, POCKET MAP A12

20 Cosmo Place at Taylor St #2, #3, #27, #38; Powell. 415 931 3600, lecolonialsf.com. Mon–Thurs & Sun 5.30–10pm, Fri & Sat 5.30–11pm.

Step back in time as you walk into *Le Colonial*'s lush interior, with its tiled floors, palm fronds and

Hog Island Oyster Co.

ceiling fans. Vietnamese appetizers and mains ($18–39) benefit from a subtle French influence – don't miss the *cha gio vit* (crispy duck rolls).

La Mar

MAP P.26, POCKET MAP C11
Pier 1.5, The Embarcadero Ⓜ #1, F;
Ⓑ Embarcadero. ☎ 415 397 8880,
Ⓦ lamarsf.com. Mon–Thurs 11.30am–
2.30pm & 5.30–9.30pm, Fri & Sun
11.30am–10pm.

This upscale, popular Peruvian spot right next to the bay is known for its half-dozen varieties of *cebiche* ($16–19), but its *anticuchos* (grilled skewers) are equally tasty. Portions are on the small side, so prepare to order several items.

Michael Mina

MAP P.26, POCKET MAP C11
252 California St at Battery St Ⓜ #1, #10,
#12, F, J, K, L, M, N, T; Ⓑ Embarcadero.
☎ 415 397 9222, Ⓦ michaelmina.net/
restaurants/san-francisco-bay-area/
michael-mina. Mon–Fri 11.30am–2pm
& 6–9pm (Fri until 10pm), Sat & Sun
5.30–10pm.

You'll be hard-pressed to find a more adventurous – or expensive – menu in San Francisco than at this five-star New American restaurant, which is operated by the namesake (and brand name) chef. The selection of mains (dinner set menu only; $135–195) is ever-changing, but the legendary butter-poached Maine lobster is a near-constant.

Pearl's Deluxe Burgers

MAP P.26, POCKET MAP A12
708 Post St at Jones St Ⓜ #2, #3,
#27, #38; Ⓑ Powell. ☎ 415 409 6120,
Ⓦ pearlsdeluxe.com. Mon–Thurs
11am–10pm, Fri & Sat 11am–midnight,
Sun noon–9pm.

One of the top budget burger spots in town, *Pearl's* features a host of patties, from beef and turkey, to veggie and even buffalo ($11–20). The cramped size of the room hasn't kept pace with its popularity, however, so bring patience along with a hearty appetite.

Cebiche at La Mar

Sam's Grill

MAP P.26, POCKET MAP B12
374 Bush St at Belden Place Ⓜ #2, #3, #8,
#30, #45; Ⓑ Montgomery. ☎ 415 421 0594,
Ⓦ samsgrillsf.com. Mon–Fri 11am–9pm.

Known for its Hang Town Fry (essentially a bacon and oyster omelette, $22), and abrupt staff who sometimes look as if they were waiting tables when this old-time fish house first opened in 1867, *Sam's* is one of the city's quintessential seafood destinations.

Sanraku

MAP P.26, POCKET MAP A12
704 Sutter St at Taylor St Ⓜ #2, #3, #27;
Ⓑ Powell. ☎ 415 771 0803, Ⓦ sanraku.
com. Mon–Sat 11am–10pm, Sun 4–10pm.

With a sushi bar, main dining room and quietly classy decor, *Sanraku* is a longtime favourite among San Francisco devotees of sushi, udon and *donburi*; even the salads are sublime. Mains around $16–21, while sushi platters are $27 and up.

Schroeder's

MAP P.26, POCKET MAP C11
240 Front St at California St Ⓜ #1, F,
J, K, L, M, N, T; Ⓑ Embarcadero. ☎ 415
421 4778, Ⓦ schroederssf.com. Mon–Fri
11.30am–10pm, Sat 4–10pm.

A meal at *Schroeder's*, which dates back to the 1890s, may well constitute San Francisco's most classic German experience: think ham hocks, schnitzel, two-litre boots of German Pilsner, and even live polka performances on some Fridays. Mains cost $16–25.

Sears Fine Food

MAP P.26, POCKET MAP A12
439 Powell St at Post St Ⓜ #8, #30, #45; Ⓑ Powell. Ⓣ 415 986 0700, Ⓦ searsfinefood.com. Mon–Thurs & Sun 6.30am–9.30pm, Fri & Sat 6.30am–10pm.
Instead of queuing up with the hordes waiting for tables outside this civic institution almost every morning, walk inside and find a stool at one of the dining counters. Once seated, order *Sears'* signature breakfast dish: 18 little Swedish pancakes for $12.50 (10,000-plus made daily), served until 3pm.

The Slanted Door

MAP P.26, POCKET MAP C11
Ferry Building Marketplace, 1 Embarcadero Ⓜ #2, #6, #14, #21, #31, F, J, K, L, M, N, T; Ⓑ Embarcadero. Ⓣ 415 861 8032, Ⓦ slanteddoor.com. Mon–Sat 11am–2.30pm & 5.30–10pm, Sun 11.30am–3pm & 5.30–10pm.
Assuming you've made a reservation well in advance, expect to enjoy one of the city's top dining experiences at this bay-side French-Vietnamese stalwart. Mains cost $23–48.

Wayfare Tavern

MAP P.26, POCKET MAP B11
558 Sacramento St at Leidesdorff St Ⓜ #1, #8, #10, #12; Ⓑ Montgomery. Ⓣ 415 772 9060, Ⓦ wayfaretavern.com. Mon–Wed 11am–10.30pm, Thurs & Fri 11am–11pm, Sat 11.30am–11pm, Sun 11.30am–10pm.
Elegant and bustling, this corner spot dishes out delightful plates of New American-meets-California cuisine, including meat, fish and vegetable dishes, all $18–52. There's also a raw food bar where oysters go for $28 per half dozen.

Bars

Benjamin Cooper

MAP P.26, POCKET MAP A13
398 Geary St at Mason St Ⓜ #2, #3, #27, #38; Ⓑ Powell. Ⓣ 415 654 5061, Ⓦ benjamincoopersf.com. Mon–Fri 5pm–2am, Sat 6pm–2am.
Trendy cocktail bar with a speakeasy vibe (you enter through an unmarked door), with only 14 bar seats and a few more off to the side. A weekly changing cocktail menu (from $13) is complemented by three types of raw oyster ($3 each).

Golden Gate Tap Room

MAP P.26, POCKET MAP A12

The Redwood Room

449 Powell St at Sutter St Ⓜ #8, #30, #35; Ⓑ Powell. ☎ 415 677 9999, Ⓦ ggtaproom.com. Daily 11.30am–2pm.
This vast beer and games hall serves over 100 beers and features shuffleboard, Skee-Ball, foosball, *Simpsons* pinball, vintage arcade games and pool tables. It's also a popular hangout for sports fans, with major events shown live via 20 huge screens.

Harry Denton's Starlight Room

MAP P.26, POCKET MAP A12
Sir Francis Drake, 450 Powell St at Sutter St Ⓜ #30, #45; Ⓑ Powell. ☎ 415 395 8595, Ⓦ starlightroomsf.com. Tues–Thurs 6pm–midnight, Fri & Sat 5pm–2am, Sun brunch 10.30am–3pm.
Be sure to arrive sharply dressed at this venerable twenty-first-floor hotel lounge. Reserve your spot for one of two brunch drag shows each Sunday, and expect a $10–15 cover charge for live entertainment on other nights.

The Redwood Room

MAP P.26, POCKET MAP A13
Clift Hotel, 495 Geary St at Taylor St Ⓜ #2, #3, #27, #38; Ⓑ Powell. ☎ 415 929 2372, Ⓦ morganshotelgroup.com/originals/originals-clift-san-francisco/eat-drink/redwood-room. Mon–Thurs & Sun 5pm–2am, Fri & Sat 4pm–2am.
Swanky, if young and posey, this landmark lounge at the *Clift Hotel* includes lightboxes on the walls that display shifting portraits of local models. Beware that the pricey $20 cocktails may have you seeing red – the room's dominant colour.

Tunnel Top

MAP P.26, POCKET MAP A12
601 Bush St at Stockton St Ⓜ #2, #3, #8, #30, #45; Ⓑ Montgomery. ☎ 415 722 6620. Mon–Thurs & Sat 4.30pm–2am, Fri 4pm–2am, Sun 5pm–2am.
This lively nightspot atop the Stockton Tunnel is known for terrific drinks, a fireplace and a fun balcony from which you can absorb the scene. DJs and/or the occasional

American Conservatory Theater

live performance (no cover) are on the calendar most weeknights.

Theatre

American Conservatory Theater (ACT)

MAP P.26, POCKET MAP A13
415 Geary St at Mason St Ⓜ #2, #3, #27, #38; Ⓑ Powell. ☎ 415 749 2228, Ⓦ act-sf.org. $25–105.
Integrating inventive staging into freshly commissioned works (and the occasional well-known play), the Bay Area's top resident theatre ensemble always seems to hit the mark. "Rush tickets" often available at noon on performance days.

Comedy

The Punch Line

MAP P.26, POCKET MAP B11
444 Battery St at Washington St Ⓜ #1, #8, #10, #12; Ⓑ Embarcadero. ☎ 415 397 7573, Ⓦ punchlinecomedyclub.com. $18–25, plus two-drink minimum.
Strangely located among the concrete environs of the northernmost Financial District, long-standing cabaret *The Punch Line* books several shows weekly featuring well-known headliners and locals on the rise.

Chinatown and Jackson Square

Today's Chinatown sits in sharp contrast to the wealthy neighbourhoods surrounding it, and its diversity continues to increase as Fujianese, Vietnamese, Korean, Thai and Laotian groups trickle in. Its pair of primary commercial streets, tourist-geared Grant Avenue and workaday Stockton Street, are home to kitsch trinket shops and noisy fish and meat markets that act as festivals for the senses. The oldest Chinatown in the US, the enclave was originally a rough-and-tumble area settled by Chinese sailors hoping to benefit from the Gold Rush, as well as Cantonese labourers who worked on the transcontinental railroad in the 1860s. A few blocks east, Jackson Square feels like a Zen garden by comparison, a small area rich in local lore where you can enjoy a glimpse of otherwise bygone nineteenth-century San Francisco architecture.

Chinatown Gate

MAP P.38, POCKET MAP B12
Grant Ave at Bush St Ⓜ #2, #3, #8, #30, #45; Ⓑ Montgomery.

Framing Grant Avenue at Chinatown's southern edge, the graceful portal of Chinatown

Chinatown Gate

Gate is the best way to approach the neighbourhood. Built in 1970, it adheres to Chinese gateway architectural standards by employing a trio of green-tiled roofs and using stone as a basic building material (rather than wooden pillars) – techniques that help make it North America's sole authentic Chinatown Gate. The distinctive, dragon-clad arch faces south according to feng shui precepts, and also features a four-character inscription – "*Tiān xià wèi gōng*" (attributed to Dr Sun Yat-sen), or "What is under heaven is for all".

Grant Avenue

MAP P.38, POCKET MAP A10–B13
Ⓜ #1, #8, #10, #12, #30, #45; cable car: California; Ⓑ Montgomery.

The ambition set forth by Chinatown Gate often falls flat as you walk up **Grant Avenue**, Chinatown's perennially popular visitor artery. While the pedestrian-heavy street features a handful of lovely portals and colourful balconies, the dense retail strip

Grant Avenue

is infamous for its disposable commercialism – if you're looking for a plastic Buddha, you've come to the right place.

Known in the nineteenth century as Dupont Street, this was a dodgy route lined with gambling halls, opium dens and bordellos ruled by rogue Chinatown gangs (*tongs*). After the near-wholesale destruction wrought by the 1906 fire and earthquake, planners renamed the thoroughfare in honour of US President Ulysses S. Grant. It's notable that, other than those locals employed here, neighbourhood residents don't seem to frequent businesses along Grant Avenue to the degree they do those one block west on Stockton Street.

Old St. Mary's Cathedral

MAP P.38, POCKET MAP B12
660 California St at Grant Ave Ⓜ #1, #8, #30, #45; cable cars: California, Powell-Hyde, Powell-Mason. ☎ 415 288 3800, Ⓦ oldsaintmarys.org. Mon–Fri 7am–2pm, Sat noon–6.30pm, Sun 8am–2.30pm.
Just inside the main doorway of **Old St. Mary's Cathedral**, you'll find a fine photo display

chronicling the damage to the city and the church at the hands of the 1906 earthquake and fire. Built in 1854 during the early heyday of then-Dupont Street's impurity, the red-brick and granite church survived the massive tremor, only to be virtually gutted by the ensuing conflagration, which melted the church bells and marble altar. However, its renovation was complete within three years.

With the 1891 dedication of the Cathedral of Saint Mary of the Assumption a mile and a half to the west, Old St. Mary's saw its visibility fall even before the 1906 calamities, but today it continues to serve the Chinatown and Nob Hill communities, while also hosting classical concerts every Tuesday at 12.30pm ($5 suggested donation).

Portsmouth Square

MAP P.38, POCKET MAP B11
Bordered by Washington, Clay and Kearny sts Ⓜ #1, #8, #10, #12, #30, #45; cable car: California.
A combination of neighbourhood living room and back yard, **Portsmouth Square** is Chinatown's primary social

Portsmouth Square

River!": a defining moment in Californian history that helped jump-start the state's Gold Rush.

The space boasts a few points of interest, including the aforementioned **flagpole** and an increasingly weathered bronze *Goddess of Democracy* statue (modelled upon a similar sculpture in Beijing's Tiananmen Square) near the playground, but is mainly worth a visit simply to absorb neighbourhood life.

gathering place for the district's old and young, where children enjoy the playground as elderly citizens meet over games of cards and Chinese chess. However, the plaza holds great importance in local lore not only as the spot where the US flag was first raised in the city in 1846, but where, two years later, San Francisco tycoon Sam Brannan cried "Gold at the American

Chinese American Telephone Exchange Building

MAP P.38, POCKET MAP B11
743 Washington St at Grant Ave Ⓜ #1, #8, #10, #12, #30, #45; cable car: California, Powell-Hyde, Powell-Mason.

Occupying the former site of Sam Brannan's *California Star* newspaper office, from which much Gold Rush hype originated in 1848, the **Chinese American**

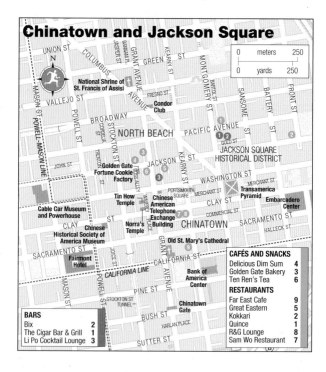

Chinatown and Jackson Square

UNION ST
COLUMBUS AVENUE
GREEN ST
BANNAM PL
JASPER PL
GRANT AVENUE
KEARNY ST
MONTGOMERY ST
BARTOL ST
SANSOME ST
BATTERY ST
FRONT ST

0 meters 250
0 yards 250

N

MASON ST
POWELL-MASON LINE
POWELL ST
VALLEJO ST
BROADWAY
CORDELIA ST
STOCKTON ST
TRENTON ST

National Shrine of
St. Francis of Assisi
FRESNO ST
Condor
Club

NORTH BEACH
PACIFIC AVENUE
❶
❶❷ GOLD ST
❷
JACKSON SQUARE
HISTORICAL DISTRICT

JOHN ST
Golden Gate
Fortune Cookie
Factory
JACKSON ST
KEARNY ST
ROSS ALLEY
❻ ❺ ❸

Tin How
Temple
WAVERLY PL
Chinese
American
Telephone
Exchange
Building
PORTSMOUTH
SQUARE
MERCHANT ST
WASHINGTON ST
CLAY ST
MERCHANT ST
Transamerica
Pyramid
Embarcadero
Center

Cable Car Museum
and Powerhouse
Norra's
Temple
❷❸
CHINATOWN
COMMERCIAL ST
SACRAMENTO ST
HALLECK ST

CLAY
ST
Chinese
Historical Society of
America Museum
GRANT AVENUE
Old St. Mary's Cathedral

SACRAMENTO ST
Fairmont
Hotel
JOICE ST
CALIFORNIA ST
CALIFORNIA LINE
MASON ST
POWELL ST
CALIFORNIA ST
Bank of
America
Center

PINE ST
STOCKTON ST
TUNNEL
Chinatown
Gate
BUSH ST
HARLAN PLACE
SUTTER ST

CAFÉS AND SNACKS
Delicious Dim Sum | 4
Golden Gate Bakery | 3
Ten Ren's Tea | 6
RESTAURANTS
Far East Cafe | 9
Great Eastern | 5
Kokkari | 2
Quince | 1
R&G Lounge | 8
Sam Wo Restaurant | 7

BARS
Bix | 2
The Cigar Bar & Grill | 1
Li Po Cocktail Lounge | 3

Telephone Exchange building is a red two-storey structure featuring three curved tile roofs punctuated by curling dragon shapes. Upon its completion in 1909, the building was home for the next forty years to phone operators who routed calls by memory – necessary at the time since Chinatown lacked telephone listings in the first half of the twentieth century. After the local phone company switched to a dialling system, the Telephone Exchange went out of business. Restored by a bank in 1960, the building soldiers on today as a financial institution.

Norra's and Tin How Temples

MAP P.38, POCKET MAP A11
109 and 125 Waverly Place at Clay St
Ⓜ #1, #8, #30, #45; cable car: Powell-Hyde, Powell-Mason. Norra's ☎ 415 362 1993. Daily 10am–4pm. Free; donations appreciated.

Along with Grant Avenue, another Chinatown street that has undergone a major transformation since the nineteenth century is Waverly Place. Once home to the majority of Chinatown brothels, these days the small side street contains the **Norra's and Tin How temples**: the former is on the third floor of no. 109, while the latter is on the fourth floor of no. 125. Norra's is named for Norlha Hotogtu, a Tibetan lama who tried to expand Tibetan Buddhism in China; Tin How, on the other hand, is a Taoist space dedicated to Mazu, the Goddess of Heaven (or "Tin Hau" in Cantonese). Norra's is less meditative and embellished than Tin How, where continually burning incense and scores of red tassels and lanterns help create a calm, reflective mood. Note that each place operates as an active temple (no photography is allowed) and appreciates modest donations from visitors.

Chinese Historical Society of America Museum

MAP P.38, POCKET MAP A11
965 Clay St at Powell St Ⓜ #1, #8, #30, #45; cable car: California, Powell-Hyde, Powell-Mason. ☎ 415 391 1188, Ⓦ chsa.org. Tues–Fri noon–5pm, Sat 11am–4pm. Free.

Located steeply uphill from the heart of Chinatown, the **Chinese Historical Society of America Museum** is a humbly sized yet rewarding repository of art, photographs and artefacts chronicling the legacy of Chinese Americans, locally and beyond. Past exhibits have examined architecture in San Francisco's Chinatown and the 1882 passing (and eventual repeal) of the infamous Chinese Exclusion Act. The museum is set in a red-brick building (designed by celebrated architect Julia Morgan) which was an earlier home to the Chinatown YWCA, evinced by the original sign that still hangs near the front entrance.

Stockton Street

MAP P.38, POCKET MAP A10–B13
Ⓜ #1, #8, #10, #12, #30, #45; cable car: Powell-Hyde, Powell-Mason.

Tin How Temple

The Barbary Coast

Resolutely tame Jackson Square wasn't always so smart– far from it, in fact. This compact area was known as the **Barbary Coast** in San Francisco's earliest decades – a notorious stronghold of dance halls, cabarets and bordellos that brought in hordes of sin-seeking visitors. This neighbourhood of iniquity first sprung to life as hundreds of ships, abandoned by would-be prospectors flocking to the **Sierra Nevada** foothills in search of gold-dusted riches, were converted into floating hotels, bars and stores, before eventually being mulched into landfill. Once Australian roughnecks took over the area's blocks from Chilean immigrants, the Barbary Coast's reputation for vice and violence kicked into high gear, fuelled in part by the frequent "shanghai'ing" of young men into involuntary servitude aboard ships docked in the bay. Having stoutly survived the 1906 **earthquake** and **fire**, some of the brick buildings along Pacific Avenue (then nicknamed Terrific Street) became San Francisco's first **jazz clubs**, the *Hippodrome* at no. 555 flourishing in particular with the sounds of musicians from New Orleans' Storyville. However, the Barbary Coast era ended abruptly in 1917 when police, citing California's Red Light Abatement Act, passed four years prior, barricaded the area and shuttered almost every establishment immediately.

If Grant Avenue represents Chinatown's pandering side, **Stockton Street** is the district's more sincere main drag, where public housing tenements loom overhead and the pavements overflow with a swirl of locals shopping for staples and herbs. It may be sensory overload for some – the aromas spilling out of certain fish markets certainly aren't for the faint of nose – but the half-dozen or so blocks of Stockton Street that course through Chinatown are the real chaotic deal. Step into one of the numerous lively markets lining the street for a staggering variety of fresh fruits and vegetables, all at fairly reasonable prices.

Golden Gate Fortune Cookie Factory

MAP P.38, POCKET MAP A11
56 Ross Alley at Jackson St Ⓜ #1, #8, #10, #12, #30, #45; cable car: Powell-Hyde, Powell-Mason. ☏ 415 781 3956. Daily 9am–6pm. Free.

Between Stockton Street and Grant Avenue, find narrow Ross Alley and follow your nose to the **Golden Gate Fortune Cookie Factory**, where employees have been cramming this small space to crank out 20,000 fresh fortune cookies daily by hand since 1962. Bakers pull dough off a hot press and place a fortune on one side before shaping each cookie over a steel rod. A 40-count bag of the light, sweet delicacies costs less than $5, but prepare to be charged 50 cents if you want to take a photograph while inside the factory.

Cable Car Museum and Powerhouse

MAP P.38, POCKET MAP A11
1201 Mason St at Washington St Ⓜ #1, #10, #12, #30, #45; cable car: Powell-Hyde, Powell-Mason. ☏ 415 474 1887, ⓦ cablecarmuseum.org. Daily April–Sept 10am–6pm; Oct–March 10am–5pm. Free.
Located on the western edge of Chinatown, right on the Powell-

Hyde cable-car line, the **Cable Car Museum and Powerhouse** provides a compelling peek into the world of late-nineteenth-century industry by peeling back the curtain on San Francisco's signature cable cars and the ten miles of track along which they trundle. Despite its name, the huge building is first and foremost a working powerhouse – head downstairs for a rare look at the revolving sheaves (enormous gears) that help keep the cars moving through the intersection of Washington and Mason streets directly above.

Numerous displays upstairs interpret the history of these famous, hill-conquering vessels in the city, from their initial appearance on San Francisco streets in 1873 on through their placement on the National Register of Historic Places nearly a century later, a triumph preceded by almost two decades of grassroots civic activism. There's also a gift shop.

Jackson Square Historical District

MAP P.38, POCKET MAP B11
Bordered by Pacific Ave, Battery, Washington and Montgomery sts Ⓜ #1, #8, #10, #12; Ⓔ Montgomery.

Although its raucous heyday came and went in the early 1900s, small **Jackson Square Historical District** (so named by the interior designers who moved into this tiny neighbourhood in the 1960s) is worth a stroll to view the only buildings in the Downtown area to escape harm in the hugely destructive earthquake and fire of 1906. The north side of **Jackson Street** consists of simple, low-slung buildings dating from the 1850s, while many structures on the south side of the street, which were built a decade or so later, feature some hints of Victorian ornamentation. One block north is leafy **Pacific Avenue**, the epicentre of Barbary Coast excess (see box); these days, it's home to a more wholesome mix of advertising agencies, law offices, and trendy interior and graphic design studios.

Cable Car Museum and Powerhouse

Cafés and snacks

Delicious Dim Sum

MAP P.38, POCKET MAP A11
752 Jackson St at Stockton St Ⓜ #1, #8, #10, #12, #30, #45; cable car: Powell-Hyde, Powell-Mason. Ⓣ 415 781 0721. Mon, Tues & Thurs–Sun 7am–6pm.
Don't miss this tiny, hole-in-the-wall nook (takeaway only) where thick beef, pork and shrimp dumplings are kept fresh and warm in layered steamers. You can feast well for $10.

Golden Gate Bakery

MAP P.38, POCKET MAP A11
1029 Grant Ave at Pacific Ave Ⓜ #1, #8, #10, #12, #30, #45. Ⓣ 415 781 2627, Ⓦ goldengatebakery.com. Daily 8am–8pm.
Queue up at this notable Chinese bakery for its fluffy *dan tat* (egg tarts) – about $2 each – although there's plenty else here worth sampling, including delectable cocktail buns (sweet, coconut-filled pastries). Just don't be surprised if the place is closed for "vacation".

Ten Ren's Tea

MAP P.38, POCKET MAP B11
949 Grant Ave at Jackson St Ⓜ #1, #8, #10, #12, #30, #45; cable car: Powell-Hyde, Powell-Mason. Ⓣ 415 362 0656, Ⓦ tenren. com. Daily 9am–9pm.

Dumplings at Delicious Dim Sum

This famed Taiwanese tea emporium is best for by-the-pound purchases and freshly brewed cups to drink on site. Several different flavoured varieties of iced tea (with gloopy tapioca balls an optional inclusion) are also on offer.

Restaurants

Far East Cafe

MAP P.38, POCKET MAP B12
631 Grant Ave Ⓜ #1, #8, #10, #12, #30, #45; Ⓑ Montgomery. Ⓣ 415 982 3245. Daily 11.30am–10pm.
A neighbourhood classic since 1920, with kitsch Chinese decor, curtained mahogany booths and all the American-Chinese favourites: *kung pao* chicken, hot and sour soup and the notorious General Chou's chicken (deep-fried chicken smothered in thick, sweet sauce). Mains are around $9–16.

Great Eastern

MAP P.38, POCKET MAP B11
649 Jackson St at Kearny St Ⓜ #1, #8, #10, #12, #30, #45; Ⓑ Montgomery. Ⓣ 415 986 2500, Ⓦ greateasternsf.com. Mon–Fri 10am–11pm, Sat & Sun 9am–11pm.
One of Chinatown's more popular restaurants – even before Barack Obama dropped in for a takeaway lunch order in 2012 – the elegant *Great Eastern* specializes in geoduck clams, sautéed squab and dim sum. Most mains hover around the $20 mark.

Kokkari

MAP P.38, POCKET MAP C11
200 Jackson St at Front St Ⓜ #1, #10, #12, F; Ⓑ Embarcadero. Ⓣ 415 981 0983, Ⓦ kokkari.com. Mon–Thurs 11.30am–2.30pm & 5.30–10pm, Fri 11.30am–2.30pm & 5.30–11pm, Sat 5–11pm, Sun 5–10pm.
Expect pricey but top-rate Greek cuisine in *Kokkari's* pair of splendid dining rooms, each decorated with Oriental rugs and goatskin lampshades. If it's on the menu, try the marvellous lamb and aubergine (eggplant) moussaka ($27).

Quince

MAP P.38, POCKET MAP B11
470 Pacific Ave at Montgomery St Ⓜ #1, #8, #10, #12; Ⓑ Montgomery. ☏ 415 775 8500, Ⓦ quincerestaurant.com. Mon–Thurs 5.30–9pm, Fri & Sat 5–9.30pm.

One of San Francisco's top fine-dining choices, sophisticated *Quince* features a nightly changing pair of French and Italian-inspired prix fixe menus ($210–250 per person), as well as an equally pricey list of caviar. A few à la carte options are also on offer.

Lobster garganelli at Quince

R&G Lounge

MAP P.38, POCKET MAP B11
631 Kearny St at Commercial St Ⓜ #1, #8, #10, #12, #30, #45; Ⓑ Montgomery. ☏ 415 982 7877, Ⓦ rnglounge.com. Daily 11am–9.30pm.

This gigantic, frosted-windowed restaurant has been pulling in the masses for family-style platters of seafood and other Hong Kong staples for years. Mains are reasonably priced at $18–20.

Sam Wo Restaurant

MAP P.38, POCKET MAP B11
713 Clay St Ⓜ #1, #8, #10, #12, #30, #45; Ⓑ Montgomery. ☏ 415 989 8898, Ⓦ samworestaurant.com. Mon & Sun 11am–4pm, Wed & Thurs 11am–4pm & 6pm–midnight, Fri & Sat 11am–4pm & 6pm–3am.

Laid-back Chinatown canteen since 1947, serving American-Chinese classics such as salt and pepper chicken wings ($7.99), their famed house chow mein ($12.25) and *kung pao* shrimp ($12.25).

Bars

Bix

MAP P.38, POCKET MAP B11
56 Gold St at Montgomery St Ⓜ #1, #8, #10, #12; Ⓑ Montgomery. ☏ 415 433 6300, Ⓦ bixrestaurant.com. Mon–Thurs 4.30–10pm, Fri 11.30am–2pm & 4.30–10pm, Sat & Sun 5.30–10pm.

Located down an evocative brick alley, this beautiful, Art Deco-inspired bar/restaurant exudes a good touch of glamour. Meat and fish dominate the menu (mains cost $28.50–48), and there's live jazz nightly.

The Cigar Bar & Grill

MAP P.38, POCKET MAP B11
850 Montgomery St at Pacific Ave Ⓜ #1, #8, #10, #12; Ⓑ Montgomery. ☏ 415 398 0850, Ⓦ cigarbarandgrill.com. Mon–Fri 4pm–2am, Sat 6pm–2am.

One of San Francisco's few smoker-friendly establishments (you can smoke on the heated patio, not inside), classy *Cigar Bar & Grill* has a strong Spanish vibe and a brick courtyard ideal for a drink and chat. Latin jazz, samba and merengue performances (no cover) occur regularly; there's also a late-night menu, while drinks are moderately priced.

Li Po Cocktail Lounge

MAP P.38, POCKET MAP B11
916 Grant Ave at Jackson St Ⓜ #1, #8, #10, #12, #30, #45; cable car: Powell-Hyde, Powell-Mason. ☏ 415 982 0072, Ⓦ lipolounge.com. Daily 2pm–2am.

With a sprawling list of libation options – there's certainly no shortage of colourful cocktails – this likeably grotty bar is Chinatown's best place for a drink. Make sure you try the bracing Mai Tai ($11), made with Chinese whisky.

North Beach and the hills

At one time a waterfront neighbourhood, North Beach lost its bay-side setting once the city expanded on landfill north of Francisco Street. The district grew as an Italian-American stronghold throughout the twentieth century and remains so today, with cultural and residential spillover from neighbouring Chinatown providing a twist to the city's own Little Italy. North Beach's charms are best appreciated by strolling its vibrant streets, enjoying meals in its scores of restaurants and having a few rounds in its countless bars and cafés. Looming adjacent are three prominent hills – Telegraph, Russian and Nob – each boasting promontories over the city and bay, with none finer than the view at Coit Tower.

Washington Square

MAP P.46, POCKET MAP A10
Bordered by Stockton St, Union St, Columbus Ave and Filbert St Ⓜ #8, #30, #39, #45; cable car: Powell-Mason.

By far North Beach's most notable public space, grassy **Washington Square** is a terrific place to while away time and take in the neighbourhood scene. Mornings here see elderly Chinese residents practising t'ai chi, while it's a perennially popular picnic ground and general hangout spot for locals and visitors alike. One weekend every June, the **North Beach Festival** (see page 157) commandeers Washington Square with performance stages, food and drink booths, Italian street painting and more.

A pair of **statues** here merit brief attention as well: Lillie Hitchcock Coit's ode to local firemen on the Columbus Avenue side of the park, and a monument to Benjamin Franklin donated by the local prohibitionist H.D. Cogswell. The latter features water taps (now dry) that Cogswell ambitiously hoped park visitors would use in lieu of drinking liquor.

Finally, any *Dirty Harry* enthusiasts may well recognize the square as a shooting location for

the 1971 film, where a black-gloved sniper fires from the top of a building just across Stockton Street to the east.

Saints Peter and Paul Church

MAP P.46, POCKET MAP A10
666 Filbert St at Powell St Ⓜ #8, #30, #39, #45; cable car: Powell-Mason. ☏ 415 421 0809, Ⓦ sspeterpaulsf.org/church. Mon–Fri 7.30am–12.30pm, Sat & Sun 7.30am–5pm.

Even given its decidedly unholy street number, **Saints Peter and Paul Church** is one of San Francisco's most prominent places of worship, with weekly Masses in English, Italian and Mandarin. Though its cream-coloured spires are one of North Beach's signature sights, the church's underlit interior is a bit of a letdown. Saints Peter and Paul was the target of radical anti-Catholics in the 1920s, when it was the target of several (unsuccessful) bomb attacks. In 1954, baseball great (and North Beach native) Joe DiMaggio and new wife Marilyn Monroe had their wedding pictures taken here; many decades later, DiMaggio's 1999 funeral attracted an overflowing crowd.

Coit Tower

MAP P.46, POCKET MAP B10

Ⓜ #39. ☎ 415 249 0995. May–Oct daily 10am–6pm, Nov–April daily 10am–5pm; mural tours: Wed & Sat 11am. Entry to lobby and tours free; $8 for elevator to top.

Rightfully one of San Francisco's top attractions, **Coit Tower** is the Art Deco cherry atop precipitous Telegraph Hill. Completed in 1933, this unpainted concrete pillar anchors tiny **Pioneer Park**, the south side of which is an excellent spot for a picnic. While it's likely you'll join most other visitors in queuing up for the tight-fitting lift to the top of the 210ft tower – an unimpeded, 360-degree panorama that shouldn't be missed – be sure to linger in the ground-floor lobby to view the frescoes covering the interior's base. More than two dozen artists, all students of Diego Rivera, collaborated on the government-funded Depression-era project; despite the variation in style (and quality), its numerous panels stretching around the lobby are linked by the work's thematic title, *Aspects of Life in California*.

Saints Peter and Paul Church

Greenwich and Filbert Steps

MAP P.46, POCKET MAP B10

Ⓜ #39, F.

You may not find a more evocative walk in San Francisco than along this pair of steep stairs, routed parallel to one another and clinging precariously to the east flank of Telegraph Hill. The **Greenwich Steps**, partly laid out in brick, are signed from the parking area at Pioneer Park and drop down to the Northeast Waterfront district. Along the way, look for a smartly placed bench in a cleared area just off the path, where there's also a parking meter planted for kicks.

One block south, the **Filbert Steps** are even steeper en route uphill to Pioneer Park, with the segment between Sansome and Montgomery streets laid with wooden planks; in spring, the foliage-consumed area around Napier Lane is marvellously fragrant with honeysuckle and roses. Throughout your visit, watch and listen for the noisy green parrots populating the area – the

sizeable flock, immortalised in the 2005 documentary film *The Wild Parrots of Telegraph Hill*, grows by the year.

Exploratorium

MAP P.46, POCKET MAP C10

Pier 15, the Embarcadero Ⓜ F. ☎ 415 528 4360, Ⓦ exploratorium.edu. Daily 10am–5pm (also Thurs 6–10pm & Fri 6–9pm, late June to early Sept). $29.95; youth 13–17 years $24.95; youth 4–12 years $19.95.

Relocated in 2013 from its cramped quarters behind the Palace of Fine Arts, the **Exploratorium** remains a San Francisco trademark. This participatory science museum – the first of its kind in the world – has been a top destination since its 1969 debut, due in large part to the engaging approach of its hands-on exhibits that decode principles of electricity and sound waves, among other scientific head-scratchers. Thursday-night programming is aimed towards adults, while the Exploratorium's Tactile Dome is a sensorydeprivation environment explored on hands and knees – reservations are essential, and claustrophobes may want to think twice before embarking.

Condor Club

MAP P.46, POCKET MAP B11

560 Broadway at Columbus Ave Ⓜ #8, #10, #12, #30, #45. ☎ 415 781 8222, Ⓦ condorsf.com. Mon–Thurs 4pm–2am, Fri–Sun 3pm–2am.

Although it's nothing particularly special to the naked eye today, the **Condor Club** is by far the most (in)famous of the handful of strip clubs that persevere along Broadway. This corner venue was the birthplace of the topless dancer phenomenon in June 1964, when Carol Doda became the first cocktail waitress to bare her naked breasts on the job; five years later, Doda once again broke new ground

when she began serving drinks completely nude. Today, a plaque outside the venue commemorates Doda's cultural contributions.

In 1983, the club was the unfortunate setting for a far more grisly event, when a randy dancer and bouncer climbed atop the white piano that hangs from the ceiling in the room beyond the main bar. During the pair's passionate after-hours tryst, the instrument's hydraulic system was accidentally activated and sent the piano up into the ceiling; the man was fatally crushed, but the woman survived.

Lombard Street

MAP P.46, POCKET MAP J2
Between Leavenworth and Hyde sts Ⓜ #19, #45; cable car: Powell-Hyde.

Torturing pedestrians with a 27 percent incline just as it taunts drivers with no fewer than eight hairpin turns, **Lombard Street**'s

Exploratorium

famously crooked one-way block never disappoints. The route, paved in red bricks and lined with thick hedges, was the brainchild of a local property owner in the 1920s as a means

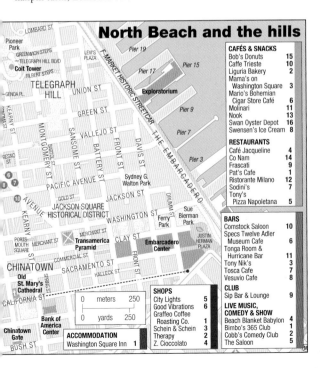

North Beach and the hills

Lombard Street

to negate the street's unforgiving gradient, and navigating its sharp turns and steep descent has since become a signature San Francisco experience; Lombard has appeared in numerous films, television shows and even driving video games. If you hope to avoid a lengthy wait in your car, arrive at the Hyde Street hilltop in early morning or, for a shimmering view of the city and bay, after dark, when traffic should be considerably lighter.

San Francisco Art Institute

MAP P.46, POCKET MAP J11
800 Chestnut St at Jones St Ⓜ #30; cable car: Powell-Hyde, Powell-Mason. ☏ 415 771 7020, Ⓦ sfai.edu. Daily 9am–7pm. Free.

San Francisco Art Institute's small campus is anchored by a squat Mission-style building that boasts one of the city's finest hidden vistas from its rear patio. Once you've sufficiently absorbed the view, find your way to the

Diego Rivera Gallery for Rivera's celebrated 1931 mural *The Making of a Fresco Showing the Building of a City*, into which the artist brilliantly inserted himself sitting with his back to the viewer in the painting's centre.

The oldest art school west of the Mississippi River, the Institute has drawn several San Francisco luminaries through its doors over the years: *Grateful Dead* guitarist and vocalist Jerry Garcia; poet, publisher and City Lights owner Lawrence Ferlinghetti; and esteemed landscape photographer Ansel Adams, who was also the founder of the school's photography department.

Macondray Lane

MAP P.46, POCKET MAP J2
Between Taylor and Leavenworth sts Ⓜ #45; cable car: Powell-Hyde, Powell-Mason.

One of a number of hillside, pedestrian-only paths scattered about San Francisco, **Macondray**

Lane on the eastern side of Russian Hill stands apart not only for its lush environs, but also for its literary association: it's widely acknowledged as the inspiration for Barbary Lane, the byway that a number of characters in Armistead Maupin's *Tales of the City* saga called home. The sloping, two-block lane is a pleasant place for a quiet stroll, and will likely be less crowded than the Greenwich and Filbert Steps.

Grace Cathedral

MAP P.46, POCKET MAP A12
1100 California St at Taylor St ⓜ #1, #27; cable car: California, Powell-Hyde, Powell-Mason. ☎ 415 749 6300, ⓦ gracecathedral. org. Mon–Wed, Fri & Sat 8am–6pm, Thurs 7am–6pm, Sun 8am–7pm; 90min tours Wed, Fri & Sat 10am. Free; tours $25.

Perched solidly atop Nob Hill, **Grace Cathedral** is a surprisingly youthful slab of neo-Gothic architecture. Although work commenced on the concrete monolith in 1928, ongoing funding struggles delayed its completion until 1964, which certainly contributed to the cathedral's somewhat jumbled final character. The Episcopal cathedral's outward design instantly recalls Notre Dame in Paris, while its massive Ghiberti doors are replicas of those at the Battistero di San Giovanni in Florence (although critics have remarked that they look horribly inappropriate here). Once inside, note how the floor labyrinth near the entrance acts as yet another direct nod to a European cathedral, France's Chartres. The pricey tour (book in advance) takes in, among other areas of the cathedral, the vestry, the gallery and, most notably, the top of the south tower, which affords grand views of the city.

Fairmont Hotel

MAP P.46, POCKET MAP A12
950 Mason St at Sacramento St ⓜ #1; cable car: California, Powell-Hyde, Powell-Mason. ☎ 415 772 5000, ⓦ fairmont.com/san-francisco.

Few structures on Nob Hill survived the 1906 earthquake and subsequent fire, but one that did was the then under construction **Fairmont Hotel**, albeit in a skeletal form. In the wake of that catastrophe, the nascent hotel's owners hired noted California architect Julia Morgan, largely for her valuable knowledge of reinforced concrete construction, which would prove to be earthquake-resistant over time. Since its 1907 opening, the Fairmont has played host to moments both crucial (meetings leading to the formation of the United Nations were held here in 1945) and infamous (Keith Richards angrily slugged Rolling Stones bandmate Ronnie Wood here in 1981), but the best reasons to drop in are to visit the lovely rooftop garden – reachable by walking through the opulent lobby and down the long, wide corridor to the right of the main desk – and for a drink at the notoriously camp *Tonga Room & Hurricane Bar* (see page 54).

Grace Cathedral

Shops

City Lights

MAP P.46, POCKET MAP B11

261 Columbus Ave at Broadway Ⓜ #8, #10, #12, #30, #45. ☎ 415 362 8193, Ⓦ citylights.com. Daily 10am–midnight.

Famed for its crucial role in establishing Beat literature as a force in the 1950s, Lawrence Ferlinghetti's City Lights remains one of the top bookstores in the West. Be sure to visit the landmark shop's upstairs poetry room, which is in a league of its own.

Good Vibrations

MAP P.46, POCKET MAP J3

1620 Polk St at Sacramento St Ⓜ #1, #19, #27, #47, #49; cable car: California. ☎ 415 345 0400, Ⓦ goodvibes.com. Mon–Thurs & Sun 10am–9pm, Fri & Sat 10am–10pm.

Helping de-stigmatize the notion of a sex shop since the late 1970s, Good Vibrations remains as popular as it's ever been. Shelves and racks stacked full of sex toys and erotica make for titillating browsing, as does the antique vibrator museum.

Schein & Schein

Graffeo Coffee Roasting Co.

MAP P.46, POCKET MAP A10

735 Columbus Ave at Filbert St Ⓜ #8, #30, #39, #45; cable car: Powell-Mason. ☎ 415 986 2420, Ⓦ graffeo.com. Mon–Fri 9am–6pm, Sat 9am–5pm.

Owned and operated by the Repetto family since 1935, this stark shop is known for its super-aromatic house-blend beans, sold over the granite counter for $17.50 a pound.

Schein & Schein

MAP P.46, POCKET MAP A10

1435 Grant Ave at Green St Ⓜ #8, #10, #12, #30, #39, #45. ☎ 415 399 8882, Ⓦ scheinandschein.com. Mon & Sun 11am–5pm, Tues–Fri 11am–6pm, Sat 10am–7pm.

With an approachable owner and a fascinating array of rare historical memorabilia and antique maps (many under $30) spanning San Francisco and far beyond, this shop is sure to grip the attention of any collector.

Therapy

MAP P.46, POCKET MAP A10

1445 Grant Ave at Union St Ⓜ #8, #30, #39, #45. ☎ 415 781 8899, Ⓦ shopattherapy.com. Daily 11.30am–7.30pm.

Seemingly a shop without focus, Therapy is nonetheless always good for an entertaining peruse. You'll enjoy picking through the boutique's smattering of men's and women's casual clothing, as well as fun greeting cards and assorted knick-knacks like camp refrigerator magnets.

Z. Cioccolato

MAP P.46, POCKET MAP A10

474 Columbus Ave at Green St Ⓜ #8, #10, #12, #30, #39, #45; cable car: Powell-Mason. ☎ 415 395 9116, Ⓦ zcioccolato.com. Mon–Thurs & Sun 11am–11pm, Fri & Sat 11am–midnight.

Wafting its sugary aromas out onto Columbus Avenue to attract passers-by, this sizeable sweets emporium sells delectable own-made fudge, chocolates and caramel popcorn (often free with any purchase), along with an enormous selection of saltwater taffy.

Cafés and snacks

Bob's Donuts

MAP P.46, POCKET MAP J3
1621 Polk St at Sacramento St #1, #19, #27, #47, #49; cable car: California. ☎415 776 3141, ⓦ bobsdonutssf.com. Daily 24hr.
Staunchly standing its ground in the face of pricier gourmet alternatives, *Bob's Donuts* remains a hugely popular round-the-clock stop for its sweet, fried treats ($1 and up). If a piping-fresh, glazed confection is your thing, this is your place.

Caffe Trieste

MAP P.46, POCKET MAP A11
601 Vallejo St at Grant Ave Ⓜ #8, #10, #12, #30, #39, #45. ☎415 392 6739, ⓦ coffee. caffetrieste.com. Mon–Thurs & Sun 6.30am–10pm, Fri & Sat 6.30am–11pm.
The West Coast birthplace of espresso in 1956, this legendary café still makes a range of bracing caffeinated cups to accompany its ever-popular Saturday mandolin sessions and opera recitals. It's rumoured that Francis Coppola liked the place so much that he wrote much of *The Godfather*'s screenplay here.

Liguria Bakery

MAP P.46, POCKET MAP A10
1700 Stockton St at Filbert St Ⓜ #8, #10, #12, #30, #39, #45; cable car: Powell-Mason. ☎415 421 3786. Tues–Fri 8am–2pm, Sat 7am–2pm.
Make a beeline for this Old World corner shop for its celebrated focaccia – choose between onion, garlic, rosemary and mushroom varieties, among others ($4–5). Bring cash and make sure that you arrive in the morning since it closes once the day's goods are gone.

Mama's on Washington Square

MAP P.46, POCKET MAP A10

Outside Molinari

1701 Stockton St at Filbert St. Ⓜ #8, #10, #12, #30, #39, #45; cable car: Powell-Mason. ☎415 362 6421, ⓦ mamas-sf.com. Tues–Sun 8am–3pm.
Justly popular all-day breakfast and brunch spot overlooking the park, especially famed for its omelettes (from $10.50), French toast (from $8.95) and eggs Benedict (from $12.50). Cash and debit cards only.

Mario's Bohemian Cigar Store Café

MAP P.46, POCKET MAP A10
566 Columbus Ave at Union St Ⓜ #8, #30, #39, #45; cable car: Powell-Mason. ☎415 362 0536. Daily 10am–11pm.
Day or night, few places are better for absorbing North Beach's vitality than a seat at this neighbourhood stalwart. Tasty focaccia sandwiches, panini and pizzas ($8–12) fill out the menu, while many simply come for the coffee, beer, wine and conviviality.

Molinari

MAP P.46, POCKET MAP A11
373 Columbus Ave at Vallejo St Ⓜ #8, #10, #12, #30, #39, #45; cable car: Powell-Mason. ☎415 421 2337. Mon–Fri 9am–6pm, Sat 9am–5.30pm, Sun 10am–4pm.

This wonderfully fragrant Italian deli is a terrific place to pick up a range of delicious cured meats to take home. It also doubles as a popular sandwich shop, so order one ($10–13) to take away and enjoy at nearby Washington Square.

Nook

MAP P.46, POCKET MAP J2
1500 Hyde St at Jackson St Ⓜ #1, #10, #12, #19, #27; cable car: Powell-Hyde. ☎ 415 447 4100, Ⓦ cafenook.com. Mon–Fri 7am–10pm, Sat 8am–10pm, Sun 8am–9pm.
A pleasant spot with outdoor tables on a signature San Francisco corner – the Powell-Hyde cable car clatters right by – *Nook* is an ideal spot to savour a cup of coffee, light meal, glass of wine, or even a $7.50 *soju* cocktail.

Swan Oyster Depot

MAP P.46, POCKET MAP J3
1517 Polk St at California St Ⓜ #1, #19, #47, #49; cable car: California. ☎ 415 673 1101. Mon–Sat 10.30am–5.30pm.
Once you score an empty stool at the long marble counter of this decidedly unfancy seafood diner, sit down and enjoy cheap shellfish, a simple bowl of chowder or – if you're feeling particularly brave – a Swan Special (shrimp cocktail and beer; $13).

Swensen's Ice Cream

MAP P.46, POCKET MAP J2
1999 Hyde St at Union St Ⓜ #19, #45; cable car: Powell-Hyde. ☎ 415 775 6818, Ⓦ swensensicecream.com. Tues–Thurs & Sun noon–10pm, Fri & Sat noon–11pm.
Swensen's original shop, here since 1948, still features twinkling lightbulbs and top-notch ice cream – make sure that you try the excellent "rocky road" (about $5.95 for two scoops). Grab several napkins since the small shop is takeaway only.

Restaurants

Café Jacqueline

MAP P.46, POCKET MAP A10
1454 Grant Ave at Union St Ⓜ #8, #30, #39, #45. ☎ 415 981 5565. Wed–Sun 5.30–11pm.
It's unlikely in North Beach that you'd expect to enjoy a splendidly fluffy soufflé amid candlelit, distinctly French environs, but *Café Jacqueline* offers precisely this

Frascati

experience. Just make sure to bring extra patience, as every soufflé ($40–60) is made to order.

Co Nam

MAP P.46, POCKET MAP J3
1653 Polk St at Clay St Ⓜ #1, #19, #27, #47, #49; cable car: California. ☎ 415 292 6161, Ⓦ conamsf.com. Tues–Thurs 11am–10pm, Fri 11am–10.30pm, Sat 10am–10.30pm, Sun 10am–10pm.

Stylish without a hint of pretence, friendly *Co Nam* concocts some of the Bay Area's most inviting Vietnamese cuisine. The kitchen's flavourful claypot medley ($17) combines chicken with heaps of vegetables over brown rice, and the *bun rieu* and *bun bo hué* (noodle soups, $14–16) are equally enticing.

Frascati

MAP P.46, POCKET MAP J2
1901 Hyde St at Green St Ⓜ #19, #45; cable car: Powell-Hyde. ☎ 415 928 1406, Ⓦ frascatisf.com. Mon–Sat 5.30–9.45pm, Sun 5.30–9pm.

Set on a vibrant Russian Hill corner, *Frascati* has been one of San Francisco's most celebrated neighbourhood restaurants for years. The menu features inventive California cuisine mains such as maple leaf duck breast ($30); be sure to request a table on the delightful balcony.

Pat's Cafe

MAP P.46, POCKET MAP J1
2330 Taylor St at Chestnut St Ⓜ #8, #30; cable car: Powell-Mason. ☎ 415 776 8735, Ⓦ patscafesf.com. Daily 7.30am–2.30pm.

Visit this friendly, informal spot to sample North Beach's best breakfasts – don't skip the banana granola pancakes or the tempting pepper-laden home fries. Lunch is equally hearty and informal, and almost everything's around or under $12.

Ristorante Milano

MAP P.46, POCKET MAP J2
1448 Pacific Ave at Hyde St Ⓜ #10, #12, #19, #27; cable car: Powell-Hyde. ☎ 415 673 2961, Ⓦ milanosf.com. Mon–Thurs 5.30–10pm, Fri & Sat 5.30–10.30pm, Sun 5–10pm.

An intimate, romantic nook not far off bustling Polk Street, *Ristorante Milano* is justifiably well known for its strong Italian wine list and, moreover, its gnocchi ($19) in an uncommonly delicious basil/gorgonzola/tomato sauce.

Sodini's

MAP P.46, POCKET MAP A10
510 Green St at Grant St Ⓜ #8, #30, #39, #45. ☎ 415 291 0499. Daily 5–10pm.

Step inside this vivacious North Beach staple, where regulars play dice at the bar and Rat Pack memorabilia dots the walls. Top choices include some of North Beach's finest gnocchi and angel hair pasta offerings (all of which cost $12–19).

Tony's Pizza Napoletana

MAP P.46, POCKET MAP A10
1570 Stockton St at Union St Ⓜ #8, #30, #39, #45; cable car: Powell-Mason. ☎ 415 835 9888, Ⓦ tonyspizzanapoletana.com. Mon noon–10pm, Wed–Sun noon–11pm.

Whether you land a table next to the brick oven at this celebrated pizza parlour or elect to go the quicker, cheaper route at the co-managed *Tony's Coal-Fired Pizza & Slice House* a couple of doors up the block, you'll think you've died and gone to pizza heaven. Come early to sample the extra-thin-crusted Margherita ($22), only 73 of which are made daily (see the menu to find out why).

Bars

Comstock Saloon

MAP P.46, POCKET MAP B11
155 Columbus Ave at Pacific Ave Ⓜ #8, #10, #12, #30, 45. ☎ 415 617 0071, Ⓦ comstocksaloon.com. Mon & Sun 4pm–midnight. Tues–Thurs 4pm–2am. Fri noon–2am, Sat 4pm–2am.

Its name a homage to the rich vein of Nevada silver that brought riches to San Francisco, Barbary Coast-styled *Comstock Saloon* offers excellent – if pricey – craft cocktails, rib-sticking pub grub (served until midnight) and hot jazz bands playing in the loft over the bar area.

Specs Twelve Adler Museum Cafe

MAP P.46, POCKET MAP B11
12 William Saroyan Place at Columbus Ave Ⓜ #8, #10, #12, #30, #45. Ⓣ 415 421 4112. Mon–Fri 4.30pm–2am, Sat & Sun 5pm–2am.

Welcoming dive *Specs* and its budget-priced drinks may be universally popular, but its bar-room is rarely as jam-packed as other stalwart public houses around North Beach. If you sit at the bar long enough, you're bound to befriend a chatty local eccentric or two.

Tonga Room & Hurricane Bar

MAP P.46, POCKET MAP A12
The Fairmont, 950 Mason St at California St Ⓜ #1; cable car: California. Ⓣ 415 772 5278, Ⓦ tongaroom.com. Wed, Thurs & Sun 5–11.30pm; Fri & Sat 5pm–12.30am.

Few luxury hotel bars can compete with this swanky tiki lounge for corny fun or happy-hour drink specials. Sham thunderstorms and a house band destroying jazz and pop

Vesuvio Cafe

standards on a thatched platform atop a small lagoon help set an ersatz, but unquestionably festive, South Seas mood.

Tony Nik's

MAP P.46, POCKET MAP A10
1534 Stockton St at Union St Ⓜ #8, #30, #39, #45; cable car: Powell-Mason. Ⓣ 415 693 0990, Ⓦ tonyniks.com. Mon–Fri 4pm–2am, Sat & Sun 2pm–2am.

This venerable watering hole's glass-brick exterior may not be the most inviting, but once inside, *Tony Nik's* stiff drinks and dimly lit vibe cement its status as one of this bar-rich neighbourhood's top places to knock a few back.

Tosca Cafe

MAP P.46, POCKET MAP B11
242 Columbus Ave at Pacific Ave Ⓜ #8, #10, #12, #30, #45. Ⓣ 415 986 9651, Ⓦ toscacafesf.com. Daily 5pm–2am.

Perhaps you'll slip into this legendary San Francisco bar for only one drink, or maybe you'll lose count of how many rounds you go through. Either way, most people in town seem to at least pass through this classy yet jovial spot where the jukebox plays nothing but opera.

Vesuvio Cafe

MAP P.46, POCKET MAP B11
255 Columbus Ave at Broadway Ⓜ #8, #10, #12, #30, #45. Ⓣ 415 362 3370, Ⓦ vesuvio.com. Daily 6am–2am.

You'd think this former Kerouac hangout would have lost its cachet in all the decades since, but it remains as good a place for a drink and lengthy philosophical discourse as any saloon in North Beach.

Club

Sip Bar & Lounge

MAP P.46, POCKET MAP A11
787 Broadway at Powell St Ⓜ #10, #12, #30, #45; cable car: Powell-Hyde, Powell-Mason. Ⓣ 415 699 6545, Ⓦ siploungesf.com. Fri & Sat 9pm–2am. No cover.

Beach Blanket Babylon

Despite the lack of a dress code, amber-hued *Sip* on the North Beach/Chinatown cusp retains an air of stylishness as DJs play mainstream hip-hop and R&B each weekend. Make sure that you visit the website to RSVP for entry.

Live music, comedy & show

Beach Blanket Babylon

MAP P.46, POCKET MAP A10
Club Fugazi, 678 Green St at Powell St Ⓜ #8, #30, #39, #45; cable car: Powell-Mason. ☎ 415 421 4222, Ⓦ beachblanketbabylon.com. $25–155.
Equal parts *Snow White*, *Saturday Night Live* and *The Daily Show*, this unflagging show – the longest-running musical revue in the US – and its extravagant wigs never seem to lose steam. It debuted in 1974 in North Beach, became a San Francisco trademark along the way and, playing seven times weekly (Wed–Fri 8pm; Sat 6pm & 9pm; Sun 2pm & 5pm), remains timely through ongoing script rewrites that lampoon current events and celebrities.

Bimbo's 365 Club

MAP P.46, POCKET MAP J1
1025 Columbus Ave at Chestnut St Ⓜ #8, #30; cable car: Powell-Mason. ☎ 415 474 0365, Ⓦ bimbos365club.com. Most tickets $12–45.
A historic venue dating from the 1930s with a plush red interior, supper club *Bimbo's* books a wide range of shows, from American indie rock and rising European acts to kitschy tribute bands playing Neil Diamond covers.

Cobb's Comedy Club

MAP P.46, POCKET MAP J2
915 Columbus Ave at Lombard St Ⓜ #8, #30; cable car: Powell-Mason. ☎ 415 928 4320, Ⓦ cobbscomedy.com. $20–35, plus two-drink minimum.
Booking major names such as Andrew Dice Clay and Jon Lovitz, as well as lesser-known touring comedians, 400-seat *Cobb's* is always a solid choice for a night of laughs. Each Monday's showcase features a hodgepodge of local comic talent.

The Saloon

MAP P.46, POCKET MAP A11
1232 Grant Ave at Vallejo St Ⓜ #8, #10, #12, #30, #45. ☎ 415 989 7666, Ⓦ sfblues.net/Saloon.html. $5 Fri & Sat.
Many claim this gritty, yet lively and friendly, dive – once a turn-of-the-century whorehouse, then a speakeasy during Prohibition – is the oldest bar in San Francisco. One thing that's not in doubt: it's the top place in town to hear blues bands playing nightly. Cash only.

The northern waterfront

From Pier 39's rowdy sea lions, Pacific Heights' masterfully preserved Victorian architecture and all the living maritime history on display at Hyde Street Pier, on through the tourist tackiness at Fisherman's Wharf and acres of open space at Fort Mason and the Presidio, there's something for nearly everyone along the city's northern waterfront. Add to this diverse list the fabled island penitentiary of Alcatraz and the spectacular rotunda of the Palace of Fine Arts, and there's little doubt that you'll at least drop into this sizeable area. And, of course, topping the chart of the northern waterfront's hit parade is the ever-wondrous Golden Gate Bridge, San Francisco's quintessential symbol of style and grace.

Alcatraz

MAP P.58, POCKET MAP K1
Accessible via ferry from Pier 33 (Ⓜ #8, #39, F); frequent departures; included in price of tour ☎ 415 981 7625, Ⓦ alcatrazcruises.com. Early March to early Nov 8.45am–3.50pm; early Nov to early March 9.10am–1.55pm. Day tour $37.25, night tour (Thurs–Mon: early March to early Nov 5.55pm & 6.30pm, early Nov to early March 4.20pm) $44.25.

Alcatraz

With over one million visitors ferried annually to this former stockade, the bleak island of **Alcatraz** clearly continues to stir public imagination. Originally built as a US Army prison in 1912, it became the country's most infamous federal penitentiary in 1934, incarcerating America's highest-profile criminals. Nonetheless, the maximum-security fortress – surrounded by frigid, churning waters that made escape nigh on impossible – turned out to be financially unsound and was abandoned in 1963. Six years later, a group of Native Americans staged a peaceful occupation, citing an agreement denoting that federal lands not in use should revert to their original ownership. Within two years, though, the US government claimed that Alcatraz's working lighthouse deemed it active; in 1972, the island became part of the new Golden Gate National Recreation Area. A compelling audio tour guides you through the prison's grim environs, with several free ranger presentations also available.

Fisherman's Wharf

MAP P.58, POCKET MAP J1–K1

Ⓜ #8, #19, #30, #39, #47, #49, F; cable car: Powell–Hyde, Powell–Mason.
Its once-mighty fishing industry rendered virtually obsolete, **Fisherman's Wharf** has long since taken on the thankless role of San Francisco's dockside amusement park of sorts – a gaudy collection of cheap souvenir retailers, tacky street performers and decent (if horribly overpriced) seafood restaurants. Numerous bay cruises depart from Piers 39, 41 and 43 several times daily, and a couple of worthwhile attractions do exist here (see below), but you'll be hard-pressed to find actual fishermen, let alone many remnants of their trade. A sure pick for laughs is the motley crew of barking sea lions that – assuming they haven't migrated elsewhere along the Pacific coast in search of a better selection of herring – congregate in an unceasing cacophony on the floating platforms between piers 39 and 41.

Aquarium of the Bay

MAP P.58, POCKET MAP K1
Pier 39 Ⓜ #8, #39, #47, F. ☏ 415 623 5300, Ⓦ aquariumofthebay.com. Check website for current hours. $24.95, children (4–12) $14.95.

Although major sea life enthusiasts will want to head 100-plus miles down the Pacific coast to the world-renowned Monterey Bay Aquarium, the **Aquarium of the Bay** certainly fits the bill for convenience and cost. Its top draws are a fun river otter exhibit and a pair of 300ft viewing tunnels allowing up-close encounters with beautiful leopard sharks, graceful bat rays and lumbering giant sea bass. Behind-the-scenes tours are available for an additional $15–25, including one that allows participants to feed pails of (dead) squid to the marine animals on display in the viewing tunnels.

Musée Méchanique

MAP P.58, POCKET MAP J1

Musée Méchanique

Pier 45 Ⓜ #39, #47, F. ☏ 415 346 2000, Ⓦ museemechanique.org. Mon–Fri 10am–7pm, Sat & Sun 10am–8pm. Free.
The Wharf's top destination for old-time fun is the **Musée Méchanique**, where an abundant collection of vintage arcade machines summons every coin in your pocket. Many of the Musée's 200-plus, painstakingly maintained mechanical games – ranging from 1920s hand-operated baseball games with tiny figurines, to antique love-testers and player pianos, to Galaga and Ms. Pac Man – are relics from Playland-at-the-Beach, San Francisco's bygone seaside amusement park. The Musée's highest-profile Playland refugee is Laffing Sal, a towering funhouse freak whose roaring guffaw often reverberates around the giant shed.

Aquatic Park

MAP P.58, POCKET MAP J1
Bordered by Jefferson, Hyde and Beach sts Ⓜ #19, #30, #47, #49, F; cable car: Powell–Hyde.
Part of the low-key but captivating San Francisco Maritime National

Aquatic Park

was the primary dumping ground for much of the city's rubble. The grassy park has a small beach where bold swimmers take bracing dips in San Francisco Bay, and with views and benches galore, it's also a fine place for a picnic, well placed as it is at the northern terminus of the Powell-Hyde cable-car line.

Overlooking the sandy spit near the park's southwest corner, the graceful, circa-1939 Aquatic Park Bathhouse is a Streamline Moderne-styled beauty from the twilight of the Art Deco era; it's now the Maritime Museum (daily 10am–4pm; free) featuring colourful murals of fanciful sea creatures in its ground-floor lobby.

Historical Park, **Aquatic Park** is a far more attractive sight today than during the clean-up following the 1906 earthquake and fire, when it

Hyde Street Pier

MAP P.58, POCKET MAP J1

Ⓜ #19, #30, #47, #49, F; cable car: Powell-Hyde. ☎ 415 447 5000, Ⓦ www. nps.gov/safr. Daily 9.30am–5pm. Entry to the ships $10.

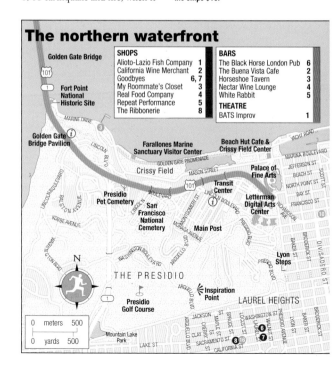

The northern waterfront

SHOPS

Alioto-Lazio Fish Company	1
California Wine Merchant	2
Goodbyes	6, 7
My Roommate's Closet	3
Real Food Company	4
Repeat Performance	5
The Ribbonerie	8

BARS

The Black Horse London Pub	6
The Buena Vista Cafe	2
Horseshoe Tavern	3
Nectar Wine Lounge	4
White Rabbit	5

THEATRE

BATS Improv	1

Hyde Street Pier and its six permanently docked ships anchor San Francisco Maritime National Historical Park with an atmospheric air. Before making your way onto the wooden-planked pier – originally used in the early decades of the 1900s to serve Sausalito ferries before the opening of the Golden Gate Bridge – step into the visitor centre at 499 Jefferson St to look at hand-rotated maps detailing the extensive changes San Francisco's shoreline has undergone since the nineteenth century.

Once out on the pier itself, purchase tickets to tour the swaying, lovingly preserved ships, the most alluring of which is 1886's Balclutha, a lanky, Scottish-constructed square-rigger that sailed around Cape Horn in the 1800s before eventually landing a Hollywood role in Mutiny on the Bounty. Another showboat

here worth a look is the stout, circa-1890 steamer Eureka, once the largest passenger vessel in the world, and formerly used as a car ferry; fittingly enough, it's now stocked with classic automobiles.

Fort Mason

MAP P.58, POCKET MAP H1
Ⓜ #19, #28, #30, #47, #49.

Having pulled duty as a defence bulkhead during California's Spanish colonial era, smelting centre and shantytown in the nineteenth century, locals' refugee camp immediately after the 1906 earthquake and fire, and troop embarkation point during World War II, **Fort Mason**'s current role as grassy public expanse and home to numerous cultural and educational organizations is decidedly more peaceful than anything that preceded it.

Upper Fort Mason is composed of hilltop parkland and a hostel (see

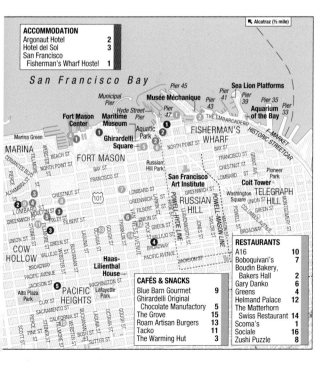

The dining room of the Haas-Lilienthal House

page 147) set in a converted Civil War barracks, behind which are a few choice bluff-side picnic areas. Lower Fort Mason, better known as the Fort Mason Center (☎415 345 7500, ⓦfortmason.org), is also well worth a visit for its varied complex of theatre companies, small galleries and museums, and Greens restaurant (see page 65), all set amid preserved warehouses and wharves.

Haas-Lilienthal House
MAP P.58, POCKET MAP H3
2007 Franklin St at Jackson St Ⓜ #1, #10, #19, #27, #47, #49. ☎415 441 3000, ⓦsfheritage.org. Tours every 20–30min Wed & Sat noon–3pm, Sun 11am–4pm. Tours $8.
San Francisco's sole Queen Anne-style Victorian home open to the public, the sprawling **Haas-Lilienthal House** was custom-built for German-born grocer William Haas in 1886, and was occupied by Haas' descendants until 1972. Today, tours offer a close look at how Pacific Heights' elite once lived. Built from sturdy redwood, the house suffered only minor damage in the catastrophic

earthquakes of 1906 and 1989, so a great deal of its original furniture remains on display, including Tiffany art-glass and stencilled leather wall panelling.

Palace of Fine Arts
MAP P.58, POCKET MAP F2
3301 Lyon St Ⓜ #28, #30.
Built for 1915's Panama-Pacific International Exhibition – a world fair that confirmed San Francisco's return to the international spotlight after the destruction the city endured nine years earlier – the **Palace of Fine Arts** perseveres as one of the Bay Area's signature architectural pieces. While its arch name suggests a grand museum of sorts, the Palace is actually an enormous open rotunda masterminded by prominent Berkeley architect Bernard Maybeck, and it was the sole structure from the Panama-Pacific Expo to avoid the wrecking ball once the event ended – chiefly because locals had become instantly smitten with its classical design. Originally constructed of wood, plaster and burlap, the monumental structure gradually

crumbled through the decades until it was recast in reinforced concrete in the 1960s. Another seismic refit completed in 2011 has the Palace and adjacent park looking better than ever, while the path circling the swan lagoon in front of the rotunda has always been a fine place for a romantic stroll.

The Presidio

MAP P.58, POCKET MAP E2

Ⓜ #1, #2, #3, #29, #30, #43, #45; PresidiGo Shuttle from Downtown. Visitor centre: 210 Lincoln Blvd at Main Post (daily 10am–5pm). ☎ 415 561 4323, Ⓦ nps. gov/prsf.

A military stronghold for more than two centuries, the **Presidio** of today plays a wide range of roles: vast open space of woodland-covered hills and windswept beaches; historic military outpost and burial ground; and, not least of all, home to scores of non-profit organizations and for-profit businesses (including a small bowling alley) that help make the 1480-acre National Park Service property financially self-sustaining.

Orient yourself at the Presidio's visitor centre, then set out for any number of destinations, including the unbeatable bay vista at Inspiration Point, the Walt Disney Family Museum, Society of California Pioneers museum and the Presidio Pet Cemetery, where you can pay respects to deceased army pets such as Frisky, Smoochy, Skippy and Moocher. A growing network of hiking and running trails also threads through the Presidio's hilly expanse.

Crissy Field

MAP P.58, POCKET MAP E3

PresidiGo Shuttle from Main Post and Letterman District.

Stretching west from near the Palace of Fine Arts to Golden Gate Bridge along San Francisco Bay, **Crissy Field** was the National Park Service's initial stab at reclamation in the Presidio once the property was relinquished by the US Army and became part of Golden Gate National Recreation Area in 1994. What was originally a salt marsh and estuary was landfilled for the 1915 Panama-Pacific International Exhibition, then used as a military airfield, evinced by the since-repurposed hangars beyond the west end of Crissy Field's huge, grassy expanse.

Finally, in the late 1990s, the ambitious, volunteer-driven project of restoring the area to something resembling its natural state got under way, and today it's a hugely popular destination – and certainly the Presidio's most visited – for walking, running, cycling, roller skating, birdwatching and windsurfing, or unleashing the pooch at the dog-friendly beach.

Fort Point National Historic Site

MAP P.58, POCKET MAP D1

Ⓜ #28. ☎ 415 556 1693, Ⓦ nps.gov/fopo. Fri–Sun 10am–5pm. Candlelight tour Sat only Nov–Feb. Entry and tours free.

Unimaginable as it may seem today, the stout brick masonry of **Fort Point** was saved only

Fort Point National Historic Site

by the ingenious architecture of the Golden Gate Bridge directly above, for until the idea of building a huge arch under the bridge's southern terminus was suggested, the fastness was set to be demolished. The US military built Fort Point in the 1850s at the mouth of San Francisco Bay to protect the rapidly growing city from potential incursions by sea, and its cannons were first mounted in 1861, the year the US Civil War began; its final army duty came during World War II, when an artillery regiment used the fort to oversee the anti-submarine net then stretching across the Golden Gate. Exhibits in the main fort highlight the roles of African American soldiers in the US military, as well as the construction of the bridge. Today, military buffs will want to book a spot on one of the fortress's winter-time candlelight tours.

Golden Gate Bridge

MAP P.58, POCKET MAP D1
Ⓜ #28. $7.50 driving toll southbound, free northbound and to pedestrians and cyclists.

Golden Gate Bridge from the Presidio

In a city rich with iconic images, few will contest that the **Golden Gate Bridge** tops the list. The 4200ft suspension bridge was originally slated to be grey, but its so-called international orange primer coat proved so popular that it has endured since the span's 1937 debut. Equal parts architectural and engineering triumph, the flexible bridge was designed to swing up to 27ft (and sag up to 10ft) in the violent gusts that can blow through San Francisco Bay's passage into the Pacific Ocean. Whether bathed in sunshine, shrouded in fog or twinkling on a clear night, the Art Deco wonder never suffers a bad day in the mirror; its best close-up vistas are from Baker Beach (see page 121) or Crissy Field (see page 61) in the Presidio, Fort Point directly below, the Marin Headlands (see page 61), the Golden Gate Bridge Pavilion (daily 9am-6pm) at the southern end and, of course, the pedestrian path on the bridge itself. Allow up to two hours for the round-trip walk next to the northbound lanes of the roadway and dress for windy conditions regardless.

Shops

Alioto-Lazio Fish Company

MAP P.58, POCKET MAP J1
440 Jefferson St at Leavenworth St Ⓜ #30, #47, F; cable car: Powell–Hyde. ☏ 415 673 5868, Ⓦ crabonline.com. Mon–Fri 6am–2pm, Sat 7am–noon.

A working fish company that's part seafood retailer and part living museum, friendly Alioto-Lazio is worth a short stop to soak up its authenticity, even if you're not looking to take a freshly caught California wild king salmon or Dungeness crab home with you.

California Wine Merchant

MAP P.58, POCKET MAP G2
2113 Chestnut St at Steiner St Ⓜ #22, #28, #30, #43. ☏ 415 567 0646, Ⓦ californiawinemerchant.com. Mon–Wed 11am–midnight, Thurs–Sat 11–1.30am, Sun 11am–11pm.

Heaven for wine aficionados, this venerable space serves as a wine bar and retailer, a handy combination that allows you to taste the varietals before you invest in a bottle or case.

Goodbyes

MAP P.58, POCKET MAP F3
3483 Sacramento St at Laurel St Ⓜ #1, #2, #3, #43. ☏ 415 674 0151, Ⓦ goodbyessf.com. Mon–Wed, Fri & Sat 10am–6pm, Thurs 10am–8pm, Sun 11am–5pm.

A terrific secondhand women's apparel boutique full of designer items at consignment prices, Goodbyes also operates an equally excellent men's shop right across Sacramento St at no. 3462, as well as a women's sale store at no. 3464 (both ☏ 415 346 6388).

My Roommate's Closet

MAP P.58, POCKET MAP H2
3044 Fillmore St at Union St Ⓜ #22, #45. ☏ 415 447 7703, Ⓦ shopmrc.com. Mon–Sat 11am–7pm, Sun noon–6pm.

Even devoted thrift-shop fashionistas will enjoy this popular women's shop in prim Cow Hollow, where all priced-to-sell

The Ribbonerie

items are brand-new overstocks from top designers.

Real Food Company

MAP P.58, POCKET MAP J2
2140 Polk St at Vallejo St Ⓜ #19, #45, #47, #49. ☏ 415 567 6900, Ⓦ realfoodco.com. Daily 8am–9pm.

Locally based grocer Real Food Company features a strong selection of organic foods and vitamins, and the wrought-iron picnic tables on its front terrace make a nice spot to enjoy items from the on-site deli.

Repeat Performance

MAP P.58, POCKET MAP H3
2436 Fillmore St at Jackson St Ⓜ #3, #10, #22, #24. ☏ 415 563 3123, Ⓦ shopsfsymphony.org/shop/Symphony-Stores.html. Mon–Sat 10am–5.30pm.

The fundraising retail arm of the San Francisco Symphony, this pricey secondhand shop sells everything from apparel, jewellery and homeware to art and books, all in excellent condition.

The Ribbonerie

MAP P.58, POCKET MAP F3
3695 Sacramento St at Spruce St Ⓜ #1, #2, #33. ☏ 415 626 6184, Ⓦ ribbonerie.com. Tues–Sat 10.30am–5.30pm.

There can't be many retailers in the world exclusively devoted to ribbons, thimbles, pincushions and the like... but even if there are, this owner-operated shop is surely one of the finest.

Cafés and snacks

Blue Barn Gourmet

MAP P.58, POCKET MAP G2
2105 Chestnut St at Steiner St Ⓜ #22, #28, #30, #43. ☎ 415 441 3232, Ⓦ bluebarngourmet.com. Mon–Fri 11am–8.30pm, Sat & Sun 11am–8pm.
A faux-rural spot in the distinctly urbane Marina district, this sandwich and salad shop is a top place to grab yourself a takeaway meal for under $15. Highlights include the spicy tuna salad with mango, sesame seeds and soba noodles.

Ghirardelli Original Chocolate Manufactory

MAP P.58, POCKET MAP J1
Ghirardelli Square, 900 North Point St at Larkin St Ⓜ #19, #30, #47, #49; cable car: Powell–Hyde. ☎ 415 474 3938, Ⓦ ghirardelli.com. Mon–Thurs & Sun 9am–11pm, Fri & Sat 9am–midnight.
Rich with the aroma of sweet waffle cones, this old-fashioned ice-cream parlour is hugely popular with groups sharing the Earthquake sundae ($39.95), essentially an eight-scoop banana split.

The Grove

MAP P.58, POCKET MAP H3
2016 Fillmore St at Pine St Ⓜ #1, #2, #3, #22. ☎ 415 474 1419, Ⓦ thegrovesf.com. Mon–Thurs 7am–11pm, Fri 7am–11.30pm, Sat 8am–11.30pm, Sun 8am–11pm.
This always-humming spot plays multiple roles well, offering everything from coffee, tea, snacks, desserts and casual meals mains $12.75–14.75) to a respectable variety of beer and wine (and even the odd soju cocktail). There's comfortable seating throughout, whether indoors near the fireplace or outdoors along Fillmore Street.

Roam Artisan Burgers

MAP P.58, POCKET MAP H2
1785 Union St at Octavia St Ⓜ #45. ☎ 415 440 7626, Ⓦ roamburgers.com. Daily 11.30am–10pm.
Customize your own burger from an extensive list of ingredients – or simply order one of the house specials ($11) – at this pleasant spot along Union Street. Bison and elk meat, sweet home-made sodas and extra-thick shakes are among the menu's unique twists.

Tacko

MAP P.58, POCKET MAP G2
3115 Fillmore St at Filbert St Ⓜ #22, #28, #43, #45. ☎ 415 796 3534, Ⓦ tackosf.com. Mon–Thurs & Sun 11.30am–10pm, Fri & Sat 11.30am–11pm.
Irrespective of whether you can remember that the name of this airy Cow Hollow taqueria indeed rhymes with "Paco", you'll be in for some of the tastiest tacos and burritos ($3.95–11.75) you'll find in this part of the city.

The Warming Hut

MAP P.58, POCKET MAP E1
Crissy Field, 983 Marine Dr. PresidiGo Shuttle from Main Post and Letterman District. ☎ 415 561 3040. Mon–Thurs 9am–6pm. Fri–Sun 9am–7pm.
As you walk or bike along Crissy Field's paths, stop at this white clapboard building near the Torpedo Wharf pier to enjoy a cheap, casual lunch at one of the neighbouring picnic tables boasting incomparable views of the Golden Gate Bridge.

Restaurants

A16

MAP P.58, POCKET MAP G2
2355 Chestnut St at Divisadero St Ⓜ #28, #30, #43. ☎ 415 771 2216, Ⓦ a16pizza. com. Mon & Tues 5.30–10pm, Wed & Thurs 11.30am–2.30pm & 5.30–10pm, Fri 11.30am–2.30pm & 5.30–11pm, Sat 11.30am–2.30pm & 5–11pm, Sun 11.30am–2.30pm & 5–10pm.

Named after a highway that crosses Italy, sleek and narrow *A16* is continually thronged for its Neapolitan-style pizzas ($18–22), while the house-cured salumi plate ($18) is another popular item that draws in the crowds.

Boboquivari's

MAP P.58, POCKET MAP H2
1450 Lombard St at Van Ness Ave
Ⓜ #19, #30, #47, #49. ☏ 415 441 8880,
Ⓦ boboquivaris.com. Daily 5–11pm.
Although it's hard to forgive its striped exterior and clown-house-inspired decor, this bi-level steakhouse (regulars call it simply Bobo's) remains the home of San Francisco's finest and most tender bone-in filet mignon ($49.95). Dungeness crab ($42.95) and iron-skillet-roasted mussels ($18.95) also feature prominently, and the desserts are uncommonly delicious.

Boboquivari's

Boudin Bakery, Bakers Hall

MAP P.58, POCKET MAP J1
160 Jefferson St at Mason St Ⓜ #8, #10, #12, #30, #39, #45; cable car: Powell-Mason. ☏ 415 928 1849, Ⓦ boudinbakery.com. Sun–Thurs 8am–8.30pm, Fri & Sat 8am–10pm.
Laid-back café serving some of the finest sourdough around, made using yeast descended from the first batch from Gold Rush times. A variety of cheap salads, sandwiches and sourdough pizzas are available, in addition to the inevitable chowder in a bread bowl.

Gary Danko

MAP P.58, POCKET MAP J1
800 North Point St at Hyde St Ⓜ #19, #30, #47; cable car: Powell-Hyde. ☏ 415 749 2060, Ⓦ garydanko.com. Daily 5pm–midnight.
The epitome of eating out in a city that seemingly can't get enough of it, a meal at five-star *Gary Danko* is completely worth the investment if you appreciate "performance food". Reserve well in advance and pack your credit card, as a five-course tasting menu costs $124.

Greens

MAP P.58, POCKET MAP H1
Fort Mason Center, Building A Ⓜ #28.

Roam Artisan Burgers

Scoma's

#10, #12, #30, #39, #45; cable car: Powell-Mason. ☎ 415 885 6116, ⓦ thematterhornrestaurant.com. Tues–Sun 5–9.30pm.

Lurking at the foot of a nondescript apartment building, this restaurant is known for its cheese, beef and chocolate fondues; its ski-lodge decor was shipped in pieces from the Swiss motherland and reassembled on site. Beef fondues for two are $51; cheese fondues for two, $45.50.

Scoma's

MAP P.58, POCKET MAP J2
Pier 47 ⓜ #47, F. ☎ 415 771 4383, ⓦ scomas.com. Mon–Thurs & Sun 11.30am–10pm, Fri & Sat 11.30am–10.30pm.

Though legendarily thronged, *Scoma's* is the best bet for a seafood meal at Fisherman's Wharf. Reserve well ahead and be aware of the pricing structure you'll be getting involved with – a plate of seafood pasta can cost up to $38.

Sociale

MAP P.58, POCKET MAP F3
3665 Sacramento St at Spruce St ⓜ #1, #2, #33. ☎ 415 921 3200, ⓦ sfsociale.com. Mon 5.30–10pm, Tues–Sat 11.30am–2.30pm & 5.30–10pm.

Set at the end of a lush pedestrian lane, and with several outdoor tables in a lovely heated courtyard, few San Francisco restaurants are more romantic than Italian-slanted *Sociale*. Whatever main you choose, begin with the fontina-stuffed fried olives starter ($11).

Zushi Puzzle

MAP P.58, POCKET MAP H2
1910 Lombard St at Buchanan St ⓜ #22, #28, #30, #43. ☎ 415 931 9319, ⓦ zushipuzzle.com. Mon–Sat 5–10.30pm.

This festive neighbourhood favourite specializes in exotic sashimi and nigiri- and maki-style sushi, all at reasonable prices – most four-piece sashimi choices cost about $11.

☎ 415 771 6222, ⓦ greensrestaurant.com. Tues–Thurs 11.45am–2.30pm & 5.30–9pm, Fri 11.45am–2.30pm & 5.30–9.30pm, Sat 11am–2.30pm & 5.30–9.30pm, Sun 10.30am–2pm & 5.30–9pm.

Inventive dinner mains on the seasonally changing menu cost from $19.50 to $28 at this delightful vegetarian spot – the first such restaurant in San Francisco (it opened in 1979). Reserve well ahead and be sure to request a window-side table for stunning bay views.

Helmand Palace

MAP P.58, POCKET MAP J2
2424 Van Ness Ave at Green St ⓜ #8, #10, #12, #30, #39, #45; cable car: Powell-Mason. ☎ 415 345 0072, ⓦ helmandpalacesf.com. Mon–Thurs & Sun 5.30–10pm, Fri & Sat 5.30–11pm.

The menu at this popular Afghan restaurant is filled with tangy and spicy staples – try the *kaddo* (caramelized pumpkin on a bed of yoghurt) or the *chapandaz* (grilled beef tenderloin). Plenty of vegetarian items are also available. Mains cost around $14–23.

The Matterhorn Swiss Restaurant

MAP P.58, POCKET MAP J2
2323 Van Ness Ave at Vallejo St ⓜ #8,

Bars

The Black Horse London Pub

MAP P.58, POCKET MAP H2
1514 Union St at Van Ness Ave Ⓜ #19, #45, #47, #49. ☎ 415 928 2414, Ⓦ blackhorselondon.com. Mon–Thurs 5pm–midnight. Fri 2pm–midnight. Sat & Sun 11am–midnight.

Although its front sign calls it a deli, the only thing vaguely deli-like about this tiny, English-style beer pub is its fine cheese plate. Shoehorn yourself in at the slim bar, sip a Chimay and enjoy a gab with the friendly bartenders. Cash only.

The Buena Vista Cafe

MAP P.58, POCKET MAP J1
2765 Hyde St at Beach St Ⓜ #19, #30, #47, F; cable car: Powell-Hyde. ☎ 415 474 5044, Ⓦ thebuenavista.com. Mon–Fri 9am–2am, Sat & Sun 8am–2am.

The local story goes that the *Buena Vista* is the North American birthplace of Irish coffee, and this ancient bar-restaurant across from Aquatic Park claims to churn out up to two thousand glasses of the house special ($10) daily.

Horseshoe Tavern

MAP P.58, POCKET MAP G2
2024 Chestnut St at Fillmore St Ⓜ #22, #28, #30, #43. ☎ 415 346 1430, Ⓦ horseshoetavern-sf.com. Mon–Fri noon–2am. Sat & Sun 10am–2am.

An anomaly along super-stylish Chestnut Street, this unpretentious tavern is a great place to play a couple of games of pool and catch a San Francisco Giants game on the TV over cheap beers or stiff cocktails.

Nectar Wine Lounge

MAP P.58, POCKET MAP G2
3330 Steiner St at Chestnut St Ⓜ #22, #28, #30, #43. ☎ 415 345 1377, Ⓦ nectarwinelounge.com. Mon–Thurs 5–10.30pm, Fri & Sat 5pm–midnight, Sun 5–10pm.

Fittingly smart and youthful for the Marina, sophisticated *Nectar Wine Lounge* wields a near-endless list of choices (at a variety of prices), augmented by a limited food menu.

White Rabbit

MAP P.58, POCKET MAP H2
3138 Fillmore St at Pixley St Ⓜ #22, #28, #43, #45; cable car: Powell-Mason. ☎ 415 993 5399, Ⓦ whiterabbitsf.com. Wed–Sun 5pm–2am.

This popular neighbourhood watering hole (originally opened in 1965 by *Jefferson Airplane*'s Marty Balin) was rebranded in 2018 with eclectic music and craft beers on tap.

Theatre

BATS Improv

MAP P.58, POCKET MAP H1
Bayfront Theater, Fort Mason Center Ⓜ #28. ☎ 415 474 6776, Ⓦ improv.org. Shows every Fri & Sat 8pm. Tickets from $17.

This groundbreaking company was one of the first to present a long-form version of the improv format; decades later, it's still one of the top ensembles in the area.

The Buena Vista cafe

South of Market

Markedly different from the city's other neighbourhoods, South of Market feels more open than much of hemmed-in San Francisco. Wide, multilane boulevards define this district's diagonal grid where the city's industrial past has been smartened up for the present: residential lofts, trendy restaurants, compelling museums and exuberant nightclubs now occupy bygone factories, workshops and even power stations. South of Market also abuts San Francisco Bay, where the southern stretch of the Embarcadero leads to the churning area around AT&T Park, a prime destination for over 40,000 fans nightly during the long months of the baseball season. Another hive of daily activity is Yerba Buena Gardens and the several museums that flank it, including the San Francisco Museum of Modern Art, reopened following an ambitious expansion project.

Cupid's Span

MAP P.70, POCKET MAP L3
The Embarcadero, between Howard and Folsom sts Ⓜ N, T; Ⓔ Embarcadero.
Certainly the most blithe element of the Embarcadero's ongoing, high-profile revitalization, 64ft-tall **Cupid's Span** wasn't without its detractors when it was first unveiled. However, as is often the case with controversial public art – a major local exception being

The ballroom at the Palace Hotel

nearby Vaillancourt Fountain (see page 29) – sceptical locals have mostly hushed up since this gigantic bow and arrow was installed a few steps from San Francisco Bay in 2002. Designed by celebrated pop-art sculptors Claes Oldenburg and Coosje van Bruggen in their characteristic-ally vivacious style, the stainless-steel work was intended to evoke San Francisco's reputation as one of the world's most romantic cities. The artists' original sketches portrayed Cupid's arrow pointed skyward, but they ultimately decided to evoke the myth of Eros shooting into the ground to make the earth fertile, artfully slanting the bow and arrow, and partially burying it atop a small knoll, to great effect.

Palace Hotel

MAP P.70, POCKET MAP B12
2 New Montgomery St at Market St Ⓜ #2, #3, #8, #9, #10, #12, #14, F, J, K, L, M, N, T; Ⓔ Montgomery. Ⓣ 415 512 1111, Ⓦ sfpalace.com.
One of San Francisco's original opulent confections, the **Palace**

Museum of the African Diaspora

Hotel was opened in 1875 as lavish evidence of San Francisco's position as the wealthiest American city west of Chicago. Thirty-one years later, the *Palace* was devastated by the post-earthquake fires that torched much of the city, so today's *Palace* actually dates from 1909, by which time its original carriage entrance had been converted into the glass-ceilinged Garden Court dining and tea room, still the hotel's grandest space. Several international dignitaries have passed through the *Palace* over the years – most notably Soviet Premier Nikita Khrushchev, who addressed a banquet crowd here on a 1959 visit, and US President Warren Harding, who died unexpectedly in room 8064 in 1923.

California Historical Society

MAP P.70, POCKET MAP B13
678 Mission St at Third St Ⓜ #2, #3, #8, #9, #10, #12, #14, #30, #45, F, J, K, L, M, N, T; Ⓑ Montgomery. ☎ 415 357 1848, Ⓦ californiahistoricalsociety.org. Tues–Sun 11am–5pm. $5.

Even if you possess only a passing interest in the Golden State's past, the **California Historical Society**'s gallery and small bookshop are worth a visit. An ongoing series of exhibitions illuminates various aspects of California's short but lively history, from photography shows documenting the state's often-overlooked rural culture to in-depth portraits of individuals who have played crucial roles in California's remarkable development.

Museum of the African Diaspora

MAP P.70, POCKET MAP B13
685 Mission St at Third St Ⓜ #2, #3, #8, #9, #10, #12, #14, #30, #45, F, J, K, L, M, N, T; Ⓑ Montgomery. ☎ 415 358 7200, Ⓦ moadsf.org. Wed–Sat 11am–6pm, Sun noon–5pm. $10.

Through temporary exhibitions built around art, artefacts and modern media, as well as educational events, author talks and its own permanent exhibits, the three-storey **Museum of the African Diaspora** traces the migration of Africans throughout the world over the centuries. The narratives of slaves' escapes to freedom, which are voiced by a variety of actors and authors (including Maya Angelou), are particularly gripping.

San Francisco Museum of Modern Art

MAP P.70, POCKET MAP B13
151 Third St at Howard St Ⓜ #8, #9, #10, #12, #14, #30, #38, #45, F, J, K, L, M, N, T; Ⓑ Powell. ☎ 415 357 4000, Ⓦ sfmoma. org. Mon, Tues & Fri–Sun 10am–5pm. Thurs 10am–9pm (late May to early Sept open until 8pm Sat). $25.

Reopened in 2016 after a major renovation, the **San Francisco Museum of Modern Art** (SFMOMA) is the largest modern

Yerba Buena Gardens

art space in the US. Towering behind the museum's signature circa-1995 structure, the newly constructed ten-storey wing stretches narrowly for two-thirds of a block, doubling SFMOMA's original exhibition space and also helping to expand its programming by up to three times (most of its vast gallery space will be taken up with changing exhibits). The airy ground-floor space along Howard Street is art-filled and admission-free, while the new Pritzker Center upstairs is the largest space devoted solely to photography at any US art museum.

Yerba Buena Gardens

MAP P.70, POCKET MAP B13
Ⓜ #8, #9, #10, #12, #14, #30, #38, #45, F, J, K, L, M, N, T; Ⓑ Powell. ☎ 415 820 3550, Ⓦ yerbabuenagardens.com. Daily 6am–10pm. Free.

Inviting and grassy, the distinctly urban glade of **Yerba Buena Gardens** serves a multitude of purposes. Helping mitigate ambient city noise is an attractive series of cascades dedicated to Martin Luther King Jr, behind which you can walk through a stone corridor to read King quotations translated into a number of languages; back towards Mission Street, a small stage regularly

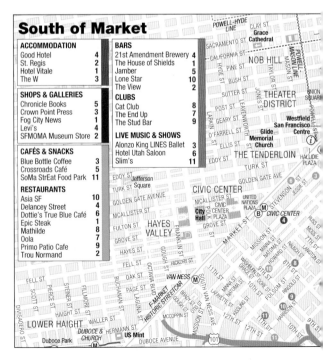

South of Market

ACCOMMODATION	
Good Hotel	4
St. Regis	2
Hotel Vitale	1
The W	3

SHOPS & GALLERIES	
Chronicle Books	5
Crown Point Press	3
Fog City News	1
Levi's	4
SFMOMA Museum Store	2

CAFÉS & SNACKS	
Blue Bottle Coffee	3
Crossroads Café	5
SoMa StrEat Food Park	11

RESTAURANTS	
Asia SF	10
Delancey Street	4
Dottie's True Blue Café	6
Epic Steak	1
Mathilde	8
Oola	7
Primo Patio Cafe	9
Trou Normand	2

BARS	
21st Amendment Brewery	4
The House of Shields	1
Jamber	5
Lone Star	10
The View	2

CLUBS	
Cat Club	8
The End Up	7
The Stud Bar	9

LIVE MUSIC & SHOWS	
Alonzo King LINES Ballet	3
Hotel Utah Saloon	6
Slim's	11

hosts free concerts between May and October (check ⓦybgfestival.org for current schedule).

Near the corner of Mission and Third streets is the **Yerba Buena Center for the Arts** (ⓣ415 978 2700, ⓦybca.org), a mixed-use space that comprises a performance theatre, art gallery and screening room for experimental films.

Yerba Buena Gardens also spreads across Howard Street, where you'll find the circa-1906 LeRoy King Carousel (daily 10am-5pm; $4) and an always-buzzing playground, as well as an ice rink, bowling alley and the Children's Creativity Museum (Wed-Sun 10am-4pm; $12; ⓦcreativity.org).

Contemporary Jewish Museum

MAP P.70, POCKET MAP B13
736 Mission St at Third St Ⓜ #8, #9, #10, #12, #14, #30, #38, #45, F, J, K, L, M, N, T; ⑥ Powell. ⓣ415 655 7800, ⓦthecjm.

org. Mon–Tues & Fri–Sun 11am–5pm, Thurs 11am–8pm. $14.

Walk up pedestrianized Yerba Buena Lane from Mission Street and look out for a massive cube lurking askew behind a church – this blue stainless-steel design quirk is a gallery within the **Contemporary Jewish Museum**'s brick home, itself a former power station. Although the museum doesn't maintain any permanent collection, its temporary exhibitions are consistently engaging: past shows have offered close looks at the history of Jewish settlement in the Bay Area and how elements of Jewish culture crept into popular black American music of the mid-twentieth century.

St Patrick Church

MAP P.70, POCKET MAP B13
756 Mission St, between 3rd and 4th sts Ⓜ #8, #9, #10, #12, #14, #30, #38, #45, F, J, K, L, M, N, T; ⑥ Powell. ⓣ415 421 3730,

ⓦ stpatricksf.org. Mon–Fri 6am–6.15pm, Sat & Sun 6am–6.45pm. Free.

On the north side of Yerba Buena Gardens lies **St Patrick Church**, a red-brick remnant of early San Francisco and its Irish Catholic community. Although the present Neo-Gothic edifice was completed in 1914, it was built on the earthquake-ravaged ruins of a church that served Irish gold miners in the 1850s. Inside, Irish green is represented by emerald Connemara marble pillars, and each of the patron saints of the 32 counties of Ireland is showcased on the grand Tiffany-style stained-glass windows.

Children's Creativity Museum

MAP P.70, POCKET MAP B13
221 4th St at Howard St ⓦ #8, #9, #10, #12, #14, #30, #38, #45, F, J, K, L, M, N, T; ⑧ Powell. ☎ 415 820 3320, ⓦ creativity. org. Tues–Sun 10am–4pm. $12.95 (under 2 years of age free).

The hands-on **Children's Creativity Museum** offers kids an innovative introduction to art and technology, with puppet theatres, magnetic storybooks, robot-coding activities, animation and music-recording

AT&T Park

studios, and sandpits designed to mimic landscapes. Rides on the LeRoy King Carousel are $3 extra.

AT&T Park

MAP P.70, POCKET MAP L4–M4
ⓦ #10, #30, #45, #47, N, T. ☎ 415 972 2400, ⓦ sfgiants.com. Tours on non-game days: June–Aug 10.30am, 11.30am, 12.30pm & 1.30pm; Sept–May 10.30am & 12.30pm, 90min, $22.

Upon opening amid great fanfare for the 2000 baseball season, red-brick-clad **AT&T Park** became an instant civic icon, helping set off a construction and real-estate boom in the China Basin/Mission Bay area that continues to this day. Purpose-built for baseball and privately funded, the San Francisco Giants' gleaming ballpark is set dramatically next to the bay, where especially well-swatted home runs to right field are fished out of the water by kayakers. The park's open outfield ensures striking views, while the action on the field has been superbly exciting of late: following a fallow period of over 50 years without a championship, the Giants earned World Series titles in 2010, 2012 and 2014. Given the team's recent success, tickets can be quite difficult (and rarely cheap) to come by, so one clever option is to queue up for a three-inning standing-room-only spot behind the right field fence, free of charge.

City Kayak

MAP P.70, POCKET MAP K1
Pier 40, the Embarcadero ⓦ #10, N, T. ☎ 415 294 1050, ⓦ citykayak.com. Check website for seasonal hours. $35/hour, $69/day.

If you'd like to give kayaking on San Francisco Bay a go, the water around **City Kayak** offers a unique perspective on the city's bay-side sights and the nearby Bay Bridge. Rent vessels and gear from the South Beach Harbor-based kayaking tour operator in the morning, when the water is often at its calmest.

Shops and galleries

Chronicle Books

MAP P.70, POCKET MAP B13
165 Fourth St at Howard St Ⓜ #8, #9,
#10, #12, #14, #30, #38, #45, F, J, K,
L, M, N, T; Ⓑ Powell. ☎ 415 369 6271,
Ⓦ chroniclebooks.com/retail-locations.
Mon–Thurs & Sun 10.30am–8.30pm, Fri &
Sat 10.30am–9.30pm.
A retail outlet for this local
publisher's wide range of books,
this entertaining shop features
everything from cookbooks by
brand-name chefs to titles devoted
to New Wave album covers, and
a variety of other items such as
vintage-style lunch pails.

Crown Point Press

MAP P.70, POCKET MAP C13
20 Hawthorne St at Howard St Ⓜ #8,
#10, #12, #14, #30, #45; Ⓑ Montgomery.
☎ 415 974 6273, Ⓦ crownpoint.com. Mon
10am–5pm, Tues–Sat 10am–6pm.
This intriguing space holds a gallery
for compelling shows by European,
Japanese and American artists (with
prints for sale), plus a working
studio and small bookshop.

Fog City News

MAP P.70, POCKET MAP C12
455 Market St at First St Ⓜ #2, #3,
#8, #9, #10, #12, #14, F, J, K, L, M, N,
T; Ⓑ Montgomery. ☎ 415 543 7400,
Ⓦ fogcitynews.com. Mon–Fri 10am–7pm,
Sat 11am–6pm.
On the face of it, this long and
narrow shopfront simply looks
like a handsome, amber-toned
newsstand. Step inside, though,
to discover a wide selection of
premium chocolate bars, as well as
greeting cards and tobacco.

Levi's

MAP P.70, POCKET MAP B13
815 Market St at Fourth St Ⓜ #9, #14, #27,
#31, F, J, K, L, M, N, T; Ⓑ Powell. ☎ 415 501
0100, Ⓦ levi.com. Mon–Sat 9am–9pm, Sun
10am–8pm.

SFMOMA Museum Store

It's worth visiting the flagship
store of this iconic brand, where
you'll find jeans (naturally) and
other apparel. Staff can be overly
assiduous at times and prices
vary wildly, but the impressive
selection compensates.

SFMOMA Museum Store

MAP P.70, POCKET MAP B13
151 Third St at Howard St Ⓜ #8, #9,
#10, #12, #14, #30, #38, #45, F, J, K,
L, M, N, T; Ⓑ Powell. ☎ 415 357 4000,
Ⓦ museumstore.sfmoma.org. Mon, Tues,
Fri & Sun 10am–6pm, Wed 10am–5pm,
Thurs 10am–9.30pm, Sat 10am–8pm.
The art store attached to the San
Francisco Museum of Modern
Art is a trove of custom prints,
creative jewellery, designer watches,
books, houseware and fun gifts
for children.

Cafés and snacks

Blue Bottle Coffee

MAP P.70, POCKET MAP A13
66 Mint St at Jessie St Ⓜ #8, #9, #14, #27,
#31, F, J, K, L, M, N, T; Ⓑ Powell. ☎ 415
252 7535, Ⓦ bluebottlecoffee.com. Daily
6.30am–7.30pm.

Tucked away in the elegant 1912 Provident Loan Association building, just off the main drag, this quirky spot offers its own roasted coffee that has taken San Francisco by storm. Cold brews also grace the menu, as do a few milk-based beverages.

Crossroads Café

MAP P.70, POCKET MAP M4
699 Delancey St at Brannan
St Ⓜ N, T. ☎ 415 836 5624,
Ⓦ delanceystreetfoundation.org/entercafe.php. Mon–Fri 7am–10pm, Sat 8am–10pm, Sun 8am–5pm.

With a small bookshop next to its kitchen, this informal offshoot of adjacent *Delancey Street* (see below) is an inviting place to enjoy an inexpensive breakfast, lunch or light dinner, either on a sofa inside or at a table in the outside courtyard.

SoMa StrEat Food Park

MAP P.70, POCKET MAP K5
428 11th St at 13th St Ⓜ #9, #12, #27, #47. Ⓦ somastreatfoodpark.com. Mon–Sat 11am–3pm & 5–9pm, Sun 11am–5pm.

This converted car park is home to a daily rotating array of food trucks selling unique concoctions such as Vietnamese-inspired mini-burgers, as well as more straightforward items like sausages and cupcakes. There's a covered beer garden, too.

Restaurants

Asia SF

MAP P.70, POCKET MAP J5
201 Ninth St at Howard St Ⓜ #12, #14, #19, F, J, K, L, M, N, T; Ⓑ Civic Center. ☎ 415 255 2742, Ⓦ asiasf.com. Dinner shows: Wed, Thurs & Sun 7.15pm; Fri 7.15pm & 9.15pm; Sat 5pm, 7.15pm & 9.15pm. $39–79.

This notorious cabaret-restaurant features transgender East Asian staff performing right in the dining room itself. Complementing the camp environs, the unusual menu is full of winning crossbreeds such

as vegan truffled soba noodles and duck quesadillas.

Delancey Street

MAP P.70, POCKET MAP M4
600 Embarcadero at Brannan
St Ⓜ N, T. ☎ 415 512 5179,
Ⓦ delanceystreetfoundation.org/enterrestaurant.php. Tues–Fri 11am–11pm, Sat & Sun 10am–11pm.

The restaurant arm of the local non-profit Delancey Street Foundation is a terrific spot for a shockingly affordable lunch or dinner (and on Sunday, brunch too). Waiting staff are usually in vocational training in an attempt to re-enter mainstream society after troubled beginnings.

Dottie's True Blue Café

MAP P.70, POCKET MAP K4
28 Sixth St at Market St Ⓜ #5, #8, #9, #14, #27, #31, F, J, K, L, M, N, T; Ⓑ Powell. ☎ 415 885 2767. Mon, Thurs & Fri 7.30am–3pm, Sat & Sun 7.30am–4pm.

Inexpensive *Dottie's* regularly packs in diners who come from all over town for extraordinary chilli cornbread and some of the best breakfasts around, including tempting specials such as chocolate-chip French toast.

Epic Steak

MAP P.70, POCKET MAP L3
369 Embarcadero at Folsom St Ⓜ N, T; Ⓑ Embarcadero. ☎ 415 369 9955, Ⓦ epicsteak.com. Mon–Thurs 11.30am–2.30pm & 5.30–9.30pm, Fri 11.30am–2.30pm & 5.30–10pm, Sat 11am–2.30pm & 5.30–10pm, Sun 11am–2.30pm & 5.30–9.30pm.

Marvellous bay-side views and a gorgeous dining room (with prices to match – there's a $17 burger on the lunch menu) compete for prominence at this waterside restaurant, where the menu deals in fish, fowl and, of course, steaks.

Mathilde

MAP P.70, POCKET MAP K4
315 Fifth St at Folsom St Ⓜ #8, #12, #27, #30, #45, #47. ☎ 415 546

SoMa StrEat Food Park

6128, Ⓦ mathildesf.com. Tues–Thurs
5.30–9.15pm, Fri & Sat 5.30–9.45pm.
With enticing Gallic mains
such as duck leg confit ($28),
tempting desserts, Sunday brunch,
and periodic violin-and-guitar
performances in its delightful
patio area, *Mathilde* is a solid
choice for Francophiles.

Oola

MAP P.70, POCKET MAP K4
860 Folsom St at Fifth St Ⓜ #8, #12, #27,
#30, #45, #47. ☎ 415 995 2061, Ⓦ oola-sf.
com. Mon & Tues 5.30–11pm, Wed &
Thurs 5.30pm–midnight, Fri 5.30pm–1am,
Sat 11.30am–3pm & 5.30pm–1am, Sun
11.30am–3pm & 5.30–11pm.
Elegant draperies and exposed
red brickwork define the decor
at this quietly sexy bistro, which
is popular with San Francisco's
beautiful elite late into the night;
the menu blends French and New
American cuisine. Main dishes cost
between $16 and $38.

Primo Patio Cafe

MAP P.70, POCKET MAP L4
214 Townsend St at Third St Ⓜ #10,
#30; #45, #47, N, T. ☎ 415 957 1129,
Ⓦ primopatiocafe.com. Mon–Sat 9am–4pm.

One of San Francisco's top
Caribbean restaurants, affordable
Primo Patio is well known for its
delectably marinated grilled jerk
chicken ($11.99) as well as its
bracingly spiced breakfasts.

Trou Normand

MAP P.70, POCKET MAP C13
140 New Montgomery St at Minna St Ⓜ #8,
#10, #12, #14, #30, #45; Ⓑ Montgomery.
☎ 415 975 0876, Ⓦ trounormandsf.
com. Mon–Fri 11.30am–3.30pm &
5.30–10.30pm, Sat 10.30am–3.30pm &
5.30–10.30pm, Sun 10.30am–3.30pm &
5.30–9.30pm.
Fashionable minimalist restaurant
in an Art Deco high-rise, with an
elegant marble bar serving forty
types of house-made charcuterie
(plates from $12), craft cocktails
and calvados, plus tables on
the back patio for pasta and
chophouse-style cuts of meat
(mains $23–29).

Bars

21st Amendment Brewery

MAP P.70, POCKET MAP L4
563 Second St at Brannan St Ⓜ #8, #10,

#12, #30, #45, N, T. ☎ 415 369 0900, Ⓦ 21st-amendment.com. Mon–Sat 11.30am–midnight, Sun 10am–midnight. Consistently popular (especially on baseball game days/nights), ballpark-adjacent *21st Amendment* regularly features around ten of its own-made craft brews on tap, along with capable pub food at reasonable prices.

The House of Shields

MAP P.70, POCKET MAP B12
39 New Montgomery St at Mission St Ⓜ #2, #3, #8, #9, #10, #12, #14, F, J, K, L, M, N, T; Ⓑ Montgomery. Ⓦ thehouseofshields. com. Mon–Fri 2pm–2am, Sat & Sun 3pm–2am.

With vintage amber-coloured panelling and a crowd ranging from dressy Downtown types swilling craft cocktails to bike messengers drinking beer, this clubby, antique tavern – routinely packed during its week-night happy hour – is as eclectic as they come.

Jamber

MAP P.70, POCKET MAP K4
858 Folsom St at Fifth St Ⓜ #8, #12, #27, #30, #45, #47. ☎ 415 273 9192, Ⓦ jambersf.com. Mon 11.30am–10pm,

The View

Tues–Fri 11.30am–midnight, Sat 3.30pm–midnight, Sun 3.30–10pm.

Industrial-feeling yet intimate, this self-described wine pub keeps nearly two dozen varieties on tap. There's also a terrific front patio and a wide selection of beer. The clever food menu includes poutine, a Canadian concoction of chips covered in cheese curds and gravy ($14).

Lone Star

MAP P.70, POCKET MAP K5
1354 Harrison St at Tenth St Ⓜ #9, #12, #27, #47; Ⓑ Civic Center. ☎ 415 863 9999, Ⓦ lonestarsf.com. Mon–Thurs 4pm–2am, Fri 2pm–2am, Sat & Sun noon–2am.

Lone Star is one of the more fun and welcoming gay bars in South of Market, with a popular patio that's slathered in antique signs and a weekday happy hour until 8pm.

The View

MAP P.70, POCKET MAP B13
Marriott Marquis, 55 Fourth St at Mission St Ⓜ #8, #9, #10, #12, #14, #30, #38, #45, F, J, K, L, M, N, T; Ⓑ Powell. ☎ 415 442 6003, Ⓦ bit.ly/TheViewBar. Mon–Wed & Sun 4pm–1am, Thurs–Sat 4pm–1.30am.

The vertigo-inducing ceiling-to-floor glass windows at this 39th-storey hotel lounge boast bird's-eye vistas over the San Francisco skyline and beyond. Arrive early to snag a window-side table.

Clubs

Cat Club

MAP P.70, POCKET MAP K5
1190 Folsom St at Eighth St Ⓜ #12, #19, #27, #47; Ⓑ Civic Center. ☎ 415 703 8965, Ⓦ sfcatclub.com. Tues 9pm–2am, Wed 9.30pm–2.30am, Thurs 9pm–3am, Fri 9.30pm–2.30am, Sat 9.30pm–3am. Free–$10.

The weekly schedule at this perennially popular nightspot spans electro, darkwave, goth, Britpop and shoegaze in two separate rooms, not to mention free karaoke every Tuesday.

The End Up

MAP P.70, POCKET MAP K4
401 Sixth St at Harrison St Ⓜ #12, #27, #47; Ⓑ Civic Center. ☏ 415 646 0999, Ⓦ facebook.com/theendup. Usually Fri 10pm–8am, Sat 10pm–6am, Sun 6am–8pm; check website for calendar and hours. $5 and up.

This local institution is most popular after-hours at weekends – especially for its all-day Sundaze party (naturally, every Sunday). The often raucous dance floor and pair of indoor bars are tempered by a mellow back patio area (where smoking is allowed).

The Stud Bar

MAP P.70, POCKET MAP K5
399 Ninth St at Harrison St Ⓜ #8, #12, #19, #27, #47; Ⓑ Civic Center. ☏ 415 863 6623, Ⓦ studsf.com. Tues & Sat 5pm–2am, Thurs & Fri 5pm–3am, Sun 5pm–midnight. Free–$8.

Open since 1966, this stalwart gay nightclub is still one of the most fun, attracting an uninhibited crowd who come for week-night comedy, karaoke and cabaret, and weekend DJs.

Live music and shows

Alonzo King LINES Ballet

MAP P.70, POCKET MAP B13
Yerba Buena Center for the Arts, 701 Mission St at Third St Ⓜ #8, #9, #10, #12, #14, #30, #38, #45, F, J, K, L, M, N, T; Ⓑ Montgomery. ☏ 415 863 3040, Ⓦ linesballet.org. $35–75.

Headed by its celebrated namesake choreographer, this contemporary troupe holds brief home seasons (usually November), when not on tour (check website for dates). Expect innovative collaborations with the likes of top musicians such as Mickey Hart and Edgar Meyer.

Hotel Utah Saloon

MAP P.70, POCKET MAP L4
500 Fourth St at Bryant St Ⓜ #8, #12,

Hotel Utah Saloon

#27, #30, #45, #47. ☏ 415 546 6300, Ⓦ hotelutah.com. Daily 11.30am–2am. Free–$15.

No longer a hotel in spite of the name, *Hotel Utah Saloon* is evocative of an earlier era. This cosy venue's tiny stage plays host to a roster of singer-songwriters and country-rock bands; regulars also pour in for the lively bar scene and tasty pub grub. Monday's open mic night is always an entertaining night out.

Slim's

MAP P.70, POCKET MAP J5
333 11th St at Folsom St Ⓜ #9, #12, #27, #47; Ⓑ Civic Center. ☏ 415 255 0333, Ⓦ slimspresents.com. $15 and up.

Slim's is one of the top mid-size venues in San Francisco for all manner of rock and international acts, although sightlines can be troubling if you find yourself behind one of its brick-walled pillars. Dinner tickets (typically an extra $24.95) include seating in the upstairs balcony, towards the rear of the room.

Civic Center and around

Not so much a neighbourhood as a political and bureaucratic powerhouse, Civic Center and its opulent complex of Beaux Arts buildings is also home to numerous cultural institutions, from San Francisco's enormous flagship library to the world-renowned Asian Art Museum. From a visitor's perspective the area is generally safe and robustly policed – all the better to take in an opera, ballet or symphony performance. However, Civic Center also reveals some of San Francisco's most maddening contradictions, for in the shadow of these monumental buildings dwells a large homeless population living apart from the city's prosperity. Though uninviting on the surface, the adjoining Tenderloin district lays claim to several excellent ethnic restaurants and top places to drink, as well as a few of the city's best live music venues.

Civic Center Plaza

MAP P.80, POCKET MAP J4
Ⓜ #5, #6, #9, #19, #21, #47, #49, F, J, K, L, M, N, T; Ⓑ Civic Center.

The landscaped centrepiece of the city's political and high-culture district, expansive **Civic Center Plaza** anchors a complex

Civic Center Plaza

of stately Beaux Arts buildings. The area represents one of San Francisco's grandest architectural achievements, although its grim side provides a striking contrast as assorted addicts and hustlers spill over from the neighbouring Tenderloin. Civic Center Plaza is a remnant of the lofty aims of early twentieth-century urban planner Daniel Burnham, who believed that employing classically influenced architecture around open space would help instil solid morals in politicians and citizens.

The plaza often hosts festivals, events and art installations that are worth a look, while the 18 flagpoles set in perfect symmetry with the entrance to City Hall across Polk Street – each flying a historic US, California or San Francisco flag – make for an interesting diversion.

City Hall

MAP P.80, POCKET MAP J4
Ⓜ #5, #6, #9, #19, #21, #47, #49, F, J, K, L, M, N, T; Ⓑ Civic Center. ☎ 415 554 6139, Ⓦ sfgov.org/cityhall/city-hall-tours. Mon–Fri 8am–8pm. Tours Mon–Fri 10am, noon & 2pm. Entry and tours free.

Imposing **City Hall** possesses a more regal presence than many state capitols, its gold-flecked dome (the fifth largest in the world) topping an elaborate interior that confirmed San Francisco's status as the pre-eminent city of the American West at the time of its opening in 1915. The behemoth structure's design incorporates more than ten acres of marble, which is best taken in from the magnificent centre staircase beneath the dome.

On the second floor and directly opposite the top of the steps, the Mayor's office was the site of San Francisco's most notorious modern-day murder, when disgruntled City Supervisor Dan White shot then-Mayor George Moscone in November 1978; moments later, White fatally wounded openly gay City Supervisor Harvey Milk on the same floor.

Main Library

MAP P.80, POCKET MAP J4
100 Larkin St at Grove St  #5, #6, #9, #19, #21, #47, #49, F, J, K, L, M, N, T; Civic Center. 415 557 4400, sfpl. org. Mon & Sat 10am–6pm, Tues–Thurs 9am–8pm, Fri noon–6pm, Sun noon–5pm. Free.

San Francisco's **Main Library** boasts a grey exterior that, despite its relative youth, smartly complements the grandiosity of Civic Center's architecture. The building's layout was skewered by some when it opened back in 1996, many of whom groused that for being such a gargantuan structure devoted to the holding of books, it seemed short on actual shelf space. Nevertheless, the library features no shortage of reading chairs and personal workspaces, and its light-flooded central atrium is lovely.

On the third floor, the **James C. Hormel LGBTQIA Center** holds a robust collection of literature and other culturally significant items, with a special emphasis on the Bay Area's contribution to the global

Marble-encased interior of City Hall

LGBTQ rights movement; it also serves as a community centre and exhibition space.

Asian Art Museum

MAP P.80, POCKET MAP J4
200 Larkin St at McAllister St #5, #6, #9, #19, #21, #47, #49, F, J, K, L, M, N, T; Civic Center. 415 581 3500, asianart.org. Tues–Sun 10am–5pm (Late March to late Sept, Thurs & Fri until 9pm). $20.

Possessing one of the top collections of Asian art and artefacts in the world, the **Asian Art Museum** could command the attention of an art enthusiast for days. The museum relocated to the former Main Library building in 2003 from a shared space in Golden Gate Park's de Young Museum (see page 117), a move that finally enabled it to showcase the best of its 17,000 works. The structure was given a major makeover by Gae Aulenti (who'd previously worked similar magic with Paris's Musée d'Orsay), as the noted Italian architect introduced much more natural light into the 1917 building's previously dim quarters. In addition to showing

Asian Art Museum

over two thousand works from its permanent collection – including the world's oldest Chinese image of the Buddha – in an extensive range of regionally specific galleries, the museum regularly hosts daily

programmes and high-profile travelling exhibitions.

War Memorial Opera House

MAP P.80, POCKET MAP J4
301 Van Ness Ave at Grove St Ⓜ #5, #6, #9, #19, #21, #47, #49, F, J, K, L, M, N, T; Ⓑ Civic Center.

The shared home of San Francisco's opera and ballet companies, the ornate **War Memorial Opera House** lays claim to hosting the signing ceremony of the United Nations charter in 1945. Given its name, the War Memorial's front arches and Doric pillars are fittingly sombre and stately, while its interior (open only for performances) features a sumptuous main lobby and 3100-seat multilevel auditorium. The main performance season for the building's original tenant, the highly regarded **San Francisco Opera** (☎ 415 864 3330, Ⓦ sfopera.

Civic Center and around

BUSH ST
SUTTER ST
COSMO PL.
HEMLOCK ST
CEDAR ST
POST ST
SHANNON ST
GEARY ST
LARKIN ST
HYDE ST
LEAVENWORTH ST
JONES ST
MYRTLE ST
O'FARRELL ST
O'FARRELL ST
ANTONIO ST
Glide Memorial Church
TAYLOR ST
MASON ST
CYRIL MAGNIN ST
OLIVE ST
ELLIS ST
THE TENDERLOIN
WILLOW ST
EDDY ST
POWELL Ⓜ
Westfield San Francisco Centre
VAN NESS AVENUE
POLK ST
TURK ST
STEVENSON ST
JESSIE ST
MISSION ST
6TH ST
GOLDEN GATE AVENUE
CIVIC CENTER
MCALLISTER ST
Supreme Court of California
Asian Art Museum
UNITED NATIONS PLAZA
FULTON ST
Main Library
MARKET STREET
7TH ST
Ⓑ CIVIC CENTER
N
Veterans Building
City Hall
CIVIC CENTER PLAZA
FRANKLIN ST
War Memorial Opera House
GROVE ST
IVY ST
Bill Graham Civic Auditorium
Louise M. Davies Symphony Hall
HAYES ST

0	meters	250
0	yards	250

com), is September to December, with a short summer run from May to July; expect avant-garde productions and crowd-pleasers alike. The season for the **San Francisco Ballet** (☎ 415 865 2000, Ⓦ sfballet.org) typically runs from January to May, with a series of popular *Nutcracker* performances staged during the Christmas season. Tickets for both the opera and ballet start at around $35.

Louise M. Davies Symphony Hall

MAP P.80, POCKET MAP J4
201 Van Ness Ave at Grove St Ⓜ #5, #6, #9, #19, #21, #47, #49, F, J, K, L, M, N, T; Ⓑ Civic Center.

Even at a glance, the **Louise M. Davies Symphony Hall** (circa 1980) and its curved frontage comes off as the architectural sore thumb amid the otherwise congruous Civic Center. The hall is home to the **San Francisco Symphony** (☎ 415 864 6000, Ⓦ sfsymphony.org), a first-rate orchestra helmed by one of the highest-profile conductors in the US, Michael Tilson Thomas.

The California native has led the ensemble to prominence through a slate of performances by twentieth-century composers during its annual September to May season, for which tickets typically command prices of $30 and upwards.

Glide Memorial Church

MAP P.80, POCKET MAP A13
330 Ellis St at Taylor St Ⓜ #9, #27, #31, #38; Ⓑ Powell. ☎ 415 674 6000, Ⓦ glide. org. Sunday services 9am & 11am.

The Tenderloin may be one of San Francisco's most infamous patches of urban grit, but its signature house of worship, **Glide Memorial Church**, perseveres as one of the beleaguered neighbourhood's most hopeful institutions. Along with providing a near-endless scope of social services for the Tenderloin's considerable population in need, the church is best known for its spirited Sunday gospel choir services, an exuberant experience for which you'll want to arrive 45 minutes early for a seat in the main sanctuary.

Glide Ensemble at the Glide Memorial Church

Shops and gallery

Jessica Silverman Gallery

MAP P.80, POCKET MAP J3
488 Ellis St at Leavenworth St Ⓜ #2, #3,
#27, #31, #38; ⓑ Powell. ☎ 415 255 9508,
ⓦ jessicasilvermangallery.com. Tues–Sat
11am–6pm.

Owner/director Silverman takes a
particularly active role at this Ellis
Street gallery, where exhibitions
of contemporary photography, art
installations and film shows by new
and established artists are the focus.
Pieces here are less pricey than at
most other galleries in the area.

The Magazine

MAP P.80, POCKET MAP J3
920 Larkin St at Geary St Ⓜ #2, #3, #27,
#38, #47, #49; ⓑ Civic Center. ☎ 415 441
7737, ⓦ themagazinesf.com. Mon–Sat
noon–7pm.

If you're on the hunt for an old
copy of *Life*, *Sports Illustrated*
or *Harper's Bazaar* – or perhaps
looking for a surprise gift for
that erotica collector in your
life – there's a solid chance you'll
track it down at this longtime
Tenderloin retailer, which stocks

The Magazine

vintage periodicals alongside
adult materials.

Modernism

MAP P.80, POCKET MAP J4
724 Ellis St at Larkin St Ⓜ #19, #27, #31,
#38, #47, #49; ⓑ Civic Center. ☎ 415 541
0461, ⓦ modernisminc.com. Tues–Sat
10am–5.30pm.

Spotlighting a far-reaching
range of works, landmark gallery
Modernism has been known since
the late 1970s for its challenging
exhibitions spanning Pop Art,
minimalism, sculpture and more.

Cafés and snacks

Saigon Sandwich

MAP P.80, POCKET MAP J4
560 Larkin St at Eddy St Ⓜ #19, #31, #47,
#49; ⓑ Civic Center. ☎ 415 474 5698. Daily
7.30am–5pm.

Grab a spot in this wee shop's
frequent queue and ponder your
bahn mi (Vietnamese sandwich)
options as you wait: barbecue
chicken, barbecue pork, meatballs
or tofu, all made to order and none
costing more than $3.75. Be sure to
top your concoction with shredded
carrot, bundles of coriander
(cilantro) or jalapeño peppers.

Taqueria El Castillito

MAP P.80, POCKET MAP J4
370 Golden Gate Ave at Larkin St Ⓜ #5,
#19, #31; ⓑ Civic Center. ☎ 415 292 7233.
Mon–Fri 10am–5.30pm.

The best bet for Mexican food
in the Civic Center/Tenderloin
area, this *taqueria* may be short on
inspiring ambience, but it more
than compensates with excellent
burritos, tacos and platters. Expect
to eat heartily for well under $10.

Restaurants

A La Turca

MAP P.80, POCKET MAP J3
869 Geary St at Larkin St Ⓜ #2, #3, #19,
#27, #38, #47, #49; ⓑ Civic Center. ☎ 415

345 1011, ⓦ alaturcasf.com. Mon–Thurs &
Sun 11am–10pm, Fri & Sat 11am–11pm.
Although it's unlikely you'll be
impressed with this restaurant's
sparse decor, you're sure to enjoy
the selection of Turkish *pides*
– baked flatbreads filled with
vegetables, meat and/or cheese –
on offer. Generously sized platter
meals (most around $13–18) make
for a slightly heartier alternative;
make sure that you don't miss the
honey-draped *künefe* dessert.

Ananda Fuara

MAP P.80, POCKET MAP J4
1298 Market St at Larkin St ⓜ #5, #6,
#9, #19, #21, #47, #49, F, J, K, L, M,
N, T; ⓑ Civic Center. ⓣ 415 621 1994,
ⓦ anandafuara.com. Tues–Sat 11am–8pm,
Sat & Sun 11am–3pm.
This affordable and popular
vegetarian restaurant casts a wide
net – a group of four could easily
sample meatless dishes spanning
the culinary styles of Mexico, the
Middle East, the American South
and South Asia. Mains are around
$12–13.

Brenda's French Soul Food

MAP P.80, POCKET MAP J4
652 Polk St at Eddy St ⓜ #19, #31, #38,
#47, #49; ⓑ Civic Center. ⓣ 415 345
8100, ⓦ frenchsoulfood.com. Mon & Tues
8am–3pm, Wed–Sat 8am–10pm, Sun
8am–8pm.
Creole hideaway *Brenda's* deals in
everything from potato hash, grits
and massive scone-like biscuits at
breakfast (and weekend brunch) to
deeply flavourful dinner mains such
as shrimp and grits in spicy tomato-
bacon gravy ($15). Leave your diet
behind and be sure to sample one
or more of the luscious beignets
(four varieties are available), and
try to arrive at an off-peak time
since this popular spot doesn't take
any reservations.

Farmerbrown

MAP P.80, POCKET MAP A13
25 Mason St at Turk St ⓜ #5, #6, #9, #14,
#27, #31, F, J, K, L, M, N, T; ⓑ Powell.

Brenda's French Soul Food

ⓣ 415 409 3276, ⓦ farmerbrownsf.com.
Mon–Wed 8am–2pm & 5–9pm, Thurs & Fri
8am–2pm & 5–10pm, Sat 10am–2.30pm &
5–10pm, Sun 10am–2.30pm & 5–9pm.
Best known for its lively all-
you-can-eat weekend brunch
($25.95), often complemented
by live music, *farmerbrown* is a
packed house most nights, full
of people of all stripes enjoying
Southern-style mains such as
crispy cornmeal catfish ($23.50)
and, of course, fried chicken with
sides ($19.50).

Lers Ros

MAP P.80, POCKET MAP J4
730 Larkin St at Ellis St ⓜ #19, #27, #31,
#38, #47, #49; ⓑ Civic Center. ⓣ 415
931 6917, ⓦ lersros.com. Daily 11am–
midnight.
Championed as one of San
Francisco's most imaginative Thai
restaurants, *Lers Ros* provides an
opportunity to try a range of lesser-
known items such as Thai curry
puff ($10.95) and garlic and pepper
rabbit ($15.95). Mainstream
favourites like five-spice duck over
rice ($12.95) and *tom yum koong*
soup ($14.95) are also present on
the extensive menu.

Shalimar

MAP P.80, POCKET MAP A13

532 Jones St at O'Farrell St 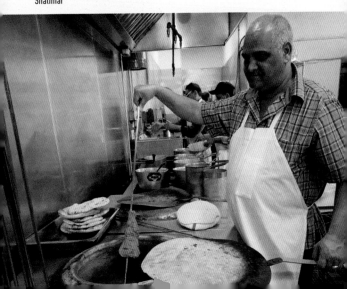 #2, #3, #27, #38; ⑧ Powell. ☎ 415 928 0333. Daily 11.30am–midnight.

Just as you'll revel in the freshly baked naan breads and exceptionally delicious (and hugely portioned) mains at this tandoori oven-heated South Asian eatery, you'll also leave smelling as if you just spent considerable time next to a campfire. It's entirely worth it, though, for the championship-calibre chicken *tikka masala* and *saag gosht* (both under $9).

Bars

Aunt Charlie's Lounge

MAP P.80, POCKET MAP A13

133 Turk St at Taylor St Ⓜ #5, #6, #9, #31, #38, F, J, K, L, M, N, T; ⑧ Powell. ☎ 415 441 2922. Mon–Fri noon–2am, Sat 10am–2am, Sun 10am–midnight.

Best known for its 1970s-themed "Tubesteak Connection" party each Thursday ($5-7), this Tenderloin gay bar also packs in plenty of punters for its frequent drag shows and cheap beer and cocktails.

Bourbon & Branch

MAP P.80, POCKET MAP A13

501 Jones St at O'Farrell St Ⓜ #2, #3, #8, #27, #31, #38; ⑧ Powell. ☎ 415 346 1735, Ⓦ bourbonandbranch.com. Daily 6pm–2am.

Gimmicky yet evocative, this unmarked tavern – look for the "Anti-Saloon League" sign outside – is a hit with locals looking to experience the world of a dimly lit, Prohibition-era speakeasy, all the way down to having to give a password at the door upon entry. Reserve online.

Edinburgh Castle

MAP P.80, POCKET MAP A13

950 Geary St at Polk St Ⓜ #2, #3, #19, #38, #47, #49; ⑧ Civic Center. ☎ 415 885 4074, Ⓦ thecastlesf.com. Daily 5pm–2am.

This long-standing Scottish-themed tavern is a perennially popular place for happy-hour pints (until 8pm), darts, pool and excellent fish and chips. "The Legendary Castle Quiz" every Tuesday is also one of the most popular pub events in the city.

Mikkeller Bar

MAP P.80, POCKET MAP A13

Shalimar

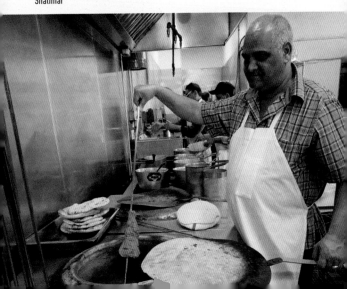

34 Mason St, between Eddy and Turk sts Ⓜ #5, #6, #9, #14, #27, #31, F, J, K, L, M, N, T; Ⓑ Powell. Ⓣ 415 984 0279, Ⓦ mikkellerbar.com. Mon–Wed & Sun noon–midnight, Thurs–Sat noon–2am. Congenial beer hall in a 1907 building, with a staggering 42 taps and a host of bottled beers from around the world. Part of the Danish Mikkeller stable, a microbrewery founded in Copenhagen in 2006.

Live music venues

Great American Music Hall

MAP P.80, POCKET MAP J4
859 O'Farrell St at Polk St Ⓜ #2, #3, #19, #31, #38; Ⓑ Civic Center. Ⓣ 415 885 0750, Ⓦ slimspresents.com/great-american-music-hall. $15 and up.
San Francisco's oldest live music venue boasts an exceptional sound system, a wraparound Victorian balcony with some of the best vantage points in the house and, above all, an inimitably warm vibe. It's one of the top spots in town for indie rock, folk and punk, as well as the occasional jazz and comedy booking.

Hemlock Tavern

MAP P.80, POCKET MAP J3
1131 Polk St at Sutter St Ⓜ #2, #3, #19, #38, #47, #49; Ⓑ Civic Center. Ⓣ 415 923 0923, Ⓦ hemlocktavern.com. Daily 4pm–2am. $5–12.
An edgy, boisterous Polk Gulch bar with a punk rock heart, the *Hemlock* offers a fantastic – and free – jukebox, bags of hot peanuts for sale (plus a floor full of empty shells), a lounge for smokers, and an intimate back room where touring and local bands love to perform.

The Warfield

MAP P.80, POCKET MAP A13
982 Market St at Sixth St Ⓜ #5, #8, #9, #14, #27, #31, F, J, K, L, M, N, T; Ⓑ Powell.

Performance at the Great American Music Hall

Ⓣ 415 775 7722, Ⓦ thewarfieldtheatre.com. $35 and up.
San Francisco's grandest rock theatre has hosted everyone from David Bowie to Spinal Tap over the years, and the 2000-plus capacity venue continues to book mid-level touring bands. The reserved-seating balcony provides a comfortable perspective, while the general-admission main floor is a festival-style standing space.

Theatre

Exit Theatre

MAP P.80, POCKET MAP A13
156 Eddy St at Taylor St Ⓜ #5, #6, #8, #9, #31, #38, F, J, K, L, M, N, T; Ⓑ Powell. Ⓣ 415 931 1094, Ⓦ theexit.org. $15–35.
Staging performances in several small theatres on one of the grottier blocks of the Tenderloin, the *Exit* is nevertheless one of the sharpest alternative theatres in town. It's a main venue for the annual *San Francisco Fringe Festival*, as well as the home of the ongoing women-centric *DIVAFest* series.

The Mission and around

Arguably San Francisco's most enthralling district, the colourful Mission is named after Mission Dolores, the city's birthplace, where a Spanish Catholic mission was founded the same summer the US declared its independence. The Mission has traditionally been a neighbourhood of immigrants: Scandinavians and Irish until the middle of the twentieth century, followed by a huge influx of Mexicans and Central Americans in the decades since. Today's Mission is most notable for its multiple identities – Latino barrio, trendy restaurant playground, epicentre for San Francisco hipster culture – so it's of little surprise that the resulting cultural mix lends the neighbourhood much of its allure. Flanking the pancake-flat Mission are Bernal Heights and Potrero Hill, a pair of sleepier, yet still intriguing, neighbourhoods whose slopes merit a wander.

Mission Dolores

MAP P.88, POCKET MAP H6
3321 16th St at Dolores St Ⓜ #22, J;
Ⓑ 16th St Mission. ☏ 415 621 8203,
Ⓦ missiondolores.org. Daily: May–Oct 9am–4.30pm; Nov–April 9am–4pm. $5 donation.

Spanish explorers founded the first edition of Mission San Francisco de Asís, better known as **Mission**

Mission Dolores

Dolores, in 1776, on this site where a now-underground creek once burbled, making it the developing city's first European settlement. The original building was replaced 15 years later by the white adobe that still stands today – San Francisco's oldest surviving structure – in the considerable shadow of the circa-1918 basilica immediately next door. Once the California missions were secularized in 1834, the squat structure soldiered on as a tavern and dance hall before again becoming a Catholic parish in 1859. It gamely survived San Francisco's pair of cataclysmic twentieth-century earthquakes, and remains the best place in the city for a glimpse of California's colonial past. A self-guided tour affords the opportunity to take in the chapel's interior of redwood beams and hand-carved pews, as well as the basilica and its lovely stained-glass windows. The final section of the tour route leads through the adjacent cemetery that figured in Alfred Hitchcock's 1959 thriller *Vertigo*.

Dolores Park

Dolores Park

MAP P.88, POCKET MAP H6
Bordered by 18th, Dolores, 20th and Church sts Ⓜ #33, J; Ⓢ 16th St Mission.

One of San Francisco's most popular greenspaces, and once the site of a Jewish cemetery, **Dolores Park** is a year-round draw for locals looking to unwind amid its rolling knolls. Sunny weekend days in particular make for a predictably thronged party scene comprising many different groups: kids enjoying the play structures at the south end of the park; Castro men tanning themselves on the southwest corner's hillside (colloquially known as Dolores Beach); football players having informal games in the flatter sections toward 18th St; various dogs zipping about; and – given its location on the edge of the Mission – groups of slouchy twenty-somethings swilling cheap beer. To the immediate south, the tame side streets along Dolores Street are occupied by a number of Victorian homes in remarkably fine condition, thanks in no small part to the firm bedrock beneath, which offered protection during the city's infamous earthquakes.

Valencia Street

MAP P.88, POCKET MAP J5–J8
Ⓜ #12, #14, #22, #27, #33, #48, #49; Ⓢ 16th St Mission and 24th St Mission.

In a city with no shortage of streets offering vibrant shopping, dining and drinking, **Valencia Street** is likely the most freewheeling – and successful – of all. Retail options along Valencia's blocks between 14th and 25th streets include thrift shops, pricey clothing boutiques, vintage furniture shops and, of course, used books and records; this is also the place to come if you're in the market for pirate supplies and artful taxidermy. To the groans of long-time neighbourhood residents, the street has been carpet-bombed in recent years with chic yet exciting restaurants, whose voguishness seems to cater to visitors from other areas. Still, plenty of *taquerias* and other casual eating alternatives persevere along (and just off) the Valencia corridor, as do some of the city's best drinking dens.

The Mission and around

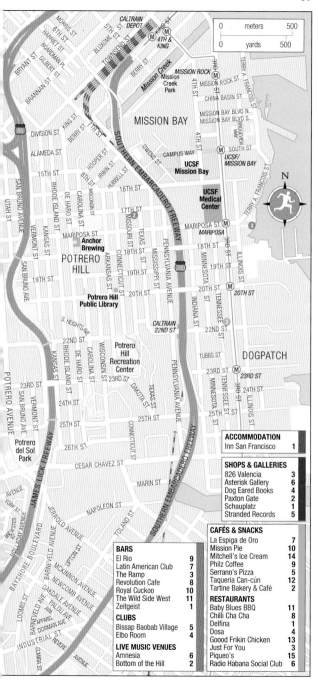

ACCOMMODATION

| Inn San Francisco | 1 |

SHOPS & GALLERIES

826 Valencia	3
Asterisk Gallery	6
Dog Eared Books	4
Paxton Gate	2
Schauplatz	1
Stranded Records	5

CAFÉS & SNACKS

La Espiga de Oro	7
Mission Pie	10
Mitchell's Ice Cream	14
Philz Coffee	9
Serrano's Pizza	5
Taqueria Can-cún	12
Tartine Bakery & Café	2

RESTAURANTS

Baby Blues BBQ	11
Chilli Cha Cha	8
Delfina	1
Dosa	4
Goood Frikin Chicken	13
Just For You	3
Piqueo's	15
Radio Habana Social Club	6

BARS

El Rio	9
Latin American Club	7
The Ramp	3
Revolution Cafe	8
Royal Cuckoo	10
The Wild Side West	11
Zeitgeist	1

CLUBS

| Bissap Baobab Village | 5 |
| Elbo Room | 4 |

LIVE MUSIC VENUES

| Amnesia | 6 |
| Bottom of the Hill | 2 |

Mission Street and 24th Street

MAP P.88, POCKET MAP J7

Ⓜ #12, #14, #22, #24, #27, #33, #48, #49, J; Ⓑ 16th St Mission and 24th St Mission.

Though dodgier in parts than boutique-lined Valencia Street to the immediate west, **Mission Street** is nonetheless an unmissable element of its namesake neighbourhood, although you'll certainly want to exercise caution between 16th and 18th streets. The thoroughfare is lined with produce markets, casual places to eat, discount clothiers and five-and-dime shops selling cheap wallets and Jesus nightlights, all with a Latin American bent. Indeed, just as Valencia Street is the Mission's epicentre of white culture, Mission Street is where the district's sizeable Mexican and Central American immigrant population comes to eat, browse and do business.

24th Street, which runs perpendicular to Mission Street, has traditionally been another earthy Latino stronghold, but many of its newer businesses skew more towards the hip and gourmet. Still, the section between Potrero Avenue and Guerrero Street is home to more *taquerias*, *panaderías* (bakeries) and "mexicatessens" than you'll find anywhere else in San Francisco.

Balmy Alley

MAP P.88, POCKET MAP K7

Between 24th, Harrison, 25th and Treat sts Ⓜ #12, #14, #27, #48, #49; Ⓑ 24th St Mission. ☎ 415 285 2287; Ⓦ precitaeyes. org. Mural tours: Sat & Sun 1.30pm; 2hr 15min. $20.

Murals are found all over the Mission – Clarion Alley between 17th, Mission, 18th and Valencia streets operates as a canvas for public art – but the best-known concentration is found on **Balmy Alley** in the neighbourhood's southern reaches. Murals here have described various aspects of Latin American heritage since the early 1970s, when artists began turning the narrow passage into an outdoor gallery of folk-art expression; the otherwise unassuming street has been the site of a dynamic rotation of colour-splashed murals ever since, with certain newer pieces putting a fine point on the Latino community's growing frustration over the ongoing gentrification of the Mission.

Located a short walk east along 24th Street at no. 2981, **Precita Eyes Mural Arts** pays for much of the creation and maintenance of Balmy Alley's artwork, while also selling maps of the neighbourhood's murals and offering a variety of mural-focused tours.

Balmy Alley

Bernal Heights

MAP P.88, POCKET MAP J8
Ⓜ #12, #14, #24, #27, #49, #67, J.

Though not one of San Francisco's destination neighbourhoods, cosy **Bernal Heights** is one of the city's most rewarding tangents for both visitors and locals. Its heart is bustling Cortland Avenue, a commercial strip packed with a host of independent businesses doing a brisk trade, while its soul is expansive Bernal Heights Park, a steeply perched greenspace offering spectacular views of San Francisco Bay, the Mission and the skylines of Downtown and South of Market, all from a uniquely southern perspective in the city.

Bernal Heights' tree-lined streets (particularly the slender ones that rise up to Bernal Heights Park north of Cortland) are delightful for aimless strolling, while a small handful of stairways are hidden amid the hillside-hugging homes between the park's peak (topped by an unattractive radio tower) and Mission Street to the west – the best are found along Eugenia Avenue and Esmeralda Corridor. Coming down the north slope of Bernal Hill, you'll stumble upon the narrow strip of Precita Park and its humble yet charming namesake mini-neighbourhood.

Potrero Hill

MAP P.88, POCKET MAP K6–L6
Ⓜ #9, #10, #19, #22, #33, #48, T.

Due east of (and far upslope from) the Mission, **Potrero Hill** offers mellow shopping and dining options, San Francisco's most beloved brewery (Anchor Brewing, see below) and unencumbered close-up views of Downtown and San Francisco Bay, making the peaceful neighbourhood a pleasant diversion for a few hours. Expect a stiff walk from the surrounding flatlands to reach Potrero's pair of quiet retail areas along 18th and 20th streets; otherwise, a few bus

Bernal Heights

lines will shuttle you uphill, while those coming by car will be pleased to find that parking options around here are strangely plentiful.

To enjoy one of the more marvellous surprise views in the city, walk to the large north-facing windows on the upstairs level of the **public library** at 1616 20th St.

Anchor Brewing

MAP P.88, POCKET MAP L6
1705 Mariposa St at Carolina St
Ⓜ #10, #19, #22. ☏ 415 863 8350,
Ⓦ anchorbrewing.com. Tours: twice daily (call for times); 90min; reservations essential. $25.

On the northwest flank of Potrero Hill, **Anchor Brewing** was founded in 1896 and struggled through a long period of difficulty following Prohibition before finally capitalizing on – some would say inspiring – the American artisan beer boom of the late twentieth century. After this, the brewery went on to become San Francisco's signature beer producer. An engaging tour tells the brewery's fascinating story and ends with a tasting of several different Anchor varieties.

Shops and galleries

826 Valencia

MAP P.88, POCKET MAP J6
826 Valencia St at 19th St Ⓜ #14, #33, #49; Ⓜ 16th St Mission. ☎ 415 642 5905, ⓦ 826valencia.org/store. Daily noon–6pm.
Swashbuckling in the classic sense of the term, this merry pirate supply shop – a business face for writer/publisher Dave Eggers' non-profit youth writing workshop in the rear of the space – stocks all manner of high-seas paraphernalia, from eye patches and gunpowder horns to hook wax, with Eggers' publications for sale too. Don't miss Pasha the Pufferfish swimming in his tank.

Asterisk Gallery

MAP P.88, POCKET MAP J7
3156 24th St at Shotwell St Ⓜ #12, #14, #48, #49; Ⓑ 24th St Mission. ☎ 415 839 9707, ⓦ asterisksanfrancisco.com/#asfgallery. Wed–Sat 11am–5pm.
Hosting a broad range of shows spanning paintings, sound-based installations, 3D drawings and photography, the small but spirited Asterisk Gallery showcases the best of San Francisco's underground talents.

Dog Eared Books

MAP P.88, POCKET MAP J6
900 Valencia St at 20th St Ⓜ #14, #33, #49; Ⓑ 24th St Mission. ☎ 415 282 1901, ⓦ dogearedbooks.com. Daily 10am–10pm.
With a prime location in the heart of Valencia's retail strip, Dog Eared is one of the Mission's top bookshops, featuring periodic author events and a range of new, secondhand and remaindered titles.

Paxton Gate

MAP P.88, POCKET MAP J6
824 Valencia St at 19th St Ⓜ #14, #33, #49; Ⓑ 16th St Mission. ☎ 415 824 1872, ⓦ paxtongate.com/paxton. Mon–Wed & Sun 11am–7pm, Thurs–Sat 11am–8pm.
There's no better place than darkly whimsical Paxton Gate for your taxidermy needs. This shop/gallery sells artfully arranged insects and stuffed mammals – some snarling, most docile – as well as jewellery and a range of succulents and cacti.

Schauplatz

MAP P.88, POCKET MAP J6
791 Valencia St at 19th St Ⓜ #14, #33, #49; Ⓑ 16th St Mission. ☎ 415 864 5665. Mon & Wed–Sat 1–7pm, Sun 1–6pm.
Packed with exceptionally preserved vintage apparel, this German-staffed boutique is one of the best places in the Mission for clothes dating from the 1970s and earlier. Prices are on the higher side, but the friendly owner may knock off a few dollars from your total.

Stranded Records

MAP P.88, POCKET MAP J7
1055 Valencia St at 21st St Ⓜ #14, #49; Ⓑ 24th St Mission. ☎ 415 647 2272, ⓦ strandedrecords.com. Daily 11am–8pm.
Having opened in 2016 in the former Aquarius space (which had been selling records since 1970), this small, independent shop remains fanatical about underground music. It's the retail arm of the archival label Superior Viaduct, based in Oakland.

Cafés and snacks

La Espiga de Oro

MAP P.88, POCKET MAP K7
2916 24th St at Florida St Ⓜ #27, #48; Ⓑ 24th St Mission. ☎ 415 826 1363. Mon–Thurs & Sat 6am–7pm, Fri 6am–7.30pm, Sun 6am–6pm.
This highly regarded *taqueria* is known for grilling some of the finest tortillas in San Francisco, so whatever you order here, make sure it includes one of the shop's famed flour or corn wraps. Everything's made to order and under $10.

Mission Pie

MAP P.88, POCKET MAP J7

2901 Mission St at 25th St Ⓜ #12, #14, #27, #48, #49; Ⓑ 24th St Mission. ☎ 415 282 1500, ⓦ missionpie.com. Mon–Fri 7am–10pm, Sat 8am–10pm, Sun 9am–10pm.

San Francisco's leading sweet pie bakery and retailer does a fervent business in its corner bakeshop, where slices ($4) and whole pies (about $27) are on offer. Variations rotate daily – expect tried-and-true favourites such as banana cream alongside left-field concoctions like ginger pear.

Mitchell's Ice Cream

MAP P.88, POCKET MAP J8
688 San Jose Ave at 29th St Ⓜ #14, #24, #49, J; Ⓑ 24th St Mission. ☎ 415 648 2300, ⓦ mitchellsicecream.com. Daily 11am–11pm.

This long-popular ice-cream shop is easy to find, particularly on warm days and most evenings – just look for the swarm of locals outside its standing-room-only storefront. All its flavours are produced on site, from rocky road and thin mint, to lychee and rum raisin; a double scoop costs under $5.

Philz Coffee

MAP P.88, POCKET MAP J7
3101 24th St at Folsom St Ⓜ #12, #14, #48, #49; Ⓑ 24th St Mission. ☎ 415 875 9370, ⓦ philzcoffee.com. Mon–Fri 6am–8pm, Sat & Sun 6.30am–8pm.

In a city obsessed with coffee, Philz regularly wins polls as San Francisco's top roaster. Along with individually made cups to enjoy here or take away, the shop also sells its variety of secret-recipe custom blends by the pound ($18).

Serrano's Pizza

MAP P.88, POCKET MAP J7
3274 21st St at Valencia St Ⓜ #14, #49; Ⓑ 24th St Mission. ☎ 415 695 1615, ⓦ serranospizza.com. Mon–Thurs & Sun 11am–midnight, Fri & Sat 11am–1am.

Featuring an almost overwhelming variety of toppings, the menu at this pizza and pasta hole-in-the-wall appeals to everyone. Oversize slices cost $4.50 and won't leave you hungry.

Taqueria Can-cún

MAP P.88, POCKET MAP J8
3211 Mission St at Fair Ave Ⓜ #12, #14,

826 Valencia

Delfina

#24, #49; Ⓑ 24th St Mission. Ⓣ 415 550 1414. Mon–Wed & Sun 11am–11.45pm, Thurs 11am–1.45am, Fri & Sat 11am–2.45am.

No San Francisco *taqueria* is more generous with avocado than this longtime standby on lower Mission St, where the home-made *horchata* (a delicious rice-cinnamon drink) helps absorb the inevitable spice incursions. The super vegetarian burrito (about $9) is rightfully legendary among the local meat-averse community.

Tartine Bakery & Café

MAP P.88, POCKET MAP J6
600 Guerrero St at 18th St Ⓜ #14, #22, #33, #49, J; Ⓑ 16th St Mission. Ⓣ 415 487 2600, Ⓦ tartinebakery.com. Mon 8am–7pm, Tues & Wed 7.30am–7pm, Thurs & Fri 7.30am–8pm, Sat & Sun 8am–8pm.

Drawing in loyalists from miles around daily, this always-thronged corner bakery concocts peerlessly flavourful pastries, tasty hot-pressed sandwiches ($13.25–14.50) and bread pudding desserts.

Restaurants

Baby Blues BBQ

MAP P.88, POCKET MAP J8
3149 Mission St at Precita Ave Ⓜ #12, #14, #27, #49; Ⓑ 24th St Mission. Ⓣ 415

896 4250, Ⓦ babybluesbbq.com. Mon–Thurs & Sun 11.30am–10pm, Fri & Sat 11.30am–11pm.

From its terrific smoked salmon salad ($14.95) and devastatingly delicious blue cheese "Lasker Burger" ($12.95), on through top-rate platters of smoked meats and a smorgasbord of spicy sauces on every table, this welcoming spot wins the gold in San Francisco's BBQ olympiad.

Chilli Cha Cha

MAP P.88, POCKET MAP J7
3166 24th St at Shotwell St Ⓜ #12, #14, #48, #49; Ⓑ 24th St Mission. Ⓣ 415 829 2960, Ⓦ chilichacha2.com. Daily 11am–11pm.

Set amid 24th Street's Mexican markets and *taquerias*, low-profile *Chilli Cha Cha* concocts Thai appetizers and mains that routinely hit the mark. Excellent curries and basil-lashed vegetable plates cost around $10 apiece.

Delfina

MAP P.88, POCKET MAP H6
3621 18th St at Guerrero St Ⓜ #14, #22, #33, #49, J; Ⓑ 16th St Mission. Ⓣ 415 552 4055, Ⓦ delfinasf.com/restaurant. Mon–Thurs 5.30–10pm, Fri & Sat 5.30–11pm, Sun 5–10pm.

Having surpassed the usual shelf life of trendy restaurants by several years, Mission mainstay *Delfina* continues to create a buzz in the neighbourhood. Try any number of inventive Cal-Ital hybrid mains, such as rosemary tagliatelle with wild boar ragu ($22).

Dosa

MAP P.88, POCKET MAP J6
995 Valencia St at 21st St Ⓜ #14, #49; Ⓑ 24th St Mission. Ⓣ 415 642 3672, Ⓦ dosasf.com/dosa-valencia. Mon–Thurs 5.30–10pm, Fri 5.30pm–11pm, Sat 11am–3pm & 5.30pm–11pm, Sun 11am–3pm & 5.30–10pm.

Named for the thin, pancake-like food in which it specializes, this highly touted South Indian restaurant remains as popular as ever. Be sure to try an *uttapam* – thicker than a *dosa* but just as mightily delicious. Expect to spend over $35 per person.

Goood Frikin Chicken

MAP P.88, POCKET MAP J8
10 29th St at Mission St Ⓜ #14, #24, #49, J; Ⓑ 24th St Mission. Ⓣ 415 970 2428, Ⓦ gooodfrickinchicken.com. Daily 11am–9pm.

You'll likely groan at *Goood Frikin Chicken*'s unfortunate name up until the moment you bite into its rotisserie half-chicken ($12), roasted with a variety of herbs and spices, and served with pillowy, olive-oil-touched pitta bread.

Just for You

MAP P.88, POCKET MAP M6
732 22nd St at Third St Ⓜ #22, #28, T. Ⓣ 415 647 3033, Ⓦ justforyoucafe.com. Mon–Fri 7.30am–3pm, Sat & Sun 8am–4pm.

You'll struggle to find something on *Just for You*'s menu that won't win you over instantly, from the home-made breads and extra-large beignets to the exceptional omelettes, pancakes and sandwiches, each around $13.

Piqueo's

MAP P.88, POCKET MAP J9
830 Cortland Ave at Gates St Ⓜ #24.

Ⓣ 415 282 8812, Ⓦ piqueos.com. Daily 5.30–10pm (till 10.30pm Fri & Sat).

Set off the beaten tourist path in Bernal Heights, *Piqueo's* warm ambience, impressive wine list and range of Peruvian *ceviches*, tapas and paellas (most $12–22) all make for a charming night out.

Radio Habana Social Club

MAP P.88, POCKET MAP J7
1109 Valencia St at 22nd St Ⓜ #12, #14, #48, #49; Ⓑ 24th St Mission. Ⓣ 415 824 7659. Daily 7.30pm–midnight. Cash only.

Drawing a mixed-bag crowd, this stalwart bolthole is always a sure bet for conviviality. Come for Cuban dinner platters (all under $10), pitchers of punch-packing sangria, and singular decor such as vintage postcards and kitschy religious icons.

Bars

El Rio

MAP P.88, POCKET MAP J8
3158 Mission St at Valencia St Ⓜ #12, #14, #27, #49; Ⓑ 24th St Mission. Ⓣ 415 282 3325, Ⓦ elriosf.com. Daily 1pm–2am.

El Rio

El Rio fulfils many roles – live music venue, LGBTQ nightspot, salsa club, burlesque performance space – but at its heart, this multi-room joint is a welcoming neighbourhood bar along one of Mission Street's liveliest stretches. Shows free to $10.

Latin American Club

MAP P.88, POCKET MAP J7
3286 22nd St at Valencia St Ⓜ #12, #14, #48, #49; Ⓑ 24th St Mission. ☎ 415 647 2732. Mon–Fri 5pm–2am, Sat 1pm–2am, Sun 2pm–2am.
This funky, longtime Mission watering hole is best in late afternoon (weekends only) and early evening, before heat-seeking crowds jam the place en masse. If you can nab one, the few tables scattered outside along the pavement are terrific for chatting and people-watching.

The Ramp

MAP P.88, POCKET MAP M6
855 Terry Francois St at Illinois St Ⓜ #22, T. ☎ 415 621 2378, Ⓦ rampsf.com. Mon–Fri 11am–9pm, Sat & Sun 10am–9pm.
While not a late-night destination, and certainly not a place you'll simply stumble upon, this bay-side bar-restaurant, which overlooks an evocative (if forgotten) part of San Francisco's shoreline, is one of the best out-of-the-way spots in the city for alfresco drinks and casual food. Live salsa bands perform every Saturday evening.

The Wild Side West

Revolution Cafe

MAP P.88, POCKET MAP J7
3248 22nd St at Bartlett St Ⓜ #12, #14, #48, #49; Ⓑ 24th St Mission. ☎ 415 642 0474, Ⓦ revolutioncafesf.com. Mon–Thurs & Sun 9am–midnight, Fri & Sat 9am–2am.
Europe and California cross paths at laidback and open-air *Revolution Cafe*, where made-to-order sandwiches and salads, draught beer, wine and *soju* cocktails fill out the menu, and an upright piano beckons anyone looking to tickle the ivories. All this, plus an eclectic array of nightly live music.

Royal Cuckoo

MAP P.88, POCKET MAP J8
3202 Mission St at Valencia St Ⓜ #12, #14, #27, #49; Ⓑ 24th St Mission. ☎ 415 550 8667, Ⓦ bit.ly/RoyalCuckoo. Mon–Thurs 4pm–2am, Fri–Sun 3pm–2am.
While it may seem kitschy on the surface, this moodily lit cocktail lounge – Hammond organist (Wednesday–Sunday) and all – is one of the better theme bars in the city. Along with a litany of house cocktails (from $10; cash only), there's also a wide range of beer and wine.

The Wild Side West

MAP P.88, POCKET MAP J8
424 Cortland Ave at Andover St Ⓜ #24. ☎ 415 647 3099. Daily 2pm–2am.
Known as the most welcoming lesbian bar in town, *The Wild Side West* has anchored Bernal Heights' bar scene since 1962. The frontier-reminiscent bar-room is decked out with heaps of Americana decor, while the multi-tiered back patio and dog-friendly garden (with plenty of seating) give visitors a glimpse of San Francisco back-yard life.

Zeitgeist

MAP P.88, POCKET MAP J5
199 Valencia St at Duboce Ave Ⓜ #6, #14, #49, #71, F, J, K, L, M, N, T; Ⓑ 16th St Mission. ☎ 415 255 7505. Daily 9am–2am.
One of the Mission's most punk-to-the-core places for a drink, *Zeitgeist* is best known for its sprawling beer

Elbo Room

garden and weekend afternoon cookouts, although its Bloody Mary ($8) is also a local legend in its own right.

Clubs

Bissap Baobab Village

MAP P.88, POCKET MAP J6
3372 19th St at Mission St Ⓜ #12, #14, #33, #49; Ⓑ 16th St Mission. ☎ 415 643 3558, Ⓦ bissapbaobab.com. Tues & Sun 5.30–10pm, Wed–Sat 5.30pm–2am. $5–10.
This Senegalese bistro becomes a West African dance hall later on, when DJs spin tunes that span the African diaspora. Dinner is worth arriving early for – try the *niebe thies* (lamb with black-eyed peas in spicy sauce, $16).

Elbo Room

MAP P.88, POCKET MAP J6
647 Valencia St at 17th St Ⓜ #14, #22, #33, #49; Ⓑ 16th St Mission. ☎ 415 552 7788, Ⓦ elbo.com. Daily 5pm–2am. $7 and up.
Although it gained notoriety as a birthplace of acid jazz and continues to host live performances (everything from punk to touring Latin American acts), the *Elbo Room* is now known more as a DJ venue. The first and third weekends of the

month see the always-fun "Saturday Night Soul Party" take place.

Live music venues

Amnesia

MAP P.88, POCKET MAP J6
853 Valencia St at 20th St Ⓜ #14, #33, #49; Ⓑ 16th St Mission. ☎ 415 970 0012, Ⓦ amnesiathebar.com. Daily 4pm–2am. Free–$10.
Bluegrass jams on Monday, jazz each Wednesday and assorted bands and DJs other nights: *Amnesia*'s booking habits elude easy categorization. The red-lit club has a broad beer selection, with $5 deals on Pabst Blue Ribbon for budget drinkers, and excellent sangria also on tap.

Bottom of the Hill

MAP P.88, POCKET MAP L6
1233 17th St at Missouri St Ⓜ #10, #19, #22. ☎ 415 626 4455, Ⓦ bottomofthehill. com. Daily 8.30pm–2am. $8 and up.
Veteran and venerated, *Bottom of the Hill* remains San Francisco's indie rock touchstone venue, where the likes of Oasis, Death Cab for Cutie and Elliott Smith played in the early days of their ascents to fame. The grotty rear patio is a smoker's haven.

The Castro and around

The rainbow flag-plastered Castro may not possess the bacchanalian atmosphere it once did, but it's a neighbourhood that clearly still knows how to have a good time. It emerged from Irish working-class origins to become San Francisco's – and perhaps America's – epicentre of LGBTQ culture by the 1970s, and today it's one of the tidiest areas of the city, a prismatic fusion of male couples parading the pavements, richly decorated retailers' windows and a general feeling of ebullience, although poignant remembrances of LGBTQ rights struggles can also be found at Harvey Milk Plaza and Pink Triangle Park. High overhead to the west, Twin Peaks and Tank Hill provide stellar vantage points over the Castro and beyond, while just south, worthwhile shopping and eating opportunities abound in the neighbourhoods of Noe Valley and Glen Park.

Castro Street

MAP P.100, POCKET MAP G5–H8
Ⓜ #24, #33, F, K, L, M, T.

The throbbing heart of the Castro is the stretch of **Castro Street** between 17th and 19th streets, a two-block strip rich with LGBTQ-friendly bars, restaurants and shops, as well as the **Castro Theatre** and, not least of all, vibrant street life. Easily reached from both Downtown and the city's southwest neighbourhoods via the Castro station along the Market Street subway, Castro Street is one of the most prominent thoroughfares of gay culture you'll find anywhere. A memorial plaque marks where avid photographer Harvey Milk opened **Castro Camera** at no. 575 in 1972, eventually using the storefront to raise his visibility as a community activist before it became campaign headquarters for his runs at a City Supervisor position later in the decade.

Castro Street is also the site of several annual community celebrations – most notably its namesake **street fair**, which is held in early October, as well as exuberant **Pride** festivities (see page 157) in late June, which attract up to half a million people.

Castro Theatre

MAP P.100, POCKET MAP H6
429 Castro St at 17th St Ⓜ #24, #33, F, K, L, M, T. ☎ 415 621 6120, Ⓦ castrotheatre. com. **Open only during film showings.**

San Francisco's finest palace of cinema, the extravagant **Castro Theatre** brings in devotees from all over the Bay Area for its varied programming and spectacular architecture. The landmark theatre opened in 1922 and was designed by Timothy Pflueger, who also masterminded Oakland's beautiful Paramount Theatre (see page 131), as well as San Francisco's City Club. Pflueger's expert grasp of the Mediterranean Revival style is on full display in the theatre exterior's flamboyant stucco and lovely window work, while the interior is just as grandiose, its enormous chandelier and busts of stately figures topping the list of ornamental excesses.

Many filmgoers like to arrive early to enjoy the pre-show Wurlitzer organ performance, while it's also worth noting Castro audiences are a notoriously animated lot – don't be surprised when on-screen heroes are cheered and villains are hissed.

GLBT History Museum

MAP P.100, POCKET MAP H6
4127 18th St at Castro St Ⓜ #24, #33, F, K, L,M, T. ☏ 415 621 1107, ⓦ glbthistory. org/museum. Mon–Sat 11am–6pm, Sun noon–5pm. $5.

Located in the heart of the Castro, the GLBT History Museum offers a poignant reminder of just how hard it was to create the successful community outside. The multimedia exhibits include Harvey Milk artefacts, historic lesbian and gay posters from the museum's extensive collection, and displays on pioneers such as José Sarria, drag queen and political activist who, in 1961, became the first openly gay candidate for public office in the US.

Harvey Milk Plaza

MAP P.100, POCKET MAP H6
Castro St at Market St Ⓜ #24, #33, F, K, L, M, T.

Serving double duty as a sunken entry to Muni's underground Castro station, concrete-and-brick **Harvey Milk Plaza** commemorates the martyred politician whose influence is felt throughout the neighbourhood he galvanized in the 1970s. The so-called Mayor of Castro Street was elected as San Francisco's first openly gay City Supervisor in 1977 and soon became one of the most prominent gay government officials in the US before his 1978 assassination at City Hall (see page 78); the New York native's story was told in the acclaimed 2008 film *Milk*, with Sean Penn portraying the fallen hero with startling accuracy. Visible for miles around, a 600-square-foot rainbow flag flutters overhead,

the work of Milk's artist friend Gilbert Baker, who came up with the design as a universal symbol for gay freedom the same year as Milk's tragic death.

Pink Triangle Park

MAP P.100, POCKET MAP G6
Market St at 17th St Ⓜ #24, #33, F, K, L, M, T. ⓦ pinktrianglepark.org.

Appropriately sitting adjacent to, but clearly apart from, the Castro's lively hubbub, solemn **Pink Triangle Park** memorializes all victims of the Holocaust who, due to sexual orientation, wore pink triangles on their concentration camp uniforms. A pink triangle rests at the centre of the three-sided park, attractively filled out with agave cacti and pink rose bushes. The space also includes 15 pink triangle-topped granite pylons, each one symbolic of one thousand LGBTQ people murdered by the Third Reich.

Pride, Castro Street

The Castro and around

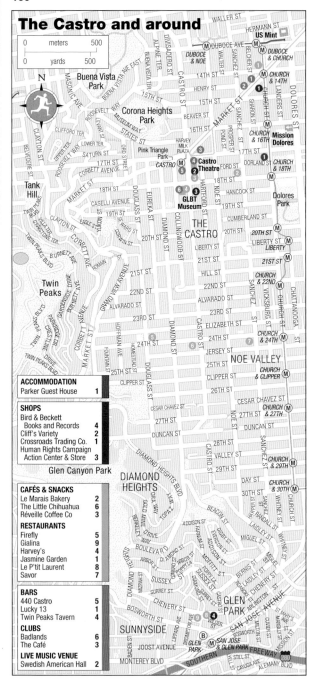

ACCOMMODATION
Parker Guest House 1

SHOPS
Bird & Beckett
  Books and Records 4
Cliff's Variety 2
Crossroads Trading Co. 1
Human Rights Campaign
  Action Center & Store 3

CAFÉS & SNACKS
Le Marais Bakery 2
The Little Chihuahua 6
Réveille Coffee Co 3

RESTAURANTS
Firefly 5
Gialina 9
Harvey's 4
Jasmine Garden 1
Le P'tit Laurent 8
Savor 7

BARS
440 Castro 5
Lucky 13 1
Twin Peaks Tavern 4

CLUBS
Badlands 6
The Café 3

LIVE MUSIC VENUE
Swedish American Hall 2

Twin Peaks

MAP P.100, POCKET MAP G7

Ⓜ #36, #37.

Looming over the Castro and Mission districts, tree-bare **Twin Peaks** may not constitute the city's highest points – that distinction goes to 925ft Mount Davidson, a short distance south – but they're certainly the most prominent. At 910ft and 904ft, the pair of promontories acts as a moisture shield during the Pacific coast's foggier months, often helping prevent thick fog from enveloping the city's eastern districts. First saucily named Los Pechos de la Chola ("Breasts of an Indian Girl") by randy Spanish settlers, the name of the rounded peaks was blandly anglicized by the time San Francisco passed into US hands. Some decades later, in the early twentieth century, Twin Peaks was the proposed home of a large amphitheatre – a grand gesture that, sadly, never came to pass.

Today, a parking area just below the north peak is a major

destination for its epic vistas; public transport riders should note, however, that Muni's 36–Teresita and 37–Corbett buses only climb partway to the summit, necessitating a bit of a hike to the gusty main lookout.

Tank Hill

MAP P.100, POCKET MAP F6

Ⓜ #33, #37.

At 650ft, **Tank Hill** offers a bird's-eye view of the surrounding districts and beyond without the tourist ruckus of its higher-profile neighbour, Twin Peaks, just to the south. Best accessed from Clarendon Avenue, the small park affords a striking vista that includes both the Golden Gate and Bay bridges; it's named for an enormous water repository that sat atop its flattened peak until 1957, after which the hilltop narrowly escaped private development. The park's grove of eucalyptus trees was planted during World War II to hide the bygone tank from wartime bomb attacks.

View from the Twin Peaks

Shops

Bird & Beckett Books and Records

MAP P.100, POCKET MAP H9
653 Chenery St at Castro St Ⓜ #23, #36, #44, J; Ⓑ Glen Park. Ⓣ 415 586 3733, Ⓦ birdbeckett.com. Mon–Thurs, Sat & Sun 11am–7pm, Fri 11am–9pm.

Its name paying homage to Charlie "Bird" Parker and Samuel Beckett, this well-stocked bookshop occupies the former Glen Park library. Author events are scheduled regularly and jazz ensembles appear on the shop's small stage every Friday and Saturday evening and Sunday afternoon; the selection of jazz LPs and CDs on hand, however, is often on the thin side.

Cliff's Variety

MAP P.100, POCKET MAP H6
479 Castro St at 18th St Ⓜ #24, #33, F, K, L, M, T. Ⓣ 415 431 5365, Ⓦ cliffsvariety.com. Mon–Sat 10am–8pm, Sun 10am–6pm.

While most San Francisco visitors surely aren't looking for a shop that sells screwdrivers and performs angled wood cuts, it's still worth roaming the aisles of this longtime

Bird & Beckett Books and Records

Castro catch-all bazaar to browse its fine selection of feather boas (sold by the yard) and toys, alongside hardware and everyday home items.

Crossroads Trading Co.

MAP P.100, POCKET MAP H5
2123 Market St at Church St Ⓜ #22, F, J, K, L, M, N, T. Ⓣ 415 552 8740, Ⓦ crossroadstrading.com. Mon–Sat 11am–8pm, Sun 11am–7pm.

Now a national chain, this Bay Area-born clothier remains one of the leading places in town for top-condition secondhand apparel (men's and women's), as well as some new items. You'll also find accessories such as hats and sunglasses here.

Human Rights Campaign Action Center & Store

MAP P.100, POCKET MAP H6
575 Castro St, between 18th and 19th sts Ⓜ #24, #33, F, K, L, M, T. Ⓣ 415 431 2200, Ⓦ shop.hrc.org. Mon–Sat 10am–8pm, Sun 10am–7pm.

One of the Castro's most venerable nonprofits, housed in Harvey Milk's old home and shop ("Castro Camera"), the HRC store sells LGBTQ-themed apparel and gifts, from T-shirts to sterling silver jewellery, plus items emblazoned with the words and images of Milk himself. All profits are donated to the Harvey Milk Foundation.

Cafés and snacks

Le Marais Bakery

MAP P.100, POCKET MAP H6
498 Sanchez St at 18th St M#22, #24, #33, F, J, K, L, M, N, T. Ⓣ 415 359 9801, Ⓦ lemaraisbakery.com. Daily 7.30am–7pm.

This Parisian-style mini-bakery chain owned by French-born Patrick Ascaso looks the part, with plenty of brass, tile, marble and wood, plus wonderful Sightglass coffee and pastries (croissants, macarons and various cakes; $2–6), as well as a breakfast and rotisserie menu (roast chicken from $15).

The Little Chihuahua

MAP P.100, POCKET MAP H7

4123 24th St at Castro St ⓦ #24, #48.
ⓣ 415 648 4157, ⓦ thelittlechihuahua.
com. Mon–Fri 11am–10pm, Sat & Sun
10am–10pm.

This amiable Cal-Mex place in
Noe Valley specializes in deeply
flavourful salsas, often spectacular
burritos ($9.45 and up) and unique
brunch items at weekends – try
the Mexican French toast – while
further items like sangria and
warm, homemade tortilla chips put
it leagues ahead of other *taquerias*
in the city.

Réveille Coffee Co

MAP P.100, POCKET MAP H6

4076 18th St at Castro St ⓦ #24, #33, F, K,
L, M, T. ⓣ 415 789 6258, ⓦ reveillecoffee.
com. Daily 7am–7pm.

Friendly neighbourhood coffee
joint with a stylish interior of
blonde wood and graphic tilework,
a bright outdoor patio and a
menu of salads and sandwiches, in
addition to its quality Colombian
coffees and tasty pastries.

Restaurants

Firefly

MAP P.100, POCKET MAP G7

4288 24th St at Douglass St ⓦ #24, #48.
ⓣ 415 821 7652, ⓦ fireflysf.com. Daily
5.30–10pm.

Sequestered upslope towards 24th
Street's western end in Noe Valley,
the delightful *Firefly* isn't a place
you'd necessarily stumble upon
by chance. Brilliant mains such as
Puerto Rican braised pork shoulder
with sweet potato–plantain mash
($28) and corn, crimini and tofu
skewers with green chile grits and
collard greens ($24) will make
you happy you found your way
here, though.

Gialina

MAP P.100, POCKET MAP H9

2842 Diamond St at Kern St ⓦ #23, #36,
#44, J; ⓑ Glen Park. ⓣ 415 239 8500,

Cliff's Variety

ⓦ gialina.com. Mon–Thurs & Sun 5–10pm,
Fri & Sat 5–10.30pm.

A mainstay on Glen Park's
restaurant scene, humbly sized
Gialina is best known for its
twelve-inch Neapolitan-style pizzas
– the chilli-fired Atomica ($15)
and pesto with chard ($16) options
are always favourites – while a
smattering of pastas and roasts fills
out the menu. No reservations are
taken, so come early or expect to
wait a while.

Harvey's

MAP P.100, POCKET MAP H6

500 Castro St at 18th St ⓦ #24, #33, F, K,
L, M, T. ⓣ 415 431 4278, ⓦ harveyssf.com.
Mon–Fri 11am–11pm, Sat & Sun 9am–2am.

Castro linchpin *Harvey's* has thrived
in its prime corner space since the
mid-1990s, with neighbourhood
denizens pouring in for dependable
mains such as sandwiches, burgers
and salads ($10 and up), plus a raft
of Bloody Mary options. There's
also stand-up comedy on Tuesdays
and happy-hour specials each
weekday (3–6pm).

Jasmine Garden

MAP P.100, POCKET MAP H5

Twin Peaks Tavern

708 14th St at Church St Ⓜ #22, F, J, K, L, M, N, T. ☎ 415 861 2682. Mon, Wed & Thurs noon–4pm & 5–9.30pm, Fri–Sun noon–4pm & 5–10pm.
Whether you come for delectably grilled five-spice chicken, soul-soothing *phô* or any other winning item on the menu, pleasant *Jasmine Garden* is sure to satisfy your Vietnamese cravings. Most mains hover affordably around the $12 mark.

Le P'tit Laurent

MAP P.100, POCKET MAP H9
699 Chenery St at Diamond St Ⓜ #23, #36, #44, J; Ⓑ Glen Park. ☎ 415 334 3235, Ⓦ leptitlaurent.net. Mon–Thurs & Sun 5.30–9.30pm, Fri & Sat 5.30–10.30pm.
Always warm and festive, *Le P'tit Laurent* in tiny Glen Park charms its clientele with some of San Francisco's finest French *plats*, including rabbit Normandy ($36) and one of the meatiest cassoulets around ($35, complete with a full duck leg). The weekly changing prix fixe "Neighborhood Menu" (Mon–Thurs & Sun, $28) is another popular dining option. Be sure to arrive a little early to make time for an *aperitif* at the small bar.

Savor

MAP P.100, POCKET MAP H7
3913 24th St at Sanchez St Ⓜ #24, #48, J. ☎ 415 282 0344, Ⓦ savorrestaurant.com. Mon–Sat 8am–10pm, Sun 8am–9pm.

There's something for everyone at this popular, inexpensive indoor-outdoor restaurant in Noe Valley, where the sprawling menu spans breakfast, lunch and dinner to include everything from omelettes and crêpes to pasta, salads and bruschetta-topped chicken (all $11–20). The heated back patio provides a calm alternative to *Savor*'s noisier interior.

Bars

440 Castro

MAP P.100, POCKET MAP H6
440 Castro St at 17th St Ⓜ #24, #33, F, K, L, M, T. ☎ 415 621 8732, Ⓦ the440.com. Daily noon–2am.
This rowdy gay bar along the Castro's eponymous main drag is an affirmed neighbourhood favourite – especially on Mondays, when the *440's* "Underwear Night" brings in regulars decked out in very little. The first Monday of the month takes the concept even further with a "Battle of the Bulges" contest (with a $150 prize).

Lucky 13

MAP P.100, POCKET MAP H5
2140 Market St at Church St Ⓜ #22, F, J, K, L, M, N, T. ☎ 415 487 1313. Daily 11am–2am.
The edge of the Castro towards Market and Church streets is home to a few straight bars, and *Lucky 13* is the best of the lot for its beer selection, pool, complimentary

popcorn, great balcony, and jukebox blasting a soundtrack of punk rock and Johnny Cash.

Twin Peaks Tavern

MAP P.100, POCKET MAP H6
401 Castro St at 17th St Ⓜ #24, #33, F, K, L, M, T. ☎ 415 864 9470, Ⓦ twinpeakstavern. com. Mon–Wed noon–2am, Thurs–Sat 8am–2am, Sun 10am–2am.

Twin Peaks Tavern is a terrific place, not only to people-watch through the first clear front windows to be installed at a gay bar in the US, but to absorb this friendly and welcoming corner spot's old-guard Castro vibe.

Clubs

Badlands

MAP P.100, POCKET MAP H6
4131 18th St at Collingwood St Ⓜ #24, #33, F, K, L, M, T. ☎ 415 626 9320, Ⓦ sfbadlands.com. Daily 2pm–2am.

The top place in the Castro for dancing, video club *Badlands* is a madhouse at weekends when the floor is jammed with shirtless men showing off their moves. The front lounge is a bit mellower, although often still buzzing.

The Café

MAP P.100, POCKET MAP H6
2369 Market St at 17th St Ⓜ #24, #33, F, K, L, M, T. ☎ 415 523 1033, Ⓦ cafesf.com. Tues–Thurs 6pm–2am, Fri 5pm–2am, Sat 3pm–2am, Sun 2pm–2am.

This longtime gay venue morphs from bar to dance club by 9pm (Thurs–Sun), when cheap covers (free–$5) and DJs bring in crowds of punters for outrageous parties like "iCandy Fridays" and Sunday's "Glamazone" drag show.

Live music venue

Swedish American Hall

MAP P.100, POCKET MAP H5
2170 Market St at Sanchez St Ⓜ #22, F, J, K, L, M, N, T. ☎ 415 861 5016, Ⓦ swedishamericanhallsf. $10 and up.

Up a few flights of stairs from humming Market Street, this evocative, dark wood-panelled venue holds no more than a few hundred concertgoers and plays host to a handful of mostly acoustic shows each month. Music is usually in the indie rock/folk vein, but there are occasional forays into other genres such as classic country.

Swedish American Hall

West of Civic Center

Spanning a motley mishmash of neighbourhoods, the sizeable area west of Civic Center extending towards Golden Gate Park is one of San Francisco's most varied. In the shadow of Civic Center sits once-grotty Hayes Valley, which has been revitalized by an influx of independent retailers and, most recently, an uncommonly high number of artisan dessert shops. Just to the west, Alamo Square and its adjacent line-up of signature Victorian houses, the "Painted Ladies", make for one of the city's most photographed perspectives. Less than a mile north, Japantown, despite its uninviting look, is a worthwhile stop for its range of Nihon-themed shops and restaurants. Finally, the Lower and Upper Haight districts, though distinct from one another, are linked by their namesake street – one of San Francisco's best for shopping, eating and drinking.

Hayes Valley

MAP P.108, POCKET MAP H4–J4
Ⓜ #21, #47, #49, F, J, K, L, M, N, T; Ⓑ Civic Center.

For decades a less than savoury area bisected by the elevated Central Freeway, **Hayes Valley** – much like the Embarcadero (see page 27) –

Hayes Valley

saw its makeover begin in the wake of 1989's Loma Prieta earthquake, which rendered the overhead monstrosity unsafe. Once the highway was torn down in the early 1990s, the neighbourhood slowly came into its own as a number of alluring boutiques, cafés and restaurants started to line Hayes, Gough and other streets in the area. Though some have criticized the compact district's flurry of gentrifying redevelopment, one universally successful element of the area's reinvention has been the flowering of **Patricia's Green**, a narrow greenspace constructed along part of the bygone freeway's path in the heart of the neighbourhood, where temporary art installations make appearances throughout the year.

Alamo Square and the "Painted Ladies"

MAP P.108, POCKET MAP H4
Bordered by Fulton, Steiner, Hayes and Scott sts Ⓜ #5, #21, #22, #24.

A pleasant hilltop park in its own right, **Alamo Square** sees great numbers of visitors for the seven colourful Victorian houses that sit directly across from the park's southeast slope. Known as the **"Painted Ladies"**, these circa-1894 Italianate homes – and the lovely view of the city's skyline and San Francisco Bay stretching behind them – have appeared on San Francisco postcards for decades. Author Alice Walker lived at number 720 until the mid-1990s, while number 722 next door, the largest of the lot, was sold in 2014 for $3.1 million.

Japantown

MAP P.108, POCKET MAP H3

Ⓜ #2, #3, #22, #38.

Its original buildings razed and redeveloped in the decades immediately following World War II, drab yet demure **Japantown** is the centre of San Francisco's tightly knit Japanese-American community. Sadly, much of the district falls victim to its late 1960s Brutalist architectural origins, but the compact area – one of only a few remaining Japantowns in the US – is nonetheless worth a wander.

Japantown's linchpin is the awkward, uninspired **Japan Center**, a three-part indoor shopping mall that's home to dozens of Japanese restaurants and shops, while the concrete Peace Pagoda, a 1968 gift from San Francisco's sister city of Osaka, is set in an outdoor plaza linking the Japan Center buildings; the tower resembles a stack of spiked pancakes, although to some its design bears a striking resemblance to an atomic bomb cloud.

Lower Haight and Duboce Park

MAP P.108, POCKET MAP H5

Ⓜ #6, #7, #22, #24, F, J, K, L, M, N, T.

Charmingly rough around the edges, but less dense and harried than the better-known Upper Haight (see below), the **Lower Haight** comprises the batch of blocks

Haight Street

along its eponymous stretch between Divisadero and Laguna streets – a laidback commercial and residential tract full of plenty of engaging places to eat, drink and browse.

Two blocks south of Haight Street and mere steps from the neighbouring Castro District, slightly inclined **Duboce Park** is one of the most popular greenspaces in the city for dog owners to let their pets run free. This pooch paradise makes for an entertaining diversion – just watch where you step, and be sure to check the grass thoroughly before you sit down.

Upper Haight

MAP P.108, POCKET MAP F5–G5

Ⓜ #6, #7, #21, #24, #33, #43, N.

Known less frequently these days by its traditional "Haight-Ashbury" name, the **Upper Haight** struggles with a major homeless youth problem, just as it continues to entice crowds for its excellent shopping, lively restaurants and bars, and delightful Victorian and Edwardian buildings. A sand dune-strewn area labelled "Wasteland" on early San Francisco maps, today's

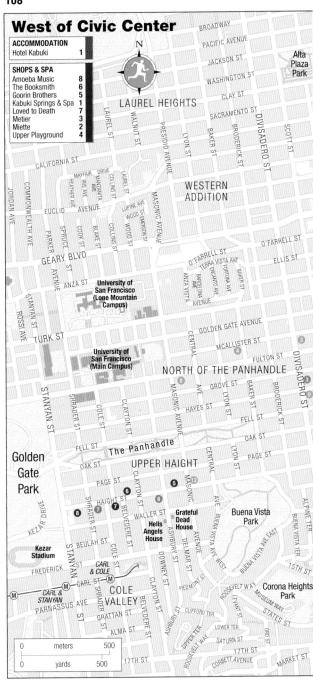

West of Civic Center

ACCOMMODATION	
Hotel Kabuki	1

SHOPS & SPA	
Amoeba Music	8
The Booksmith	6
Goorin Brothers	5
Kabuki Springs & Spa	1
Loved to Death	7
Metier	3
Miette	2
Upper Playground	4

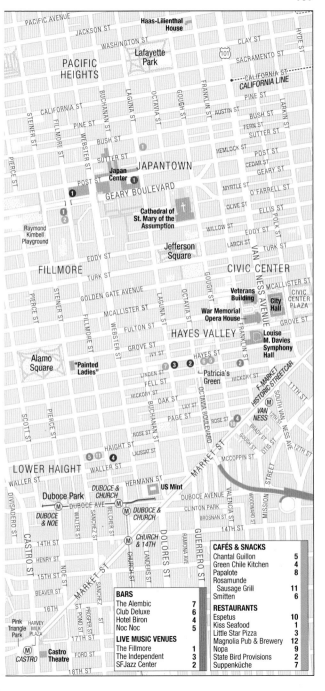

CAFÉS & SNACKS

Chantal Guillon	5
Green Chile Kitchen	4
Papalote	8
Rosamunde Sausage Grill	11
Smitten	6

RESTAURANTS

Espetus	10
Kiss Seafood	1
Little Star Pizza	3
Magnolia Pub & Brewery	12
Nopa	9
State Bird Provisions	2
Suppenküche	7

BARS

The Alembic	7
Club Deluxe	6
Hotel Biron	4
Noc Noc	5

LIVE MUSIC VENUES

The Fillmore	1
The Independent	3
SFJazz Center	2

neighbourhood shows multiple sides: to many visitors who barely stray from its namesake street's popular retail strip, it seems like a patchouli-scented carnival, its pavements emanating a combative mood that directly contradicts the district's trademark peace-and-love posturing; to others who walk its tree-lined blocks away from Haight Street, it's a pleasant residential enclave full of wonderfully restored homes.

The westernmost blocks of Haight Street – those nearest to Golden Gate Park – are its dodgiest for drug-dealing and aggressive panhandling, but provided you exercise caution, you're highly unlikely to run into trouble.

Grateful Dead and Hells Angels houses

MAP P.108, POCKET MAP G5
710 and 715 Ashbury St at Waller St Ⓜ #6, #7, #33, #43. Closed to the public.

In a neighbourhood known for rebellion – and for carrying a strong 1960s torch to this day – it's fitting that two of the Upper Haight's top sights were once inhabited by legends of that decade who were frequent targets for law

enforcement officials. Members of the **Grateful Dead** called 710 Ashbury Street home during the band's late 1960s ascent, when the San Francisco group's fame rose alongside that of Haight-Ashbury itself. Across the street, the infamous **Hells Angels** maintained ornamentally detailed number 719 as their San Francisco headquarters during the same volatile era.

The Panhandle

MAP P.108, POCKET MAP F5–G5
Ⓜ #6, #7, #21, #24, #33, #43.

Landscaped prior to the rest of Golden Gate Park, the **Panhandle** was a prime carriage ride venue before the 1906 earthquake and resultant fires turned it into a tented refuge for 30,000 families. The thin greenspace, which marks the northern edge of the Upper Haight, was nearly wiped out by a freeway proposal in the 1950s, then reached its zenith of notoriety during the neighbourhood's late 1960s heyday, when it was a hotbed for numerous hippy gatherings. Today it's run-down in parts, but its basketball courts, bike routes and running paths remain as popular as ever.

Former home of the Grateful Dead, 710 Ashbury Street

Shops and spa

Amoeba Music

MAP P.108, POCKET MAP F5
1855 Haight St at Stanyan St  #7, #33, #43, N. ☎ 415 831 1200, ⓦ amoeba.com. Daily 11am–8pm.

Widely recognized as one of the top independent music retailers nationwide, Amoeba is a bottomless well of new and used items, including vinyl, CDs, DVDs and memorabilia. Live performances (free) occur frequently on the store's sizeable stage.

The Booksmith

MAP P.108, POCKET MAP F5
1644 Haight St at Cole St Ⓜ #7, #33, #43, N. ☎ 415 863 8688, ⓦ booksmith.com. Mon–Sat 10am–10pm, Sun 10am–8pm.

While this Upper Haight mainstay is reliable for its robust and diverse book stock, it's perhaps best known for its ongoing series of prominent author visits – recent events have featured Roxane Gay and Ian Rankin. Check the website for upcoming events.

Goorin Brothers

MAP P.108, POCKET MAP G5
1446 Haight St at Masonic St Ⓜ #6, #7, #33, #43, N. ☎ 415 436 9450, ⓦ goorin. com. Mon–Fri 11am–7pm, Sat & Sun 10am–7pm.

In business locally since 1949, hat retailer Goorin Brothers has remained current through the decades, and today offers a broad scope of men's and women's caps, ranging from traditional to bold.

Kabuki Springs & Spa

MAP P.108, POCKET MAP H4
1750 Geary Blvd at Fillmore St Ⓜ #2, #3, #22, #38. ☎ 415 922 6000, ⓦ kabukisprings.com. Communal baths: daily 10am–10pm; men-only: Mon, Thurs & Sat; women-only: Wed, Fri & Sun; unisex: Tues. $25.

This Japantown spa features a full slate of treatments (including massages), but its most popular

Goorin Brothers

element is the communal bath area, which includes a steam room, dry sauna, small cold plunge pool and a larger hot soaking pool.

Loved to Death

MAP P.108, POCKET MAP F5
1681 Haight St at Cole St Ⓜ #7, #33, #43, N. ☎ 415 551 1036, ⓦ lovedtodeath.com. Daily noon–7pm.

While this gothic boutique is best known for creative taxidermy, it's also the best place in town to pick up esoteric gifts such as sword-shaped umbrellas, quill pens, decorative gator feet, Edward Gorey books, sheep brain specimens and the odd embalming rib cutter.

Metier

MAP P.108, POCKET MAP H4
546 Laguna St at Hayes St Ⓜ #5, #21, F, J, K, L, M, N, T; Ⓑ Civic Center. ☎ 415 590 2998, ⓦ metiersf.com. Tues–Sat noon–6pm.

This welcoming, diverse gallery of expensive women's clothes, jewellery and accessories features items by North American and European designers, with an emphasis on smart, limited-edition pieces.

Miette

Miette

MAP P.108, POCKET MAP H4
449 Octavia St at Hayes St Ⓜ #21, #47,
#49, F, J, K, L, M, N, T; Ⓔ Civic Center.
Ⓣ 415 626 6221, Ⓦ miette.com. Daily
11am–7pm.
Among the city's most loved sweet
shops, Miette is a feast for the
senses, where a host of delectable,
homemade sweets, cupcakes,
pastries and chocolates lines the
shelves and window display.

Upper Playground

MAP P.108, POCKET MAP H5
220 Fillmore St at Waller St Ⓜ #6, #7, #22,
N. Ⓣ 415 861 1960, Ⓦ upperplayground.
com. Daily 11am–7pm.
With its omnipresent walrus mascot
and unceasingly amusing designs –
many cleverly referencing the Bay
Area – Upper Playground remains
one of the top hip-hop clothing and
art boutiques in the city.

Cafés and snacks

Chantal Guillon

MAP P.108, POCKET MAP J4
437A Hayes St at Gough St Ⓜ #21, #47,
#49, F, J, K, L, M, N, T; Ⓔ Civic Center.
Ⓣ 415 864 2400, Ⓦ chantalguillon.com.
Daily 11am–7pm.
Named for its French expatriot
owner, *Chantal Guillon* is San
Francisco's go-to bakery for all
things macaron. Confection
flavours run the gamut from
red velvet and coffee to unusual
alternatives such as Persian rose
and guava.

Green Chile Kitchen

MAP P.108, POCKET MAP G4
1801 McAllister St at Baker St Ⓜ #5,
#21, #24, #31, #43. Ⓣ 415 440 9411,
Ⓦ greenchilekitchen.com. Mon–Thurs
10am–9.30pm, Fri 10am–10pm, Sat
9am–10pm, Sun 9am–9.30pm.
Specializing in the chilli-rich
cuisine of New Mexico, *Green
Chile Kitchen* serves incomparably
flavourful meat- and quinoa-
stuffed poblano peppers, *posole*
(stew) and a green chilli-topped
burger that swaps a grilled tortilla
for a traditional bun (all $14–19),
among the many unique dishes
on offer. The hopping corner
spot also boasts plenty of adult
libations: beer, wine, sangria (red
and white), agave margaritas and
verbena cocktails.

Papalote

MAP P.108, POCKET MAP G5
1777 Fulton St at Masonic St Ⓜ #5, #21,
#43. ☎ 415 776 0106, Ⓦ papalote-sf.com.
Mon–Sat 11am–10pm, Sun 11am–9pm.

It's hard to go wrong at Cal-Mex
powerhouse *Papalote*, where
everything on the menu, from the
carne asada nachos ($11.25) to the
marinated tofu burrito ($8.75), is in
a class of its own – especially when
the shop's championship-calibre
roasted tomato salsa is involved. The
popular *taqueria*'s tiny eating area
has room for only a few tables, so
consider coming at an off-peak time.

Rosamunde Sausage Grill

MAP P.108, POCKET MAP H5
545 Haight St at Fillmore St Ⓜ #6,
#7, #22, N. ☎ 415 437 6851,
Ⓦ rosamundesausagegrill.com/haight-
street. Mon–Wed 11.30am–10pm, Thurs–
Sat 11.30am–11pm, Sun 11.30am–9pm.

This humbly sized storefront serves
excellent grilled sausages ($8.50–
9.50) on sesame rolls, to which you
can add as many mustard varieties
as you wish. Flavours run the
gamut from all-beef knockwurst to
vegan *kielbasa*.

Smitten

MAP P.108, POCKET MAP J4
432 Octavia St at Linden St Ⓜ #21, #47,
#49, F, J, K, L, M, N, T; Ⓑ Civic Center.
☎ 415 863 1518, Ⓦ smittenicecream.com.
Mon–Wed & Sun noon–10pm, Thurs–Sat
noon–midnight.

Housed in a revamped shipping
container, *Smitten* uses customized
machines that run on liquid
nitrogen to produce each ice-
cream order (starting at around
$5) from scratch in about one
minute; flavour varieties of the
uncommonly smooth frozen treats
rotate regularly.

Restaurants

Espetus

MAP P.108, POCKET MAP J5
1686 Market St at Gough St Ⓜ #47, #49,
F, J, K, L, M, N, T; Ⓑ Civic Center. ☎ 415
552 8792, Ⓦ espetus.com. Mon–Thurs
11.30am–2.30pm & 5–10pm, Fri 11.30am–
2.30pm & 5–11pm, Sat noon–3pm &
5–11pm, Sun noon–9pm.

You'll likely spend at least $50 per
person at this Brazilian *churrascaria*,
where staff roam continuously
wielding tall skewers of filet
mignon, chicken legs, grilled
prawns and even pineapple.

Kiss Seafood

MAP P.108, POCKET MAP H3
1700 Laguna St at Sutter St Ⓜ #2, #3, #38.
☎ 415 474 2866, Ⓦ kissseafoodsf.com.
Wed–Sat 5.30–9.30pm.

Operated solely by a husband-
and-wife team, this signless,
unassuming corner spot on the
edge of Japantown has become
one of the city's most revered sushi
restaurants, although its reputation
and minuscule size make scoring a
seat very difficult. Expect to spend
upwards of $80 per person.

Little Star Pizza

MAP P.108, POCKET MAP G4
846 Divisadero St at McAllister St
Ⓜ #5, #21, #24, 31. ☎ 415 441 1118,
Ⓦ littlestarpizza.com. Mon–Thurs
5–9.30pm, Fri 4–10.30pm, Sat 3–10.30pm,
Sun 3–9.30pm.

Little Star's kitchen excels at both
thin-crust and deep-dish pizzas
($13.95–27.50), so it's no wonder
the place is one of the liveliest spots
along the Divisadero corridor. Its
name-sake pizza is a devastatingly
good deep-dish number, and
includes ricotta, feta, spinach
and other vegetables. The stellar
jukebox, meanwhile, is heavy on
American and British indie rock.

Magnolia Pub & Brewery

MAP P.108, POCKET MAP G5
1398 Haight St at Masonic Ave Ⓜ #6,
#7, #33, #43. ☎ 415 864 7468,
Ⓦ magnoliapub.com. Mon–Thurs 11am–
midnight, Fri 11am–1am, Sat 10am–1am,
Sun 10am–midnight.

This handsome and inviting corner
spot is known for its clever menu

Nopa

(try the "little gems", grapes and hazelnuts in port blue dressing, $7) and respected own-brewed beers. The kitchen stays open late and there's also plenty of alfresco seating.

Nopa

MAP P.108, POCKET MAP G5
560 Divisadero St at Hayes St #21, #24. ☎ 415 864 8643, ⓦ nopasf.com. Mon–Thurs 5pm–midnight, Fri 5pm–1am, Sat 10.30am–1am, Sun 10.30am–midnight.
Named for its North of Panhandle neighbourhood and open late nightly, this sizeable restaurant (housed in a former laundromat) is one of San Francisco's most celebrated. Choose from a diverse array of mains, including vegetable tagine ($23) and rotisserie herbed chicken with beet hummus ($27).

State Bird Provisions

MAP P.108, POCKET MAP H4
1529 Fillmore St at Geary Blvd #2, #3, #22, #38. ☎ 415 795 1272, ⓦ statebirdsf.com. Mon–Thurs & Sun 5.30–10pm, Fri & Sat 5.30–11pm.
Expect long lines at this popular spot, serving small plates of Californian fusion cuisine, dim-sum style; guinea hen dumpling with aromatic broth ($3), cauliflower falafel ($6), halibut spring roll ($14) and summer squash goat cheese toast ($7).

Suppenküche

MAP P.108, POCKET MAP H4
525 Laguna St at Hayes St #5, #21, F, J, K, L, M, N, T; ⓑ Civic Center. ☎ 415 252 9289, ⓦ suppenkuche.com. Mon–Sat 5–10pm, Sun 10am–2.30pm & 5–10pm.
Poised on the edge of Hayes Valley's precious commercial strip, *Suppenküche* is the place to go for bracing Bavarian meals, including bratwurst with sauerkraut and mashed potatoes ($19.50), potato pancakes with apple sauce ($12.50), and the like.

Bars

The Alembic

MAP P.108, POCKET MAP F5
1725 Haight St at Cole St #7, #33, #43, N. ☎ 415 666 0822, ⓦ alembicsf.com. Mon & Tues 4pm–midnight, Wed–Fri 4pm–2am, Sat noon–2am, Sun noon–midnight.
Offering a refreshing break from the dog-eared Haight scene, this small, stylish spot is serious about its liquor, with a wide selection of small-batch bourbons, ryes and gins poured by knowledgeable, friendly bartenders.

Club Deluxe

MAP P.108, POCKET MAP G5
1509 Haight St at Ashbury St #6, #7, #33, #43. ☎ 415 552 6949, ⓦ clubdeluxe. co. Mon–Fri 4pm–2am, Sat & Sun 2pm–2am.
One of the longest-operating bars along Haight Street, artful *Club Deluxe* is also one of the few places in the neighbourhood to offer live entertainment on a nightly basis ($5 cover; usually free till 9pm): bossa nova, jazz, comedy and more. Cash only.

Hotel Biron

MAP P.108, POCKET MAP J5
45 Rose St at Gough St #14, #47, #49, F, J, K, L, M, N, T; ⓑ Civic Center. ☎ 415 703 0403, ⓦ hotelbiron.com. Daily 5pm–2am.
This cosy spot doesn't offer overnight stays like its name suggests, but rather an expertly

selected wine list featuring a wide array of choices from California and far beyond. *Hotel Biron*'s rotating art shows and short menu of cheeses ($7) and olives ($6) also set it apart.

Noc Noc

MAP P.108, POCKET MAP H5
557 Haight St at Steiner St #6, #7, #22, N. ☎ 415 861 5811, ⓦ nocnocs.com. Mon–Thurs 5pm–2am, Fri 3.30pm–2am, Sat & Sun 3pm–2am.
Dimly lit *Noc Noc* is a Lower Haight fixture – a singular bar-room that suggests Alice in Wonderland on heavy hallucinogenics. There's a broad range of beers on offer, as well as wine and *sake*.

Live music venues

The Fillmore

MAP P.108, POCKET MAP H4
1805 Geary Blvd at Fillmore St #2, #3, #22, #38. ☎ 415 346 3000, ⓦ thefillmore. com. $22.50 and up.
There's hardly a performer who doesn't profess the thrill of ascending the Fillmore's stage,

SFJazz Center

graced as it's been by everyone from Led Zeppelin to Beck to Black Rebel Motorcycle Club throughout the decades. Bands on the rise and veteran favourites alike fill the beautiful ballroom nightly.

The Independent

MAP P.108, POCKET MAP G5
628 Divisadero St at Hayes St #5, #21, #24. ☎ 415 771 1421, ⓦ theindependentsf. com. $12 and upwards.
Booking acts across a host of genres – hip-hop, international folk, rock and electronic among them – this understated mid-sized club with friendly staff and crystal-clear sound is one of the leading venues on San Francisco's music scene.

SFJazz Center

MAP P.108, POCKET MAP J4
201 Franklin St at Fell St #21, #47, #49, F, J, K, L, M, N, T; ⓔ Civic Center. ☎ 866 920 5299, ⓦ sfjazz.org. $25 and up.
Opened in 2013 adjacent to the city's opera, ballet and symphony halls, this dynamic venue – its capacity is adjustable from 350 to 700 – was designed with jazz's unique acoustics in mind. Major names such as Brad Mehldau, Bill Frisell and Béla Fleck are regularly booked for four-night residencies.

Golden Gate Park and beyond

Extending over three miles to the city's – and continent's – edge, Golden Gate Park is one of North America's finest urban parks. The 1017-acre greenspace was transformed in the late nineteenth century from heaps of sand dunes to become a grassy, forested triumph of park design, its footpaths, meadows, knolls and lakes providing a natural counterpoint to its eastern end's heavily visited museums. The park bisects the city's pair of sprawling western neighbourhoods, the Richmond and the Sunset, which constitute the mild-mannered residential heart of San Francisco's summer fog belt and contain a handful of worthwhile restaurants for intrepid visitors. The city's spectacular northwesterly corner holds a number of enchanting sights as well, including Sutro Heights Park and Lands End, while the popular San Francisco Zoo brings a stream of visitors to the city's distant southwest reaches.

Conservatory of Flowers

MAP P.118, POCKET MAP E5

Ⓜ #5, #21, #33, #44, N. Ⓣ 415 831 2090, Ⓦ conservatoryofflowers.org. Tues–Sun 10am–6.30pm (last entry 6pm). $8.

Surrounded by gorgeous gardens and topped with a grand dome, the whitewashed **Conservatory of Flowers** takes on a dreamlike appearance in both sun and fog. The elegant building – Golden Gate Park's oldest – was an indirect gift from California's wealthiest individual, San Jose philanthropist James Lick, whose estate sold it to the city of San Francisco after his death in 1876. In the time since, it has endured fires, earthquakes, severe storm damage and even explosions to remain one of the most visited attractions in the park, its steamy rooms full of plants from the lowland and highland tropics; there's also a cooler aquatic plant room with impressive gargantuan Victoria water lilies.

California Academy of Sciences

MAP P.118, POCKET MAP E5

Ⓜ #5, #44, N. Ⓣ 415 379 8000, Ⓦ calacademy.org. Mon–Sat 9.30am–5pm, Sun 11am–5pm. $35.95.

Among the largest natural history museums found anywhere in the world, the **California Academy of Sciences** occupies an adventurously designed building in the heart of Golden Gate Park. The Academy's previous home was torn down in 2005 to make way for the current eco-friendly structure by Italian architect Renzo Piano – take the lift to the Living Roof, where native Bay Area plants provide natural insulation while preventing rainwater from draining to waste. Among the building's brilliant exhibits, the most compelling is the glass **Rainforests of the World** dome, where a circular walkway climbs gradually amid flora and fauna native to Borneo, Madagascar, Costa Rica and other tropical locales. Further highlights include a planetarium, aquarium, African penguins and a ceiling-suspended pendulum that gracefully demonstrates the Earth's rotation.

de Young Museum

MAP P.118, POCKET MAP E5

Ⓜ #5, #44, N. ☏ 415 750 3600, Ⓦ deyoung.
famsf.org. Mid-April to late Nov: Tues–
Thurs, Sat & Sun 9.30am–5.15pm, Fri
9.30am–8.30pm; late Nov to mid-April:
Tues–Sun 9.30am–5.15pm. $15.

The **de Young Museum** is known
for its rotation of temporary
art, fashion and photography
exhibitions, as well as its copper-
coloured structure, topped with
a twisting tower that affords an
exceptional vista over Golden Gate
Park and around. The museum's
permanent collection includes over
one thousand American paintings
encompassing Spanish Colonial,
Impressionist, and Arts and
Crafts styles, among others, while
sprinkled throughout the site are
four artworks from contemporary
artists – most notably Gerhard
Richter's massive black-and-white
piece *Strontium*, which incorporates
digitally manipulated photographs
to create a mural of sorts in the
main atrium.

Japanese Tea Garden

MAP P.118, POCKET MAP E5

Ⓜ #5, #44, N. ☏ 415 752 1171,
Ⓦ japaneseteagardensf.com. Daily: March–
Oct 9am–6pm; Nov–Feb 9am–4.45pm. $8,
free before 10am on Mon, Wed & Fri.

The oldest of its kind in the US,
the **Japanese Tea Garden** was
created for Golden Gate Park's
1894 California Midwinter
International Exposition and
remains one of the most serene
hideaways in the city, provided
you arrive before hordes of visitors
descend to take in its meticulously
groomed plants and miniature
trees. Footpaths wind through
the lovely five-acre fantasyland of
foliage, revealing thickets of bonsai
and cherry trees, colourful carp
swimming in pools, a steep moon
bridge and an enormous bronze
Buddha. Tea and fortune cookies
(which made their American debut
here in 1915) are available to enjoy
in the delightful teahouse.

San Francisco Botanical Garden

MAP P.118, POCKET MAP D5–E5

Ⓜ #7, #44, N. ☏ 415 661 1316,
Ⓦ sfbotanicalgarden.org. Open daily
7.30am; Check website for closing times. $8.

The 75-acre **San Francisco
Botanical Garden** is a

Japanese Tea Garden

GOLDEN GATE PARK AND BEYOND

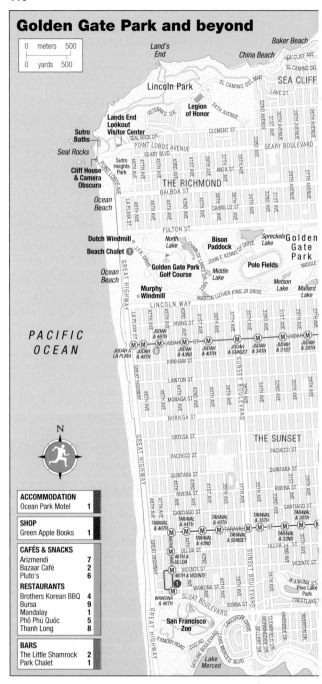

Golden Gate Park and beyond

| 0 | meters | 500 |
| 0 | yards | 500 |

Land's End
Baker Beach
China Beach
SEA CLIFF AVE
EL CAMINO DEL
SEA CLIFF

Lincoln Park

Legion of Honor

EL CAMINO DEL MAR
LAKE ST

Lands End Lookout Visitor Center
VETERANS DR
34TH AVENUE
32ND AVENUE
31ST AVENUE
28TH AVENUE

Sutro Baths
SEAL ROCK DR
CLEMENT ST
GEARY BOULEVARD

POINT LOBOS AVENUE

Seal Rocks
Sutro Heights Park
GEARY BLVD
45TH AVE
43RD AVE
41ST AVE
39TH AVE
37TH AVE
35TH AVE
33RD AVE

Cliff House & Camera Obscura
POINT LOBOS AVE
4TH AVE
ANZA ST
29TH AVENUE
27TH AVENUE

THE RICHMOND
BALBOA ST

Ocean Beach
46TH AVE
42ND AVE
40TH AVE
38TH AVE
36TH AVE
34TH AVE
32ND AVE
31ST AVE

CABRILLO ST

FULTON ST

Dutch Windmill
North Lake
Bison Paddock
Spreckels Lake
Golden Gate Park

Beach Chalet
L.F.K. DRIVE
CHAIN OF LAKES DR E of POST
JOHN F. KENNEDY DRIVE
MIDDLE

Golden Gate Park Golf Course
Middle Lake
Polo Fields

Ocean Beach
Murphy Windmill
Metson Lake
Mallard Lake

MARTIN LUTHER KING JR DRIVE

LINCOLN WAY
43RD
41ST AVE
39TH AVE
35TH AVE
33RD AVE
31ST AVE
29TH AVE
27TH AVE

IRVING ST

JUDAH & 46TH
JUDAH ST
JUDAH & 43RD
JUDAH & 40TH
JUDAH & SUNSET
JUDAH & 34TH
JUDAH & 31ST
JUDAH & 28TH

PACIFIC OCEAN

JUDAH & LA PLAYA
JUDAH & 48TH
KIRKHAM ST

LA PLAYA ST
48TH AVE
46TH AVE
LAWTON ST
42ND AVE
40TH AVE
38TH AVE
SUNSET BOULEVARD
34TH AVE
32ND AVE
30TH AVE
28TH AVE

MORAGA AVE

NORIEGA ST

N

ORTEGA ST

PACHECO ST
THE SUNSET
PACHECO ST

QUINTARA ST
QUINTARA ST
31ST AVE
29TH AVE

47TH AVE
45TH AVE
43RD AVE
41ST AVE
39TH AVE
37TH AVE
35TH AVE
33RD AVE
RIVERA ST
RIVERA ST

GREAT HIGHWAY

SANTIAGO ST
SANTIAGO ST

TARAVAL & 46TH
TARAVAL & 44TH
TARAVAL & 42ND
TARAVAL & 40TH
TARAVAL & SUNSET
TARAVAL & 35TH
TARAVAL & 32ND
TARAVAL & 30TH

ULLOA ST
ULLOA ST
SUNSET BOULEVARD

WAWONA & 46TH
VICENTE ST
46TH & VICENTE
WAWONA ST AVE
34TH AVE
38TH AVE
VICENTE ST

WAWONA ST
Pine Lake
CRESTLAKE

San Francisco Zoo
SLOAT BOULEVARD
YORBA ST

LAKESHORE DRIVE
CLEARFIELD DR
MOONRIDGE DR
HAVENSIDE DR
RIVERTON DR

ARMORY ROAD
ZOO RD
ZOO ROAD
SKYLINE BOULEVARD
LAKE MERCED BLVD
GELLERT DR

Lake Merced

ACCOMMODATION
Ocean Park Motel 1

SHOP
Green Apple Books 1

CAFÉS & SNACKS
Arizmendi 7
Bazaar Café 2
Pluto's 6

RESTAURANTS
Brothers Korean BBQ 4
Bursa 9
Mandalay 1
Phô Phú Quôc 5
Thanh Long 8

BARS
The Little Shamrock 2
Park Chalet 1

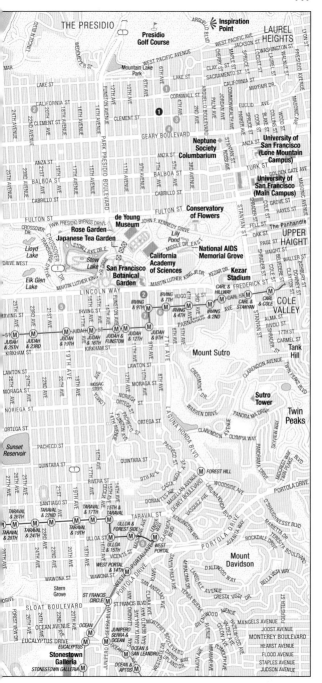

Sutro Baths ruins

horticulturalist's delight, although its tranquil groves will appeal to anyone looking for a quiet retreat. The park-within-a-park is home to over eight thousand plants from around the world, including everything from Andean wax palms and Australian Lilly Pilly trees to Himalayan magnolias and, of course, California coastal redwoods. Also of particular note is the wonderfully aromatic Garden of Fragrance and the Rhododendron Garden, the latter reaching peak bloom in spring.

Dutch and Murphy Windmills

MAP P.118, POCKET MAP A5 & A6
Dutch Windmill: Ⓜ #5, #18, #31. Murphy Windmill: Ⓜ #18, N.

Unlikely as it may seem, a pair of resplendent windmills anchors the far western end of Golden Gate Park. At the park's northwest corner sits the **Dutch Windmill**, constructed in 1902 and surrounded by the sublime Queen Wilhelmina Tulip Garden; its more stark counterpart, the **Murphy Windmill** (circa 1907) at the park's southwest corner, underwent

a marathon refurbishment that finally saw completion in 2012 and returned the previously derelict structure to glory. Originally built to pump water throughout the park, the colossal windmills now exist purely for aesthetic purposes and form a striking sight when viewed from Ocean Beach across the Great Highway.

Sutro Heights Parkand around

MAP P.118, POCKET MAP A4
Ⓜ #5, #18, #31, #38. ☎ 415 750 0415, Ⓦ giantcamera.com. Camera Obscura: daily 11am–5pm. $3.

San Francisco's desolately beautiful far northwest corner remains a realm apart from the rest of the city. The area is watched over by captivating **Sutro Heights Park**, which sits atop a tall bluff and offers a fine vantage point over the huge white Cliff House (where you'll find a pair of pricey restaurants) and the crashing Pacific below. Behind the Cliff House, restored circa 1907, a promenade landing leads to **Camera Obscura**, a relic that uses a rotating mirror to angle light into its darkened quarters and reveal a panorama of the area, including birds on guano-covered Seal Rock just offshore. Uphill from the Cliff House is the National Park Service's **Lands End Lookout Visitor Center** (Mon–Fri 9am–5pm, Sat & Sun 9am–6pm; ☎ 415 426 5240, ⓦ parksconservancy.org), far below which loom the evocative ruins of Sutro Baths, a once-enormous bathhouse that met its end in a 1966 fire, long after it had been permanently shuttered. Beyond the ruins, a lengthy cave (accessible at lower tides) leads through to a pocket-sized cove.

Legion of Honor

MAP P.118, POCKET MAP B4
100 34th Ave at El Camino del Mar Ⓜ #1, #18. ☎ 415 750 3600, ⓦ legionofhonor. famsf.org. Tues–Sun 9.30am–5.15pm. $15.
Although its heroic hilltop setting threatens to upstage its holdings, the palatial **Legion of Honor** fine arts museum is well worth a visit for its remarkable collection of Rodin sculptures, hailed as one of the best outside Paris. Its grand entrance courtyard features a cast of *The Thinker*, while inside the stately building, three airy courts bathed in natural light contain numerous plaster, marble and, especially, bronze works by the masterful French sculptor. Back outside and somewhat hidden to the side of the car park, look out for American sculptor George Segal's grimly poignant memorial *The Holocaust*.

Baker Beach

MAP P.118, POCKET MAP C3
Ⓜ #29.
San Francisco's most spectacular strand is the Presidio's **Baker Beach**, epically sited in the shadow of the towering Golden Gate Bridge. The stretch of sand here is ideal for a languid stroll, although certain visitors have gotten a shock upon encountering the occasional nude sunbather at the beach's northern end. Given the notoriously moody weather along the Northern California coast, Baker Beach sees swarms of people on days of full sun (rare here in summer); the rest of the time, however, it's a pleasantly mellow spot to spend a quiet afternoon.

San Francisco Zoo

MAP P.118, POCKET MAP B9
Sloat Blvd and Great Highway Ⓜ #18, #23, L. ☎ 415 753 7080, ⓦ sfzoo.org. Daily: March–Oct 10am–5pm; Nov–Feb 10am–4pm. $20.
Home to nearly 200 species, **San Francisco Zoo** is Northern California's most diverse. The menagerie, adjacent to the sea, is set near the far southwest corner of the city, with roughly seven hundred animals spread across seven distinct sections: the so-called Children's Zoo just inside the main entrance is one of the most visited, where meerkats, prairie dogs and farm animals await, as does a restored carousel. Elsewhere, lemurs, chimpanzees and monkeys are always a major draw, as is the compound of gorillas. The lion and tiger enclosures, meanwhile, have received significant security improvements after a Siberian tiger escaped from its pen to fatally maul a visitor in 2007.

Legion of Honor

Shop

Green Apple Books

MAP P.118, POCKET MAP E4
506 Clement St at Sixth Ave Ⓜ #1, #2, #38,
#44. ☎ 415 387 2272, Ⓦ greenapplebooks.
com. Daily 10am–10.30pm.

This Inner Richmond stalwart
is one of San Francisco's better
general-purpose bookstores, highly
respected for its selection and
curation – be sure to seek out the
"Books That Will Never Be Oprah's
Picks" section.

Cafés and snacks

Arizmendi

MAP P.118, POCKET MAP E6
1331 Ninth Ave at Irving St Ⓜ #6,
#7, #43, #44, N. ☎ 415 566 3117,
Ⓦ arizmendibakery.com. Tues–Fri
7am–7pm, Sat & Sun 7.30am–6pm.

Arizmendi devotees pour in for the
aromatic bakery's daily rotation
of artisanal breads and inventive
vegetarian pizzas, served whole
($24) or by the slice ($3). Visit the
website for that day's menu.

Bazaar Café

MAP P.118, POCKET MAP D4
5927 California St at 22nd Ave Ⓜ #1, #29,
#38. ☎ 415 831 5620, Ⓦ bazaarcafe.com.
Daily 9am–10pm.

Mild-mannered *Bazaar Café* in the
Outer Richmond offers light meals
(soups, salads, sandwiches, bagels,
etc – all well under $10), beer and
wine, and, perhaps best of all, a
delightful rear garden. Local folk
singer-songwriters perform several
nights weekly.

Pluto's

MAP P.118, POCKET MAP E6
627 Irving St at Seventh Ave Ⓜ #6,
#7, #43, #44, N. ☎ 415 753 8867,
Ⓦ plutosfreshfood.com. Daily 11am–10pm.

Custom salads (about $8.50) are a
popular speciality at this informal
Inner Sunset spot, although the
soups, made-to-order sandwiches
and comfort-food sides like mac
'n' cheese might be a better choice
under foggy conditions.

Restaurants

Brothers Korean BBQ

MAP P.118, POCKET MAP E4
4128 Geary Blvd at Sixth Ave Ⓜ #2, #38,
#44. ☎ 415 387 7991. Mon–Thurs 5–11pm,
Fri–Sun 11am–11pm.

Groups and families descend on this
Inner Richmond mainstay to feast
on marinated meats and countless
side dishes; certain tables have
sunken *hibachis* built right in so that
you can cook the meats yourself.
Expect to spend at least $25 each.

Bursa

MAP P.118, POCKET MAP E8
60 West Portal Ave at Vicente St Ⓜ #48, K,
M, T. ☎ 415 564 4006, Ⓦ bursasf.com. Mon,
Wed–Thurs & Sun 11am–9pm, Fri & Sat
11am–10pm.

An easy Muni streetcar ride from
anywhere along Market Street,
Bursa in charming West Portal
excels at Mediterranean favourites:
falafel salad ($13), *beyti* (lamb and
ground beef wrapped in *lavash*,
$17) and the more than half a
dozen kebabs on offer ($16–28) all
hit the mark.

Mandalay

MAP P.118, POCKET MAP E3
4348 California St at Sixth Ave Ⓜ #1, #2,
#44. ☎ 415 386 3895, Ⓦ mandalaysf.com.
Mon–Thurs 11.30am–2.30pm & 5–9.30pm,

Green Apple Books

Park Chalet

Fri & Sat 11.30am–2.30pm & 5–10pm, Sun 11.30am–10pm.

Few items at *Mandalay* exceed $15 and there's rarely a wait for a table on weeknights, making it one of the smarter options in the city for affordable, authentic Burmese cuisine. Don't leave without sampling the *balada*, a crispy pancake starter.

Phô Phú Quôc

MAP P.118, POCKET MAP D6
1816 Irving St at 19th Ave #7, #28, #29, N. ☎ 415 661 8869, ⓦ ppqsf.com. Daily 11am–11pm.

Regulars of all stripes call this beloved, no-frills Vietnamese noodle house simply "PPQ", routinely stopping in to cut the chill of San Francisco evenings with enormous bowls of the restaurant's signature beef or seafood *phô* (under $10).

Thanh Long

MAP P.118, POCKET MAP A6
4101 Judah St at 46th Ave #7, #18, N. ☎ 415 665 1146, ⓦ thanhlongsf.com. Tues–Thurs & Sun 5–9.30pm, Fri & Sat 5–10pm.

Thanh Long was the city's first Vietnamese restaurant in the early 1970s; it's become increasingly French-inspired and upscale in the years since. The dining room is bedecked in a soothing mix of blonde-wood panelling and earth tones. Most mains cost around $15–25.

Bars

The Little Shamrock

MAP P.118, POCKET MAP E6
807 Lincoln Way at Ninth Ave #6, #7, #43, #44, N. ☎ 415 661 0060. Mon–Thurs 3pm–2am, Fri 2pm–2am, Sat & Sun 1pm–2am.

Loads of Irish pubs litter the Sunset and Richmond districts, and with its fireplace, natty sofas, free popcorn and $5 pints, the *Little Shamrock* – San Francisco's second-oldest tavern, by many accounts – is the most comfortable. Cash only.

Park Chalet

MAP P.118, POCKET MAP A5
1000 Great Highway at John F. Kennedy Dr #5, #18, #31. ☎ 415 386 8439, ⓦ parkchalet.com. Mon–Thurs noon–9pm, Fri noon–10pm, Sat 11am–10pm, Sun 11am–9pm.

Though often overrun for weekend brunch ($28), this popular destination at the western edge of Golden Gate Park is ideal for pints of its own-made beer, either inside the airy bar or on the attractive rear lawn.

Oakland and Berkeley

Often characterized as earthier counterpoints to sophisticated San Francisco, Oakland and Berkeley are the undisputed cultural and academic centres of the East Bay, counterbalancing their famed cross-bay neighbour with greater open space, more frequent sunshine and, despite several pockets of poshness, an overall lower cost of living. Oakland wears its perennial underdog status with pugnacious pride, and while it's historically had its share of troubled areas, a closer look at the Bay Area's second city reveals superb shopping and dining options, as well as a buzzing bar scene. Immediately north, chin-stroking Berkeley is an internationally recognized hive of intellectualism and home to the flagship campus of the University of California, the city's long-held penchant for progressive thought serving as a point of pride for liberals and a punchline for conservatives.

Lake Merritt

MAP P.126, POCKET MAP B20
AC Transit #11, #12, #26, #72; ⓑ 19th St/
Oakland and Lake Merritt.

The natural focus of central Oakland and the first designated wildlife refuge in the US, **Lake Merritt** is not the landlocked body of water its name suggests,

Oakland viewed across Lake Merritt

but a tidal lagoon connected to San Francisco Bay by saltwater channels. Its three-mile perimeter is ringed by paths heavily used by walkers and runners, while a necklace of 3400 individual lights makes the lake an enticing after-dark sight too. Occupying Lake Merritt's northwest shore, Lakeside Park is home to both a boat/canoe rental facility and Children's Fairyland, a gentle amusement park aimed at tots.

Oakland Museum of California

MAP P.126, POCKET MAP B21
1000 Oak St at 10th St, Oakland. AC Transit #11, #14, #26; ⓑ Lake Merritt. ☎ 510 318 8400, ⓦ museumca.org. Wed & Thurs 11am–5pm, Fri 11am–9pm, Sat & Sun 11am–6pm. $15.95.

The highly respected **Oakland Museum of California** is the city's top visitor attraction, its three floors telling the ongoing saga of the Golden State through a robust collection of nearly two million objects, as well as engaging temporary exhibits detailing

Berkeley campus and the Campanile

subjects as diverse as the Gold Rush and baseball. The circa-1969 complex, though composed primarily of dull grey concrete, gracefully integrates its indoor and outdoor spaces, and is topped by a lovely terraced sculpture garden affording fine views of Lake Merritt.

Chabot Space & Science Center

MAP P.126, POCKET MAP C21
10,000 Skyline Blvd, Oakland. AC Transit #339. ☎ 510 336 7300, ⓦ chabotspace.org. Wed–Sun 10am–5pm. $18.

Nestled high amid parkland in the forested hills overlooking Oakland, **Chabot Space & Science Center** is the top public observatory in the Bay Area. Though its educational programmes are largely aimed at kids, there's plenty here to command adults' attention, including Space Race paraphernalia, absorbing astronomy exhibits and a trio of giant telescopes best enjoyed after dark. Stop to linger at the mesmerizingly undulating wave sculpture hovering over the main lobby.

Campanile

MAP P.126, POCKET MAP B15
AC Transit #1, #7, #51B; ⓑ Downtown Berkeley. ⓦ visit.berkeley.edu/ campus-tourscampanile-tour. Mon–Fri 10am–3.45pm, Sat 10am–4.45pm, Sun 10am–1.30pm & 3–4.45pm. $3.

Sather Tower, better known as the **Campanile** for its similarity to Venice's Campanile di San Marco, has been the defining symbol of the University of California at Berkeley since the tower's completion in 1914. The third-tallest bell-and-clock tower in the world is set amid a grid of deciduous trees well upslope on the lovely, bustling hillside campus – home to over 35,000 students – and stands 307ft tall. The views from its observation platform, set two-thirds of the way up and reached by a lift and stairs, reveal predictably spectacular views of a sizeable chunk of the Bay Area.

UC Berkeley Art Museum

MAP P.126, POCKET MAP B15
2155 Center St at Oxford St, Berkeley. AC Transit #1, #7, #51B; ⓑ Downtown Berkeley. ☎ 510 642 0808, ⓦ bampfa. berkeley.edu. Wed, Thurs & Sun 11am–7pm, Fri & Sat 11am–9pm. $12.

One of the largest university-operated institutions of its kind in the US, the **UC Berkeley Art Museum** opened the doors of

OAKLAND AND BERKELEY

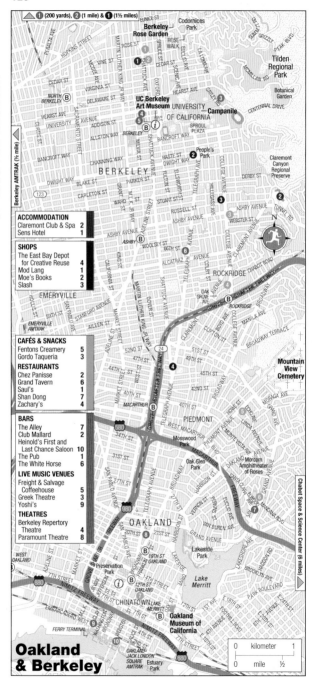

ACCOMMODATION
Claremont Club & Spa 2
Sens Hotel 1

SHOPS
The East Bay Depot
 for Creative Reuse 4
Mod Lang 1
Moe's Books 2
Slash 3

CAFÉS & SNACKS
Fentons Creamery 5
Gordo Taqueria 3

RESTAURANTS
Chez Panisse 2
Grand Tavern 6
Saul's 1
Shan Dong 7
Zachary's 4

BARS
The Alley 7
Club Mallard 2
Heinold's First and
 Last Chance Saloon 10
The Pub 1
The White Horse 6

LIVE MUSIC VENUES
Freight & Salvage
 Coffeehouse 5
Greek Theatre 3
Yoshi's 9

THEATRES
Berkeley Repertory
 Theatre 4
Paramount Theatre 8

Oakland
& Berkeley

its new home in early 2016 with an all-encompassing exhibit on architecture. Since debuting in 1970, the museum has hosted exhibitions that have often skewed towards conceptual and avant-garde performance art, although more orthodox shows based around photography and Asian art have also appeared regularly. The new space is also home to the Pacific Film Archive, which screens works from its extensive collection in a pair of state-of-the-art theatres.

Berkeley Rose Garden and Rose Walk

MAP P.126, POCKET MAP B14
1200 Euclid Ave at Eunice St, Berkeley. AC Transit #65. Dawn to dusk. Free.

It's worth spending an hour or more winding through the Berkeley Hills, where custom-designed homes cling to hillsides along twisting streets that follow the contours of the land. The terraced **Berkeley Rose Garden**, home to over 100 varieties of rose and featuring a vine-draped pergola, is a delightful spot for a stroll or picnic, while less than a quarter of a mile south along Euclid Avenue, **Rose Walk** is a lovely pedestrian path – one of dozens in the Berkeley Hills – flanked by fine early twentieth-century homes.

Tilden Regional Park

MAP P.126, POCKET MAP C14
AC Transit #65, #67. ☎ 510 544 2747, ⓦ ebparks.org/parks/tilden.

One of the larger links in a lengthy chain of parks covering the East Bay's hills, inviting **Tilden Regional Park** above Berkeley is a much-loved destination for its wide scope of attractions and recreation opportunities. The park's unique amusement is Redwood Valley Railway (Mon–Fri 11am–5pm, Sat & Sun 11am–6pm; $3), a miniature steam locomotive railroad that runs along 1.25 miles of narrow-

gauge track threading through an area of redwood trees. Tilden's two thousand acres also feature a botanical garden (free) and antique carousel ($3), swimming at Lake Anza (May–Sept only; daily 11am–6pm; $3.50), scores of hiking trails, and the Little Farm (daily 8.30am–4pm; free), where visitors of all ages can hand-feed pigs, goats and other animals.

Grizzly Peak Boulevard

MAP P.126, POCKET MAP C14

If you've got your own wheels, snake your way up (and up) to **Grizzly Peak Boulevard** for the top sunset vista in the Bay Area. The twisting road begins near Tilden Regional Park and winds south above the University of California campus and along the spine of the Berkeley Hills to Oakland, where it eventually meets Skyline Boulevard. Numerous pullouts along the west side of the route reward southbound travellers with magnificent lookouts which, on the clearest of days, extend far over the yawning Pacific in the distance.

UC Berkeley Art Museum and Pacific Film Archive

Shops

The East Bay Depot for Creative Reuse

MAP P.126, POCKET MAP B18
4695 Telegraph Ave at 47th St, Oakland. AC Transit #1, #12, #18; ⊜ MacArthur. ☎ 510 547 6470, ⓦ creativereuse.org. Daily 11am–6pm.

Though this budget emporium of recycled goods is geared toward teachers and artists, any thrift-store enthusiast will want to browse its range of candles, books, homeware and containers – to say nothing of all manner of art and school supplies.

Mod Lang

MAP P.126, POCKET MAP A14
6328 Fairmount Ave at Kearney St, El Cerrito ⊜ El Cerrito Plaza. ☎ 510 486 1880, ⓦ modlang.com. Mon–Wed, Fri & Sat 11am–7pm, Sun noon–6pm.

Two BART stops north of Downtown Berkeley, you'll find this veteran record shop aimed at buyers of UK and European imports and American indie rock. It's excellent for new and used vinyl, especially seven-inch singles, which are priced at $5 and upwards.

Moe's Books

MAP P.126, POCKET MAP B15
2476 Telegraph Ave at Haste St, Berkeley. AC Transit #1, #51B, #52; ⊜ Downtown Berkeley. ☎ 510 849 2087, ⓦ moesbooks. com. Daily 10am–10pm.

Enter under this longtime shop's signature red-and-white striped awning to browse four storeys of new and used titles covering nearly every imaginable genre at all price levels. Collectors will want to head up to the top floor for an impressive array of rare and fine arts books.

Slash

MAP P.126, POCKET MAP C16
2840 College Ave at Russell St, Berkeley. AC Transit #49, #51B. ☎ 510 665 5994, Mon–Sat 11am–7pm, Sun noon–6pm.

Visit this terrific shop for a wide selection of pricey women's and men's (but mostly women's) jeans in a staggering range of colours and sizes. The knowledgeable, amiable staff will help find which cut and look suits you the best.

Cafés and snacks

Fentons Creamery

MAP P.126, POCKET MAP C18
4226 Piedmont Ave at Glenwood Ave, Oakland. AC Transit #12. ☎ 510 658 7000, ⓦ fentonscreamery.com. Mon–Thurs 11am–11pm, Fri & Sat 9am–midnight, Sun 9am–11pm.

The alleged birthplace of rocky road ice cream, this legendary parlour remains a civic favourite for its heaped $10 sundaes made from unusual flavours (eg coffee cookie dream, butter brickle) and unique seasonal selections (apple pie, maple nut, etc).

Gordo Taqueria

MAP P.126, POCKET MAP C16
2989 College Ave at Ashby Ave, Berkeley. AC Transit #49, #51B. ☎ 510 204 9027, ⓦ gordotaqueria.co. Daily 10am–10pm.

Mostly dealing in hefty burritos ($4.85–7.85) that always hit the spot, this barely decorated *taqueria* has been the top choice for casual Mexican food in its Elmwood neighbourhood for decades. The menu is austere: burritos, tacos, quesadillas.

Restaurants

Chez Panisse

MAP P.126, POCKET MAP B14
1517 Shattuck Ave at Vine St, Berkeley. AC Transit #7, #18. ☎ 510 548 5525, ⓦ chezpanisse.com. Mon–Sat, seatings begin at 5.30pm & 8pm.

Since opening in 1971, renowned *Chez Panisse* has launched not only a micro-neighbourhood (Berkeley's so-called Gourmet Ghetto), but also the very notion of California

Grand Tavern's dining room

cuisine itself. Seatings occur in two sets every evening and feature nightly changing four-course prix fixe menus ($100–125).

Grand Tavern

MAP P.126, POCKET MAP C19
3601 Grand Ave at Mandana Blvd, Oakland. AC Transit #12, #26, #57. ☎ 510 444 4644, Ⓦ grandtavern.net. Mon–Thurs 5–10pm, Fri 5pm–midnight, Sat 10am–midnight, Sun 10am–10pm.

Set in a former residential home along Oakland's appealing Grand Avenue, this gastropub draws in diners from both sides of the bay for its inventive new American cuisine (try the lamb burger on Afghani flatbread), craft cocktails and robust beer and wine lists. Mains range from $19–29.

Saul's

MAP P.126, POCKET MAP B14
1475 Shattuck Ave at Vine St, Berkeley. AC Transit #7, #18. ☎ 510 848 3354, Ⓦ saulsdeli.com. Mon–Thurs & Sun 8am–9pm, Fri & Sat 8am–10pm.

Saul's has been a culinary and cultural cornerstone of the East Bay Jewish community for decades, and the menu proves it: fried matzo and eggs ($10.25) in the morning, meaty sandwiches ($12.50–19.50) in the afternoon and stuffed cabbage rolls ($16.50) at night. Monday nights see live klezmer music.

Shan Dong

MAP P.126, POCKET MAP B21
328 10th St at Webster St, Oakland. AC Transit #11, #14, #26 B 12th St/Oakland City Center. ☎ 510 839 2299, Ⓦ sd.222.to. Tues–Thurs & Sun 10am–9.30pm, Fri & Sat 10am–10pm.

Specializing in delectable American Chinese cuisine (with a few Sichuan specialties also available), and justly acclaimed for its hand-pulled noodles, no-nonsense *Shan Dong* in Oakland's somewhat grotty Chinatown runs laps around most other Bay Area Chinese restaurants. Most mains, such as the spicy platter of sesame paste noodles, are under $10.

Zachary's

MAP P.126, POCKET MAP C17
5801 College Ave at Oak Grove Ave, Oakland. AC Transit #51A, #51B; Ⓑ Rockridge. ☎ 510 655 6385, Ⓦ zacharys. com. Mon–Thurs & Sun 11am–10pm, Fri & Sat 11am–10.30pm.

Heinold's First and Last Chance Saloon

The East Bay's most celebrated purveyor of Chicago-style deep-dish pizza, *Zachary's* varieties run the gamut from meat-packed to vegan; they're stuffed with any number of ingredients and are decadently splashed with tomato sauce. A 14-incher feeds at least four people and costs $32.25–33.40.

Bars

The Alley

MAP P.126, POCKET MAP C20
3325 Grand Ave at Elwood Ave, Oakland.
AC Transit #12, #26, #57. ☎ 510 444 8505.
Mon 6pm–midnight, Tues–Thurs 5pm–2am,
Fri & Sat 4pm–2am, Sun 6pm–2am.
Playing almost any song you can think of, veteran piano man/human jukebox Rod Dibble provides brilliant entertainment at this convivial Grand Lake bar (Tues–Sat 9pm–2am). It's a patently funky place, full of hidden nooks and hemmed in by walls slathered with vintage business cards.

Club Mallard

MAP P.126, POCKET MAP A14
752 San Pablo Ave at Washington Ave,
Albany. AC Transit #18, #72. ☎ 510 524 8450. Mon–Fri 2pm–2am, Sat & Sun noon–2am.
There's something for everyone at this zealously decorated two-storey tavern just outside Berkeley: great jukeboxes, five pool tables, a pair of lush outdoor patios and baseball on the television.

Heinold's First and Last Chance Saloon

MAP P.126, POCKET MAP A21
48 Webster St at Embarcadero West,
Oakland. AC Transit #31, #72. ☎ 510 839 6761, ⓦ facebook.com/heinolds.
Mon–Thurs & Sun noon–11pm, Fri & Sat noon–1am.
Built from the timber remains of a whaling vessel in 1880 and still illuminated by its original gas lights, affable *Heinolds'* on Oakland's old waterfront is in many ways a time warp. Aim for a stool at the sharply slanted bar, which was tilted along with the floor by the 1906 earthquake.

The Pub

MAP P.126, POCKET MAP A14
1492 Solano Ave at Santa Fe Ave,
Albany. AC Transit #18. ☎ 510 525 1900,
ⓦ schmidtspub.com. Mon–Wed & Sun noon–midnight, Thurs–Sat noon–1am.
Officially called *Schmidt's Pub*, but flagged on its front sign as simply *Pub*, this warm and welcoming tavern set in a converted Craftsman home along Albany's main drag is a favourite haunt of local artists and intellectuals.

The White Horse

MAP P.126, POCKET MAP B17
6551 Telegraph Ave at 66th St, Oakland.
AC Transit #1, #18; Ⓢ Ashby. ☎ 510 652 3820, ⓦ whitehorsebar.com. Mon–Thurs 3pm–2am, Fri–Sun 1pm–2am.
Located virtually right on the Oakland–Berkeley boundary, the East Bay's oldest gay bar is as much of an exuberant dive as ever. Come for stiff drinks, "Drag King" shows ($5 cover charge), a cosy fireplace and covered patio.

Live music venues

Freight & Salvage Coffeehouse

MAP P.126, POCKET MAP B15
2020 Addison St at Milvia St, Berkeley.
AC Transit #1, #49, #51B; Ⓑ Downtown
Berkeley. ☎ 510 644 2020, Ⓦ thefreight.
org. $5 and up.

A coffee house in spirit at least, this nonprofit and all-ages venue brings in devotees of folk, jazz, bluegrass and other traditional musical styles to its spacious room nightly.

Greek Theatre

MAP P.126, POCKET MAP C15
2001 Gayley Rd, Berkeley. AC Transit #51B,
#52, F; Ⓑ Downtown Berkeley. ☎ 510
548 3010, Ⓦ thegreekberkeley.com. $45
and up.

Modelled upon the amphitheatre in Epidauros, Greece, this spectacular 8500-capacity outdoor venue, which is set far uphill on the University of California campus, plays host to a variety of concerts at weekends between April and October.

Yoshi's

MAP P.126, POCKET MAP A21
510 Embarcadero West at Washington St,
Oakland. AC Transit #31, #72. ☎ 510 238
9200, Ⓦ yoshis.com. $20 and up.

The Bay Area's pre-eminent jazz club boasts a popular Japanese restaurant and the sharpest sound system you'll experience anywhere. Major artists play multi-night residencies and span genres beyond jazz, including world, blues, funk and more.

Theatres

Berkeley Repertory Theatre

MAP P.126, POCKET MAP B15
2025 Addison St at Shattuck Ave,
Berkeley. AC Transit #1, #49, #51B;
Ⓑ Downtown Berkeley. ☎ 510 647 2900,
Ⓦ berkeleyrep.org. $29–97.

Tony Award-winning Berkeley Rep has premiered several plays that have gone onto Broadway or been turned into films. Its pair of centrally located theatres are routinely packed, with half-off discounts available to anyone under 30 and free guided presentations and discussions held before and after select performances.

Paramount Theatre

MAP P.126, POCKET MAP B20
2025 Broadway at 21st St, Oakland. AC
Transit #11, #12, #72; Ⓑ 19th St/Oakland.
☎ 510 465 6400, Ⓦ paramounttheatre.com.
$40 and up.

Seating nearly 3500, this Art Deco beauty hosts a broad spectrum of events: symphony and ballet performances, African-American comedy showcases and more. Its monthly "Paramount Movie Classics" series, which screens favourites such as *Casablanca* for $3-5, often plays to capacity.

Paramount Theatre

Around the Bay Area

Outside the urban core of San Francisco, Oakland and Berkeley, the Bay Area's extraordinary natural beauty comes into even sharper focus. Strong conservation efforts have resulted in an astonishing amount of sprawl-mitigating open space for this continually growing region of seven million residents – a legacy that's resulted in an extensive network of state parks, National Park Service entities and dozens of other preserves. North and south of San Francisco, the Pacific coastline remains remarkably unspoilt from sublime Point Reyes to wildlife-rich Año Nuevo, while north of San Francisco Bay, the wine-producing domains of Sonoma and Napa counties continue to exert a magnetic pull on travellers and locals alike. Sausalito, Angel Island and Muir Woods are all accessible daily via public transport from San Francisco, but you'll need a car to reach the other destinations highlighted here.

Marin Headlands

MAP P.134
Ⓜ #76. Ⓦ nps.gov/goga/marin-headlands. htm.

Portions of the wild heath known as the **Marin Headlands** were saved from private development by a grassroots preservation campaign in the 1960s, and the area's rugged shoreline and hills have been in the public's hands ever since. The Headlands' considerable charms range from remote **Point Bonita Lighthouse** and windswept **Rodeo Beach** to the **Marine Mammal Center** (2000 Bunker Road, Fort Cronkhite, Sausalito; daily 10am–4pm; free; Ⓦ marinemammalcenter.org), a rehabilitation facility for injured seals and other types of pinniped.

Dozens of miles of stunning hiking trails thread the Headlands, with one of the most thrilling views of the Golden Gate Bridge and San Francisco available by climbing steep **Slacker Hill** via the Coastal Trail; equally stunning vistas are available travelling by car along

Conzelman Road, which can be easily reached off US-101.

Sausalito

MAP P.134
Golden Gate Transit ferry from San Francisco's Ferry Building. Bay Model Visitor Center: 2100 Bridgeway at Marinship Way; ☎ 415 332 3871. Summer: Tues–Fri 9am–4pm, Sat & Sun 10am–5pm; rest of year: Tues–Sat 9am–4pm. Free.

At one time a rough-and-tumble fishing town, then a major wartime shipbuilding centre, attractive **Sausalito** became a bourgeois haven in the twentieth century's latter half; today its hill-hugging real estate is among Marin County's most valuable. The tiny town's ferry landing along main commercial drag Bridgeway helps make Sausalito a popular day-trip, but the thoroughfare's shopping and dining aren't particularly special, although its views of San Francisco across the water certainly are.

About one mile north of central Sausalito's tourist hubbub, the US Army Corps of Engineers' **Bay Model Visitor Center** is a unique diversion offering a working hydraulic model of San Francisco Bay – simulated tidal shifts, miniature Golden Gate Bridge and all.

Angel Island State Park

MAP P.134

Ferries from Tiburon and San Francisco. Daily 8am–sunset. ☏415 435 5390, ⓦwww.parks.ca.gov/AngelIsland. Park entry $3; round-trip ferry $15-19.50; bicycle rental $15/hour, $60 a day.

Encompassing most of San Francisco Bay's largest island, **Angel Island State Park** makes for one of the Bay Area's best day-trips. Most visitors come to picnic, tour the island's historic buildings, cycle its paved perimeter road and hike to the peak of 788ft Mount Livermore for a stunning, unimpeded panorama of the bay. Ferries arrive at Ayala Cove, adjacent to the park's visitor centre, snack bar (the island's only food and beverage service) and bike rental facility; those wishing to stay overnight can advance-book one of the nine backcountry campsites spread around the island ($30/night; ⓦreserveamerica.com).

Muir Woods National Monument

MAP P.134

1 Muir Woods Rd, Mill Valley; Shuttle from Sausalito Ferry Terminal. ☏415 388 2595, ⓦnps.gov/muwo. Daily: late Jan to early March 8am–6pm; early March to mid-Sept 8am–8pm; mid-Sept to mid-Oct 8am–7pm; mid-Oct to early Nov 8am–6pm; early Nov to early Jan 8am–5pm. $10.

Along with Alcatraz (see page 56), the Bay Area's highest-profile National Park Service property is **Muir Woods National Monument**, home to one of the region's few remaining stands of old-growth redwood trees; arrive early to beat the inevitable crowds and enjoy the groves at their most tranquil. Paved and unpaved paths wind between the sky-scraping giants, while the easy Redwood Creek Trail traces its namesake stream for a few miles between Muir Woods and the tiny coastal community of **Muir Beach**, home to the marvellous *Pelican Inn* (see page 146).

Also leading out of Muir Woods are a few routes that connect with the tangled web of trails clinging to the wooded slopes of **Mount**

Rodeo Beach at the foot of the Marin Headlands

Around the Bay Area

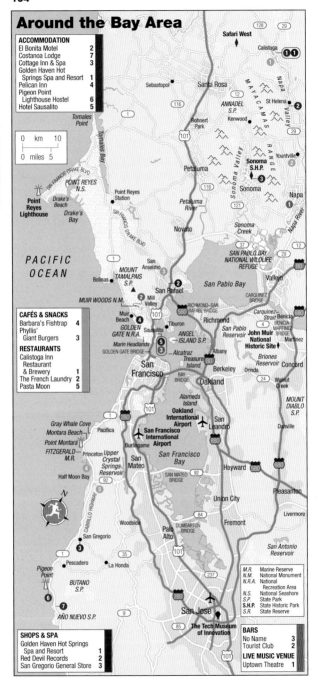

ACCOMMODATION

El Bonita Motel	2
Costanoa Lodge	7
Cottage Inn & Spa	3
Golden Haven Hot Springs Spa and Resort	1
Pelican Inn	4
Pigeon Point Lighthouse Hostel	6
Hotel Sausalito	5

CAFÉS & SNACKS

Barbara's Fishtrap	4
Phyllis' Giant Burgers	3

RESTAURANTS

Calistoga Inn Restaurant & Brewery	1
The French Laundry	2
Pasta Moon	5

SHOPS & SPA

Golden Haven Hot Springs Spa and Resort	1
Red Devil Records	2
San Gregorio General Store	3

BARS

No Name	3
Tourist Club	2

LIVE MUSIC VENUE

Uptown Theatre	1

M.R. Marine Reserve
N.M. National Monument
N.R.A. National Recreation Area
N.S. National Seashore
S.P. State Park
S.H.P. State Historic Park
S.R. State Reserve

Tamalpais, the Bay Area's most revered mountain. If you'd rather enjoy Tamalpais' views without breaking a sweat, drive Ridgecrest Boulevard to the car park 230ft below the 2571ft summit.

Point Reyes National Seashore

MAP P.134

☎ 415 464 5100, ⓦ nps.gov/pore. Free. Further afield than Marin County's more heavily visited greenspaces, 71,000-acre **Point Reyes National Seashore** trumps them all for biodiversity, sheer size and, in many of its areas, a true sense of wilderness. Reached by descending 308 steps from the visitor centre (itself half a mile from the car park), **Point Reyes Lighthouse** commands an epic vista from the windiest spot on the entire Pacific coast; its free after-dark tours are highly recommended (check website for schedule). Top day-hikes lead to blustery **Tomales Point** at the northern tip of the peninsula (nine miles return), where herds of tule elk wander; along the undulating **Coast Trail** from Palomarin to Alamere Falls (eight miles return), one of the few waterfalls in the state to tumble directly onto beach sand; and to sparsely visited Kelham Beach via the gentle **Bear Valley Trail** (11 miles return). The preserve's desolately beautiful beaches, edged by bluff-topped cliffs, yawn for miles and are among the cleanest in California.

Sonoma

MAP P.134

Though more than a shade touristy, the small community of **Sonoma** remains likeable, and is known for its proximity to scores of nearby wineries, as well as its pleasant town square and well-preserved colonial architecture. Sonoma enjoyed momentary notoriety when its settlers revolted against Mexico in 1846 to make the town

Point Reyes National Seashore

California's capital, a designation that lasted all of three weeks before the nascent territory was subsumed by the US. This episode is one of many captured at **Sonoma State Historic Park** (daily 10am–5pm; $3; ☎ 707 938 9560, ⓦ www.parks.ca.gov), which flanks Sonoma Plaza in a scattered batch of sites – the most notable of which is the confusingly named **Mission San Francisco Solano de Sonoma**, the northernmost link in California's chain of 21 Franciscan missions.

Safari West

MAP P.134

3115 Porter Creek Rd, Santa Rosa ☎ 707 579 2551, ⓦ safariwest.com. Daily tours: spring to autumn 9am, 10am, 1pm, 2pm & 4pm; winter 10am and/or 2pm. $83–115. It's about an hour's drive north from Sonoma to reach Porter Creek Road's junction with Franz Valley Road, the improbable home of private African bird and mammal refuge **Safari West**. Three-hour guided tours survey the hilly, 400-acre spread in African-style jeeps and on foot, providing encounters with species including lanky African spoonbills, blue wildebeests, mud-loving warthogs, and, of course, familiar safari suspects such as cheetahs, zebras and giraffes – all nearly half a world away from their natural sub-Saharan habitats. Meals, as well as overnight lodging in well-appointed tents ($275–425), are also available.

Napa Valley

MAP P.134

Napa Valley's legend first gained steam in global viticulture and oenophile circles when Calistoga winery Chateau Montelena toppled the powerhouse French producers in the Paris Wine Tasting of 1976 (a story adapted for the 2008 film *Bottle Shock*). The ensuing decades have seen a glut of wineries sprout from the valley's rich soil, making this narrow basin and its glimmering vineyards not only a major tourist destination, but a veritable luxury brand name. Today, seemingly just as many exclusive restaurants and resorts line Napa Valley's main traffic artery, CA-29 (which leads through the prim communities of **Yountville** and **St Helena**), and

John Muir National Historic Site

its less-travelled counterpart to the east, Silverado Trail, as do a smattering of wineries. **Calistoga**, the valley's northernmost community, remains its most down-to-earth and enjoyable destination, where mud-bath spas mingle with charming bistros.

John Muir National Historic Site

MAP P.134

4202 Alhambra Ave, Martinez ☎ 925 228 8860, ⓦ nps.gov/jomu. Daily 10am–5pm. Free.

Amid acres of fruit orchards on the edge of the Contra Costa County community of Martinez sits captivating **John Muir National Historic Site**, the former home of the father of America's conservation movement. Muir spent his last 24 years (1890–1914) residing in the wonderfully preserved knoll-top Italianate Victorian home here, penning in his second-floor "scribble den" umpteen articles and books that were instrumental in the creation of Yosemite and other national parks – and, eventually, the National Park

Service itself. Climb to the cupola atop the 14-room mansion to ring the big bell and enjoy a view of the pretty ranch, which is full of choice picnic spots.

The Tech Museum of Innovation

MAP P.134
201 S Market St at Park Ave, San Jose
☎ 408 294 8324, ⓦ thetech.org. Daily 10am–5pm. $24.

Bringing a splash of colour to unspirited downtown San Jose, the tangerine-and-blue **Tech Museum of Innovation** is one of the Bay Area's most interactive. The huge, purpose-built structure attracts families who come to experience a jet-pack simulator, build and test miniature wind and water turbines, watch films in the IMAX theatre, and have portraits drawn by a pen-wielding robot. True tech nerds can read a historical timeline of microprocessors and learn how silicon is made from sand in over 300 steps.

Half Moon Bay

MAP P.134
Eleven months of the year, a reasonable number of visitors stream into the most sizeable town on the San Mateo coast, **Half Moon Bay**, to stroll Victorian architecture-lined Main Street and the long, sandy beach just west of town. October, however, sees the community come alive, as Bay Area families enjoy petting zoos and rides at regional farms, with the month's festivities centred on the two-day **Half Moon Bay Art and Pumpkin Festival** (check website for exact dates; free; ☎ 650 726 9652, ⓦ pumpkinfest.miramarevents. com), an annual fête featuring the famed "World Championship Pumpkin Weigh-off".

Pescadero

MAP P.134
Set two miles inland, peaceful **Pescadero** is a slow-paced hamlet

Northern elephant seals in Año Nuevo State Park

with a handful of inviting markets and places to eat. On the edge of town you'll find congenial **Harley Farms Goat Dairy** (205 North St; Jan & Feb: Mon–Thurs 11am–3pm, Fri–Sun 10am–4pm; rest of year: daily 10am–5pm; free; ☎ 650 879 0480, ⓦ harleyfarms.com), where 200 goats help produce award-winning cheese.

Año Nuevo State Park

MAP P.134
☎ 650 879 2025 (park), ☎ 800 444 4445 (guided walk reservations), ⓦ www.parks. ca.gov/anonuevo. 8.30am–sunset. Parking $10; guided walks $7.

One of the most enthralling places to visit along San Mateo County's wild coast is pinniped skirmish site **Año Nuevo State Park**, where the beaches become breeding grounds for lumbering northern elephant seals each winter. Call to reserve a spot on one of the guided park walks, which are the only way to watch the 4000-pound males bloodily jostle for siring supremacy. Please note that the following listings are all between **15 and 75 miles** from San Francisco.

Shops and spa

Golden Haven Hot Springs Spa and Resort

MAP P.134

1713 Lake St, Calistoga ⓣ 707 942 8000, ⓦ goldenhaven.com. Daily 8.30am–10pm.
Refreshingly unpretentious, *Golden Haven* offers massages ($59–125), hot pools ($59 with 25min massage), overnight lodging (see page 146) and – uniquely – hot mud baths ($89–99) in its quiet Calistoga compound. Visit the website for discount offers.

Red Devil Records

MAP P.134

894 Fourth St at Lootens Place, San Rafael ⓣ 415 457 8999, ⓦ reddevilrecords.net. Mon–Fri 11am–7pm, Sat & Sun 11am–6pm.
Small but spirited, Red Devil deals mostly in vinyl, and is a terrific shop for rare collectibles, as well as reasonably priced copies of David Bowie and Marvin Gaye classics.

San Gregorio General Store

MAP P.134

7615 Stage Rd, San Gregorio ⓣ 650 726 0565, ⓦ sangregoriostore.com. Mon–Thurs 10.30am–6pm, Fri 10.30am–7pm, Sat 10am–7pm, Sun 10am–6pm.
This thriving business is the centre of life in this town of approximately 300, selling clothing, groceries and eclectic gifts and home items. The lively bar is also popular with day-trippers, with blues, folk and Americana bands performing every weekend afternoon.

Cafés and snacks

Barbara's Fishtrap

MAP P.134

281 Capistrano Rd, Half Moon Bay ⓣ 650 728 7049, ⓦ barbarasfishtrap.com. Mon–Thurs & Sun 11am–8pm, Fri 11am–8.30pm, Sat 11am–9pm.
Serving some of the tastiest clam chowder ($5–10) on the Pacific coast, always-thronged *Barbara's Fishtrap* sits on stilts over Half Moon Bay's waters. If you'd rather not wait for a table, visit the takeaway window next to the restaurant's entrance.

Phyllis' Giant Burgers

MAP P.134

2202 Fourth St, San Rafael ⓣ 415 456 0866, ⓦ phyllisgiantburgers.com. Daily 11am–9pm.
Modest *Phyllis'* remains the best place in Marin County to get a top-notch burger that's not served atop a bone china plate. A juicy half-pound slab costs a mere $6.75, with chicken, turkey and veggie variants available, as well as clever twists such as teriyaki and pesto burgers.

Restaurants

Calistoga Inn Restaurant & Brewery

MAP P.134

1250 Lincoln Ave, Calistoga ⓣ 707 942 4101, ⓦ calistogainn.com. Mon–Fri 11.30am–9.30pm, Sat & Sun 11am–9.30pm.
Occupying a choice riverside spot complete with delightful patio, this circa-1882 landmark is known for generously portioned plates of paella ($30) and smoked baby back ribs ($28); award-winning beers are brewed in the adjacent water tower.

The French Laundry

MAP P.134

6640 Washington St, Yountville ⓣ 707 944 2380, ⓦ thomaskeller.com/tfl. Mon–Thurs 5–8.45pm, Fri–Sun 11am–12.30pm & 5–8.45pm.
Twice topping UK trade magazine *Restaurant*'s "World's 50 Best Restaurants" list (the only US entry to do so), celebrity chef Thomas Keller's 60-seat Gallic-American fixture – fittingly, it's housed in a former French laundry – offers two tasting menus ($310) daily, neither of which uses the same ingredient more than once. Reservations are taken up to two months in advance.

Pasta Moon

MAP P.134

315 Main St, Half Moon Bay ⓣ 650 726 5125, ⓦ pastamoon.com. Mon–Thurs 11.30am–2pm & 5.30–8.45pm, Fri 11.30am–2pm & 5.30–9.15pm, Sat noon–3pm & 5.30–9.15pm, Sun noon–3pm & 5.30–8.45pm.

With a refined yet easy-going vibe, *Pasta Moon* specializes in earthy Italian cuisine incorporating San Mateo County-grown seasonal ingredients. The spaghetti *puttanesca* ($26) is a seafood-lover's dream, while the pizzas ($19–22) are equally delicious.

Bars

No Name

MAP P.134

757 Bridgeway, Sausalito ⓣ 415 332 1392, ⓦ thenonamebar.com. Daily 11am–2am.

This friendly, refreshingly lowbrow bar is the best place to get a sense of what's left of bohemian Sausalito, including heavy pours, live music several nights weekly and a pleasant rear garden patio where smoking is allowed.

Calistoga Inn Restaurant & Brewery

Tourist Club

MAP P.134

30 Ridge Ave, Mill Valley ⓣ 415 388 9987, ⓦ touristclubsf.org. Check website for hours.

A 0.7-mile hike from trailheads along Panoramic Highway leads to this private, volunteer-staffed mountainside retreat, where the outdoor deck overlooking Muir Woods opens to the public on scattered weekend afternoons throughout the year. Come for drinks, light snacks and an unforgettable view.

Live music venue

Uptown Theatre

MAP P.134

1350 Third St at Franklin St, Napa ⓣ 707 259 0123, ⓦ uptowntheatrenapa.com. $20 and up.

Restored to its original 1937 glory, this resplendent Art Deco venue (a former cinema) now plays host to a series of well-known names, with an emphasis on acts (Boz Scaggs, David Sedaris, Lisa Loeb) sure to appeal to Napa Valley's less rambunctious audiences.

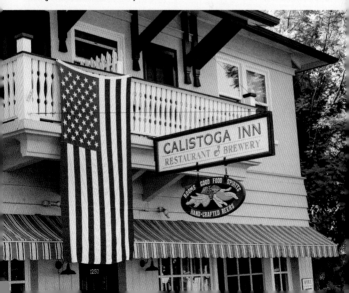

ACCOMMODATION

Phoenix Hotel

Accommodation

Unless you come to buy property or enjoy five-star meals twice or more daily, you can expect your greatest expense in San Francisco and the Bay Area to be your accommodation. Once you make peace with the fact that you're likely to shell out $200 and upwards nightly for a place to sleep, however, you can enjoy availing yourself of the region's raft of fun, stylish and memorable overnight options in a range of neighbourhoods and settings – from living the lavish high life at the *St. Regis* in resolutely urban South of Market (see page 143), to stunning Pacific Ocean views at pastoral *Pigeon Point Lighthouse Hostel* (see page 147). The sample rates listed here indicate the lowest price rack rates for a double room during the Bay Area's April–October high season, so as you plan your visit, consider coming in March or November, when the weather remains mostly agreeable and room rates are (often substantially) lower. Always reserve as far in advance as possible, and book online for the best deals – ⓦ hotels.com, ⓦ priceline.com and ⓦ expedia.com regularly offer cut-price rates – keeping in mind that all rooms in San Francisco proper are subject to the city's fourteen percent occupancy tax, plus 1–1.5 percent Tourism Improvement District fee, on top of the room rates listed here.

Downtown and the Embarcadero

HYATT REGENCY MAP P.26, POCKET MAP C11. 5 Embarcadero Center (Drumm St at California St) ⓜ #2, #6, #14, #21, #31, F, J, K, L, M, N, T; ⓑ Embarcadero ☏ 415 788 1234, ⓦ sanfranciscoregency.hyatt.com. Known among Mel Brooks fans as the place where the funnyman cracked up in the 1977 film *High Anxiety*, the Hyatt Regency's open ground floor is like no other – at over 42,000 square feet, it's on record as the world's largest atrium lobby. The dizzying sight of the inverted terraces high above is the apogee of this hotel's wonderfully whimsical design, which also features hundreds of hypo-allergenic rooms (many with excellent views), BART access steps from the front entrance and a revolving bar-restaurant, the *Regency Club*, topping off the building. **$379.**

HOTEL UNION SQUARE MAP P.26, POCKET MAP A13. 114 Powell St at Ellis St ⓜ #8, #30, #45, F, J, K, L, M, N, T; ⓑ Powell ☏ 415 397 3000, ⓦ hotelunionsquare.com. San Francisco's first boutique hotel is a delightful spot for anyone looking to stay Downtown amid a splash of Art Deco style. It's set next to a pair of Powell Street cable-car lines, and its interior boasts distressed brick walls, countless mosaics, clever design and platform beds in the well-appointed rooms and plush suites. Fans of San Francisco classic *The Maltese Falcon* will want to book the Dashiell Hammett Suite. **$332.**

WESTIN ST. FRANCIS MAP P.26, POCKET MAP A12. 335 Powell St at Geary St Ⓜ #8, #30, #45, F, J, K, L, M, N, T; Ⓑ Powell ☎ 415 397 7000, Ⓦ westinstfrancis. com. This lavish hotel has made national headlines often throughout the decades: a young starlet staying in Fatty Arbuckle's suite died suddenly in 1921, Al Jolson passed away here in 1950 while playing poker, and an attempt was made on President Gerald Ford's life just outside the hotel in 1975. Rooms in the main building (which dates back to the early twentieth century) are outfitted with chandeliers and vaulted ceilings, while those in the more modern tower offer exceptional views. $420.

North Beach and the hills

WASHINGTON SQUARE INN MAP P.46, POCKET MAP A10. 1660 Stockton St at Filbert St Ⓜ #8, #30, #39, #45; cable car: Powell-Mason ☎ 415 981 4220, Ⓦ wsisf. com. Overlooking its namesake square in the heart of North Beach, this charming inn is one of the finest places to stay in the city's Italian quarter. Rooms are coloured in neutral shades of taupe and cream, with some featuring cushioned seating next to bay windows. The friendly, unobtrusive staff lay out excellent coffee (and in late afternoon, complimentary wine) in the lobby, and while rooms vary in size and few feature bathtubs, all are en suite. $199.

The northern waterfront

ARGONAUT HOTEL MAP P.58, POCKET MAP J1. 495 Jefferson St at Hyde St Ⓜ #19, #30, #47, #49, F; cable car Powell-Hyde ☎ 415 563 0800, Ⓦ argonauthotel.com. Occupying a former warehouse space in the circa-1907 Cannery complex, the *Argonaut* is a markedly hushed place to stay considering its location at the terminus of the Powell-Hyde cable-car line on the fringe of Fisherman's Wharf. The hotel's design mixes exposed brick with a predictably anchor-happy nautical theme to great effect, while extra amenities such as complimentary yoga accessories and a pet-friendly policy will appeal to many guests. $489.

HOTEL DEL SOL MAP P.58, POCKET MAP H2. 3100 Webster St at Greenwich St Ⓜ #22, #28, #30, #43, #45 ☎ 415 921 5520, Ⓦ jdvhotels.com/hotels/california/san-francisco/hotel-del-sol. A one-time motor lodge since mutated into a tropical-themed boutique inn, *Hotel del Sol* offers an update on 1950s California motel chic. Cheerily coloured rooms and suites feature walk-in closets, but relatively small bathrooms by US standards. Apart from free parking, this Cow Hollow inn's unique amenity is its family-friendly saltwater outdoor pool, as well as its hammock-laden courtyard ringed by grass and palm trees. $379.

South of Market

GOOD HOTEL MAP P.70, POCKET MAP K4. 112 Seventh St at Mission St Ⓜ #14, #19, #21, F, J, K, L, M, N, T; Ⓑ Civic Center ☎ 415 621 7001, Ⓦ haiyi-hotels.com/thegoodhotel. Eco-friendly and stylish, the *Good Hotel* is equipped with fun touches like a photo booth and chalkboard wall, as well as more practical amenities such as wi-fi, pet treats and bicycles to pedal around town – all complimentary. Over forty of its 117 rooms surround a courtyard, with each bed made entirely from reclaimed wood. The Asian Art Museum and other Civic Center sights are just a short walk across Market Street. $185.

ST. REGIS MAP P.70, POCKET MAP B13. 125 Third St at Mission St Ⓜ #8, #9, #10, #12, #14, #30, #38, #45, F, J, K, L, M, N, T; Ⓑ Powell ☎ 415 284 4000, Ⓦ stregissanfrancisco.com. The *St. Regis* practically sets its own standard for opulence, and few other San Francisco hotels can compete with it for unadulterated luxury – something its stratospheric nightly rates confirm. The forty-storey tower's interior is gracefully designed with curved fixtures and striking art pieces, while its rooms and suites are bedecked in soothing visual tones and infinitely soft linens. $711.

HOTEL VITALE MAP P.70, POCKET MAP C11. 8 Mission St at Embarcadero Ⓜ #2, #6, #14, #21, #31, F, J, K, L, M, N, T; Ⓑ Embarcadero ☎ 415 278 3700,

ⓦ jdvhotels.com/hotels/california/san-francisco/hotel-vitale. Boasting a choice bay-side location very near the Ferry Building (see page 28), as well as elegant touches both major (a rooftop spa with soaking tubs) and minor (lavender sprigs hanging off room doors), *Hotel Vitale* is a sumptuous delight. Bathrooms are clad in limestone and include oversize shower heads, while guest rooms are decorated in soft whites and blues, and are well insulated to filter Embarcadero noise. **$495.**

THE W MAP P.70, POCKET MAP B13. 181 Third St at Howard St ⓜ #8, #9, #10, #12, #14, #30, #38, #45, F, J, K, L, M, N, T; ⓑ Powell ⓣ 415 777 5300, ⓦ wsanfrancisco.com. Located across Third Street from Yerba Buena Gardens, and virtually next door to the San Francisco Museum of Modern Art, the showy *W* is as hyperbolic as ever – look no further than its room-type names, which range from Spectacular and Fantastic to Extreme Wow Suite. It includes a spa, multiple bars and restaurants, a nightclub-like VIP air, and terrific views over South of Market and beyond. **$469.**

Civic Center and around

PHOENIX HOTEL MAP P.145, POCKET MAP J4. 601 Eddy St at Larkin St ⓜ #19, #31, #38, #47, #49; ⓑ Civic Center ⓣ 415 776 1380, ⓦ phoenixsf.com. Billing itself as "San Francisco's rock 'n' roll hotel" after long being a favourite local stopover for bands on tour, the *Phoenix* brings a sunny Sunset Strip vibe to the Tenderloin's inner-city grit. This mid-century motor lodge has

been freshened up in recent years, with a bar-restaurant, *Chambers*, the latest addition. Most uniquely of all, there's an outdoor courtyard swimming pool with a mural on the bottom. Guest rooms are swathed in tropical colours and include works by local artists, while free parking and complimentary weekday passes to Kabuki Springs & Spa (see page 111) also sweeten the deal. **$242.**

HOTEL VERTIGO MAP P.145, POCKET MAP J3. 940 Sutter St at Leavenworth St ⓜ #2, #3, #27, #38; ⓑ Powell ⓣ 415 885 6800, ⓦ haiyi-hotels.com/hotelvertigosf. Situated where the Tenderloin begins to rise toward Nob Hill – an area known to unwitting locals as "the TenderNob" – this six-storey inn mixes contemporary elegance with a traditional French feel. The signature inner stairwell will be instantly recognizable to anyone who's seen Alfred Hitchcock's legendary thriller, from which the hotel takes its name. Just be prepared for lots of orange, for whether it's accenting curtains, chairs or pillows, or in the form of nasturtium petals scattered in the bathroom sink, it appears in some capacity in many of the 102 rooms. **$285.**

The Mission and around

INN SAN FRANCISCO MAP P.88, POCKET MAP J6. 943 S Van Ness Ave at 20th St ⓜ #12, #14, #49; ⓑ 16th St Mission, 24th St Mission ⓣ 415 641 0188, ⓦ innsf.com. The Mission may be woefully short on accommodation options, but this sizeable B&B almost makes up for it single-handedly. It stretches across a pair of lovingly restored Victorian houses (built

---

B&Bs and apartment rental

We list a small handful of the region's top **B&Bs**, but for a more robust selection, contact Bed & Breakfast San Francisco (ⓣ 415 899 0060, ⓦ bbsf.com). Another increasingly popular alternative to hotels is short-term **apartment or house rental**; ⓦ airbnb.com is the best for choice, affordability and ease, while other resources include ⓦ roomorama.com and ⓦ homeaway.com. Note, however, that a 2017 ruling forcing all hosts to register with the city is expected to reduce the number of listings substantially (hosts can only rent their permanent residence, and no one can rent more than one unit).

in 1872 and 1904), with the older structure topped by a roof terrace claiming terrific views over the neighbourhood. All but two rooms across the complex are fitted with private bathrooms, and while the decor can be a bit fussy here and there, the redwood hot tub in the garden is a smart feature. **$165.**

The Castro and around

PARKER GUEST HOUSE MAP P.100, POCKET MAP H6. 520 Church St at 17th St ⓜ #22, #33, F, J, K, L, M, T ☎ 415 621 3222, ⓦ parkerguesthouse.com. The top place to stay around the Castro, the 21-room *Parker Guest House* is popular with LGBTQ visitors, but equally welcoming to straight guests. This yellow B&B is housed in a pair of converted Edwardian mansions that front lush gardens and a beautiful fountain-splashed patio. Inside, a sun room, living room with fireplace and piano all make for a relaxed stay; there's even a sauna to enjoy. Guest rooms, meanwhile, are fitted with tiled bathrooms and down bedding. **$189.**

West of Civic Center

HOTEL KABUKI MAP P.108, POCKET MAP H3. 1625 Post St at Laguna St ⓜ #2, #3, #38 ☎ 415 922 3200, ⓦ jdvhotels.com/kabuki. With its mid-rise tower one of the more appealing buildings in Japantown, *Hotel Kabuki* stands apart by offering a variety of in-room spa treatments; guests who book online receive passes for free entry to nearby Kabuki Springs & Spa (see page 111). Several of the 200-plus rooms and suites have a Japanese-style soaking tub, while all include marble and tile bathrooms. The impeccably designed Traditional Japanese Suite features a sunken living room, shoji screens and a bamboo-and-sand garden. **$259.**

Golden Gate Park and beyond

OCEAN PARK MOTEL MAP P.118, POCKET MAP B9. 2690 46th Ave at Wawona St ⓜ #18, #23, L ☎ 415 566 7020, ⓦ www. oceanparkmotel.com. If you're looking to stay far from San Francisco's urban hubbub but still within the city proper, the Streamline Moderne-styled *Ocean Park Motel* is an ideal choice. Opened in 1937, it's the oldest Art Deco motel in town, with classic touches such as nautical porthole windows overlooking smartly landscaped lawns. The outdoor hot tub is a welcome amenity, while its location makes for easy visits to the beach and San Francisco Zoo (see page 121). **$165.**

Oakland and Berkeley

CLAREMONT CLUB & SPA MAP P.126, POCKET MAP C16. 41 Tunnel Rd, Berkeley; AC Transit #49, E ☎ 510 843 3000, ⓦ fairmont.com/claremont-berkeley. One of Northern California's highest-profile hotels, the whitewashed *Claremont* has been luring overnight guests to the East Bay since it opened in 1915. Lined by palm trees, the majestic hillside complex (much of which sits on Oakland land, although its address is in Berkeley) is visible for miles around, and includes an extensive range and numerous tennis courts. Rooms are appropriately comfortable and relaxed, with many boasting not only favourable rates compared to San Francisco, but also splendid views of the bay and beyond. **$299.**

SENS HOTEL MAP P.126, POCKET MAP B14. 1538 Shattuck Ave at Vine St, Berkeley; AC Transit #7, #18 ☎ 510 548 9930, ⓦ senshotelberkeley.com. A charming find along North Berkeley's main drag, this brick-clad inn is steps from *Chez Panisse* (see page 128) and other epicurean delights, including the aromatic *Vanne Bistro* on its ground floor. While rooms here fall well short of luxurious, all feature cherrywood armoires, writing tables and other attractive touches, and a handful are equipped with balconies. **$177.**

Around the Bay Area

EL BONITA MOTEL MAP P.134. 195 Main St (CA-29), St Helena ☎ 707 963 3216, ⓦ elbonita.com. Old roadside motel in the heart of Napa Valley done up to hotel standard, with outdoor pool and hot tub. El

Bonita started life as a religious retreat in the 1940s before becoming a motel in the 1950s – it still retains its chic Art Deco style. Surrounded by a 2.5-acre garden, the charming rooms here come with flatscreen TVs, microwaves and fridges. Antique-filled St Helena is eighteen miles from Napa itself (and just nine miles from the *French Laundry*, page <?>), and makes an excellent base for exploring the Wine Country. **$155**

COSTANOA LODGE MAP P.134. 2001 First St E, Pescadero ☎ 650 879 1100, Ⓦ costanoa.com. A self-contained nature resort set along the southern end of the gorgeous San Mateo County coastline, lovely *Costanoa Lodge* woos visitors from the Bay Area and beyond to enjoy its wealth of offerings: a full-service spa, *Cascade Bar & Grill*, personal barbecue grilling stations, and a host of accommodation choices ranging from cosy lodge guestrooms and surprisingly plush cabins to rustic, canvas-walled tent bungalows. It's well placed for visits to Año Nuevo State Park (see page 137), while the lively coastal city of Santa Cruz is less than 25 miles down CA-1. **Lodge rooms $207, cabins $199, tented bungalows $100.**

COTTAGE INN & SPA MAP P.134. 310 First St E, Sonoma ☎ 707 996 0719, Ⓦ cottageinnandspa.com. Its canopied corridors echoing the architectural style of Mission San Francisco Solano de Sonoma (located at the end of the block), this bucolic inn is accented by a handful of burbling courtyard fountains, making it a tranquil escape from nearby Sonoma Plaza's bustling parade of restaurants and bars. An on-site spa centre and passes for complimentary local wine-tasting sessions help make for a romantic getaway, as do the nine alluring rooms and suites (all television-free to encourage guests to unplug), smartly supplied with in-room continental breakfast, candles, flowers and chocolate. **$215.**

GOLDEN HAVEN HOT SPRINGS SPA AND RESORT MAP.134. 1713 Lake St, Calistoga ☎ 707 942 8000, Ⓦ goldenhaven.com. Although the rooms at this motel will never be confused with those at Napa Valley's poshest spa resorts, they're nonetheless tidy and quite comfortable; several are fitted with an in-room hot tub ($80 extra), as well as king bed and vaulted ceiling. *Golden Haven's* spa (see page 138) offers mud baths and is one of the best-value in the region, while the entire complex is located a few minutes' drive from Lincoln Avenue, Calistoga's prime tourist centre. **$215.**

PELICAN INN MAP P.134. 10 Pacific Way, Muir Beach ☎ 415 383 6000, Ⓦ pelicaninn. com. An oddity in West Marin, the cosy *Pelican Inn* – with its slightly undulating floors, snug rooms and period furnishings – harks back to sixteenth-century England and makes for a wonderfully unique overnight destination less than twenty miles from San Francisco. Several of the inn's seven fussy rooms are equipped with drapery-clad four-poster beds, but the true charm of the place rests not only in its location (a short walk from Muir Beach's subdued strand) but in its strikingly authentic Tudor-style pub, complete with dartboard, low ceiling and strong list of beers. **$240.**

HOTEL SAUSALITO MAP P.134. 16 El Portal, Sausalito ☎ 415 332 0700, Ⓦ hotelsausalito.com. Designed to evoke the French Riviera, this sixteen-room inn sits just a few steps from both main drag Bridgeway and the local ferry landing; marvellous views over San Francisco Bay and beyond are available from the rooftop terrace. Many of the classily understated rooms are painted in mild taupes and include iron beds, while others are done up with brighter tones and feature painted armoires. Complimentary pastries and beverages are available to guests each morning. **$175.**

Hostels

The San Francisco Bay Area is home to a number of hostels aimed at budget travellers – we list the best options in terms of location, value and amenities.

San Francisco's steep accommodation rates make hostels attractive to an even greater percentage of visitors than in other US cities, so be sure to make a reservation well in advance. Note that *Pigeon Point Lighthouse* and *San Francisco Fisherman's Wharf* are affiliates of Hostelling International and therefore may charge a nominal daily surcharge (usually $3) to non-members; both hostels allow a maximum stay of fourteen nights per calendar year.

PIGEON POINT LIGHTHOUSE HOSTEL MAP P.134. 210 Pigeon Point Rd, Pescadero ⓣ 650 879 0633, ⓦ norcalhostels.org/ pigeon. This coast-side hostel is one of the more popular budget accommodation options in the Bay Area, and for ample reason: it's sequestered in a set of four buildings beneath a towering lighthouse. Along with access to nearby cove beaches and tidepools, guests are privy to full kitchen facilities, inviting lounges and – most spectacularly of all – a hot tub with a panoramic vista over the Pacific. It's a short drive to both Año Nuevo State Park and Pescadero (see page 137), as well as terrific hiking at Butano State Park. **Dorms $30, doubles $82.**

SAN FRANCISCO FISHERMAN'S WHARF HOSTEL MAP P.58, POCKET MAP H1. Building 240, Fort Mason M#19, #28, #30, #49 ⓣ 415 771 7277, ⓦ sfhostels.org/ fishermans-wharf. Although its name is somewhat misleading – it's actually set within Fort Mason, a bit west of Fisherman's Wharf proper – this is one of the top hostels in San Francisco, and certainly the most dramatically situated. It's perched on a bluff high above the bay in a Civil War-era barracks, with nearly 200 beds available in both mixed and single-sex dorms; room capacities range from six to twelve people. The hostel's considerable amenities include free continental breakfast, a huge kitchen, an outdoor deck and stunning views across San Francisco Bay. **Dorms $44, doubles and twins $126.**

USA HOSTEL MAP P.26, POCKET MAP A13. 711 Post St at Jones St M#2, #3, #8, #27, #38; ⓢ Powell ⓣ 415 440 5600, ⓦ usahostels.com/locations/ san-francisco. More expensive than other hostels in San Francisco, but worth it for its excellent central location, fun vibe and wealth of complimentary amenities: laundry facilities and supplies, billiards and table football in the sizeable lounge, a spacious kitchen with all-you-can-make pancakes each morning and movies in the fifty-seat on-site theatre. Dorm rooms include only four beds at most, while the attentive staff are happy to book tours and excursions to attractions in the area such as Muir Woods and the Wine Country. **Dorms $49, private rooms (double/two twin bunks) $155.**

ESSENTIALS

San Francisco's iconic cable cars

Arrival

By plane

The San Francisco Bay Area is served by three major airports. **San Francisco International** (SFO; ☎ 650 821 8211, ⓦ flysfo.com), located about 15 miles south of Downtown San Francisco in San Mateo County, is the largest of the lot and operates a comprehensive schedule of international and domestic flights. A direct **BART** train ride from SFO whisks passengers to Powell station near Union Square (29min, $8.95). If you require door-to-door service, note that blue **SuperShuttle** (☎ 800 258 3826, ⓦ supershuttle.com) vans depart several times each hour from SFO's upper level, charging $17 for a drop-off within San Francisco (they also operate out of OAK); **American Airporter** (☎ 415 202 0733, ⓦ americanairporter.com) offers a similar service at SFO for $17.

If you're with others or simply too exhausted to care, **taxis** at SFO are an option; they charge $50–70 for the 25-minute drive to Downtown San Francisco (not including the customary 15 percent tip). The usual crop of **rental car** agencies is based in a huge facility just north of SFO and is reached from passenger terminals via a tram shuttle (free).

Oakland International (OAK; ☎ 510 563 3300, ⓦ oaklandairport.com) is largely geared towards domestic flights and more compact than SFO, and isn't much further from Downtown San Francisco. From OAK, board BART's airport connector tram, then transfer to a BART train at Coliseum/Oakland Airport station to reach Downtown San Francisco (38min, $10.20). For a taxi to Downtown San Francisco expect to pay a base rate of $75–95 (not including 15 percent tip).

Isolated **Norman Y. Mineta San Jose International** (SJC; ☎ 408 392 3600, ⓦ flysanjose.com) is best suited for South Bay visitors as it's a long way from San Francisco itself.

By train

Amtrak (☎ 800 872 7245, ⓦ amtrak.com) trains stop short of serving San Francisco directly, only making it as far as the East Bay. An efficient BART connection is available from the rail network's Richmond station, with slower Amtrak bus links (included in fare) to select points around central San Francisco available at Emeryville.

By bus

San Francisco's new Transbay Transit Center, just south of Mission Street from Second to Beale streets, (transbaycenter.org) should be opening in 2018. **Greyhound** (☎ 800 231 2222, ⓦ greyhound.com) buses should be using the new terminal. **Megabus** (☎ 877 462 6342, ⓦ us.megabus.com) currently drops passengers at the Caltrain station at 700 Fourth St and King St.

Greyhound's **Oakland** terminal is adjacent to Downtown at 2103 San Pablo Ave at Castro St, less than half a mile from BART's 19th St / Oakland station, while Megabus uses BART's West Oakland station (on 7th St) as its drop-off point.

By car

The **Bay Bridge** ($4–6 toll, depending on time and day) and its newly opened span between Oakland and Yerba Buena Island serves as the sole car route into San Francisco from the east, while the **Golden Gate Bridge** ($7.50 toll) is the only way into the city from the north. A pair of freeways, **I-280** and **US-101**, offers bridgeless (and free) access to San Francisco from the south.

Getting around

If you're planning an extended stay in the Bay Area and expect to ride public transport regularly, or even if you'll be using multiple services during a shorter visit, it may pay to get a stored-value **Clipper card** (☏ 877 878 8883, ⓦ clippercard.com). The electronic card is available for $3 via vending machines on the concourse of Market Street Subway stations and is currently accepted by all major Bay Area transport agencies (excluding Blue & Gold Fleet ferries), making for easy, seamless transfers between Muni and BART, among others – although only a trivial fare discount applies with its use.

Visit ⓦ 511.org for schedules, journey planners and real-time departure information to help you navigate Bay Area buses, trains, cable cars and ferries.

By bus or train

San Francisco Municipal Railway (☏ 511, ⓦ sfmta.com) – commonly known as **Muni** – operates the city's buses, light rail and cable cars. Its buses in particular can fall victim to San Francisco's notorious traffic congestion, while an insufficient number of available transport vehicles at peak times often gnarls the system up too. Seven Muni Metro light rail train lines operate throughout the city, including the above-ground F-Market, a popular line that runs restored vintage streetcars between the Castro and Fisherman's Wharf; the other six lines use the Market Street Subway before sprouting to the surface for journeys to outer neighbourhoods.

The basic **fare** for all Muni buses and Muni Metro trains is $2.75, with free transfers good for 90 minutes from initial boarding. **Muni Passports**, meanwhile, are well-suited for city visitors and allow unlimited rides on Muni buses, trains and cable cars; they're available to buy in one- ($21), three- ($32) or seven-day ($42) denominations.

Reliably timed and comfortable, electrically powered **BART** (Bay Area Rapid Transit; ☏ 511, ⓦ bart.gov) trains are best for excursions along Market Street and to the Mission district, Oakland, Berkeley and the Bay Area's two main airports. **Fares** are determined by journey length and range from $1.95 (within San Francisco) to $12.05.

AC Transit (☏ 511, ⓦ actransit. org) buses ply East Bay streets, with certain routes well connected to BART stations; the basic fare is $2.25. **Caltrain** ($3.75–13.75, depending on length of journey; ☏ 800 660 4287, ⓦ caltrain.com), which terminates at its own depot at Fourth and King streets in Mission Bay, is geared toward Peninsula and South Bay commuters and holds little use for most visitors.

By cable car

No visit to San Francisco is complete without riding one of the city's three **cable car** lines, which tackle some of the city's most vertiginous hills with grace and aplomb. Two **Powell Street** lines (Powell-Mason and Powell-Hyde) connect Downtown with the northern waterfront, while the **California Street** line rattles over Nob Hill en route to Van Ness Avenue from Market Street. A single-ride (no-transfer) fare is $7. Queues can often be long, but there are ways to avoid them (see box).

By ferry

Provided that the weather is cooperative and skies aren't too foggy, a **ferry** ride on San Francisco Bay will treat you to incomparable views of the city and surrounding region, which can take on a unique perspective from the water. Major carriers include: **Blue & Gold Fleet** (☎415 705 8200, ⊛blueandgoldfleet.com), which offers regular services between San Francisco and Sausalito (25–35min, $12.50 one-way) and also offers several pleasure cruises on the bay; **Golden Gate Ferry** (☎415 455 2000, ⊛goldengateferry.org), which is best for trips to Larkspur (30–50min, $11) and Sausalito (30min, $11.75) in Marin County; and **San Francisco Bay Ferry** (☎415 705 8291, ⊛sanfranciscobayferry.com), which serves Oakland and Alameda in the East Bay (20–30min, $6.60) and Vallejo in the North Bay (60–80min, $13.80).

By taxi

Though they've earned a dodgy reputation among locals for substandard overall service, **taxis** are plentiful around Downtown San Francisco and, to a somewhat lesser degree, in the city's prime destination neighbourhoods; be aware, however, that it can be a tormenting experience trying to hail one once the city's bars close at 2am, or in rainy weather. If you need to arrange a pick-up, your best bet is **National and Veterans Cab** (☎415 321 8294). Expect to pay $18 for a ride from Yerba Buena Gardens to North Beach, or $23 from Union Square to the Mission (not including tip).

By car

With an unceasing array of transport vehicles, pedestrians and cyclists to contend with – to say nothing of other cars – **driving** in San Francisco requires surgical focus, particularly if you're unfamiliar with the city's idiosyncratic layout or sheepish about hills. Parking, too, can often become diabolical and/or expensive, especially Downtown. City law requires curbing your car's wheels on hills: into the curb if pointing downhill, away if uphill.

These caveats aside, if you're up for the challenge you'll find that all the usual **car rental companies** do business at SFO and in the city proper: leading companies include Enterprise (⊛enterprise.com) and Budget (⊛budget.com). Visit ⊛511.org for real-time traffic updates.

By bicycle

San Francisco's **cycling** community is a zealous bunch – this is where Critical Mass got its start, after all. If you'd like to join the two-wheeled throng in the numerous bicycle lanes threading the city's streets, try one of **Blazing Saddles**' (⊛blazingsaddles.com/san-francisco) seven locations around the central part of the city, where daily rentals start at $32.

City tours

Given its walkability, it's little surprise that San Francisco's most compelling **city tours** are enjoyed on foot. Some of the best are offered by **San Francisco City Guides** (⊛sfcityguides.org; free) and cover specific neighbourhoods, sights and historic topics such as Chinatown, the *Palace Hotel* and "Alfred Hitchcock's San Francisco". Other top choices include **Cruisin' the Castro** (☎415 255 1821, ⊛cruisinthecastro.com; $30), which tells the story of the district's transformation from working-class Irish neighbourhood to gay stronghold, and **Victorian Home Walk** (☎415 252 9485, ⊛victorianhomewalk.com; $25), on which you'll learn to distinguish the difference between a Queen Anne, Italianate and San Francisco Stick in Pacific Heights and Cow Hollow. As for bus tours, try **City Sightseeing San Francisco** (☎415 440 8687, ⊛city-sightseeing.us; $31 and up), whose red open-top double-decker buses trundle along several routes around the city.

Directory A-Z

Cinemas

A handful of top **cinemas** continue to thrive in this enthusiastic film city, including the venerable Castro Theatre (see page 98), Embarcadero Center Cinema at 1 Embarcadero Center (☎ 415 352 0835, ⊕ landmarktheatres.com) in the Financial District, and AMC Kabuki 8, 1881 Post St at Fillmore St (☎ 415 346 3243, ⊕ amctheatres.com). Oakland's **Paramount Theatre** (see page 131) is also worth visiting for its monthly "Paramount Movie Classics" series. Expect to pay anywhere from $11 to $16, with tickets available in advance for selected theatres at ⊕ movietickets. com and ⊕ fandango.com.

Consulates

Australia: 575 Market St at Second St; ☎ 415 644 3620, ⊕ usa.embassy.gov.au.
Canada: 580 California St at Kearny St; ☎ 415 834 3180, ⊕ canadainternational.gc.ca.
Ireland: 100 Pine St at Front St; ☎ 415 392 4214, ⊕ dfa.ie/irish-consulate/sanfrancisco.
UK: 1 Sansome St at Market St; ☎ 415 617 1300, ⊕ www.gov.uk/world/usa.

Crime and personal safety

Though not known as a particularly dangerous place for **crime**, San Francisco, like any major US city, requires all the usual precautions to maintain **personal safety**: keep your wits about you at all times, avoid poorly lit places at night, try not to use ATMs after dark (especially if alone) and carry your wallet in your front pocket, or your handbag across your body. In terms of especially dodgy areas – and this is by no means a complete list – much of the **Tenderloin** is quite rough at any hour, while across Market Street, Sixth Street between Market and Howard streets is also nowhere for visitors to linger, even at midday. The **Mission** has its unsavoury areas as well: take extra care along Mission Street between 14th and 19th streets, and, though increasingly gentrified, along 24th Street between Mission Street and Potrero Avenue. Downtown **Oakland** and **Berkeley** are fairly safe, though again you'll want to exercise extra caution after dark.

If you're confronted anywhere on the street, remain calm, hand over anything of value, then dial ☎ 911 or find the nearest police station.

Electricity

US **electricity** runs on 110V AC – plugs have two flat parallel pins, while some contain a third round one. Certain devices such as hairdryers and curling irons brought from outside North America require both a plug adaptor and a voltage transformer, while dual voltage devices like laptop computers, cameras, MP3 players and most mobile phones only require a plug adaptor.

Health

Given that fees for **health care** in the US can be shockingly high, it's best that foreign visitors organize some kind of insurance cover before visiting. Should you require emergency medical attention, dial ☎ 911 and expect a swift response; you'll be billed later. For situations not requiring an ambulance, find any San Francisco hospital with walk-in emergency facilities – a few of the best located are Saint Francis Memorial Hospital, 900 Hyde St at Pine St (☎ 415 353 6000); California Pacific Medical Center, 45 Castro St at Duboce St (☎ 415 600 6000); and San Francisco General Hospital, 1001 Potrero Ave at 22nd St (☎ 415 206 8000).

You can attend to minor ailments by visiting one of Walgreens' **24hr pharmacies**: 459 Powell St at Sutter St (☎415 984 0793); 498 Castro St at 18th St (☎415 861 3136); or 1344 Stockton St at Broadway (☎415 981 6274). Note that doctor and dentist appointments can be difficult to schedule at short notice and will require quite an outlay – count on owing at least $100–200 (if not more) for one consultation.

Internet

You're never far from **internet** access in this tech-savvy region. If you're toting your own laptop, it's worth noting that most local **cafés** offer wi-fi for the price of a single beverage (though some may limit your access to an hour or two), and, thanks to Google, there are free wi-fi hotspots throughout the city (look for #SFWiFi). All 28 **San Francisco Public Library** branches also offer free wi-fi – visit ⓦsfpl.org for locations. Libraries also offer computers with internet access for 15 minutes on a first-come first-served basis, while due to the prevalence of smartphones and laptops, only a very scarce number of cafés still have computers for temporary use.

LGBTQ travellers

San Francisco has been synonymous with **gay** culture since the 1940s, when soldiers suspected of being homosexual disembarked from World War II duty in the port city and remained, rather than return home to face likely stigma; within three decades, the Castro district (see page 98) was wearing its out-and-proud heart on its rainbow-coloured sleeve. Gay residents now populate many neighbourhoods throughout the city, while Oakland is more and more becoming the Bay Area's centre of **lesbian** culture. Local resources on LGBTQ life include *Gloss* magazine (ⓦglossmagazine.net), ⓦsfqueer.com for austerely presented event listings, and the GLBT History Museum, 4127 18th St at Collingwood St (see page 99) in the Castro, which presents historical exhibits, talk programmes and art showings.

Media

The Bay Area is one of the largest **media** markets in the US, and while coverage can often veer towards provincial, the region's populace is seemingly just as likely to seek out independent and public broadcasting outlets for news and analysis as it is to dial into corporation-run networks. Though beleaguered in recent years by sharp cutbacks, the city's major print and online news source remains the *San Francisco Chronicle* and its online arm (ⓦsfgate.com), although *The Mercury News* (ⓦmercurynews.com), published in San Jose, has a solid reputation among many. The city's alternative paper, *SF Weekly* (ⓦsfweekly.com), soldiers on and is best for entertainment listings and muckraking local coverage.

Bay Area **radio**, meanwhile, is a mixed bag of news and sports chat, all manner of music and publicly funded offerings; for a smart slant on local news, tune in to KALW 91.7 FM (ⓦkalw.org) and KQED 88.5 FM (ⓦkqed.org/radio). Of course, all the major US television networks have Bay Area outlets: Fox (channel 2), NBC (3 and 11), CBS (5) and ABC (7).

Money

San Francisco is famously **expensive** – second perhaps only to New York in terms of major North American cities. Assuming you stay in hotels, accommodation will be your biggest outlay (easily over $200 a night in high season), although a meal for two with wine at one of San Francisco's finest restaurants will rival the cost of a night's stay. Add in taxi and transport costs, performance tickets, attraction entry fees and $12 craft cocktails, and you're looking at a potential bottom line that could have even the least budget-conscious traveller seeing red by visit's end.

Plastic is often the most efficient means of payment, especially if your card doesn't charge foreign transaction fees. **ATMs** and their attendant withdrawal fees ($3 and up) pepper many city blocks, though, and it's always a good idea to keep US dollars on hand for the odd bar or lowbrow restaurant that doesn't accept cards.

Visit Currency Exchange International, 343 Sansome St at Bush St, Suite 100 (Mon–Fri 9am–5pm; ☎ 415 677 4040, Ⓦ ceifx.com), if you need to make any **foreign currency** transactions.

Phones

Check with your provider to learn if your **mobile phone** will work abroad, and find out about costs associated with calls and internet access. Prepaid phone cards, easily found at supermarkets and similar shops, can be a smart purchase, but again, consult your mobile provider in advance to see if extra charges will apply. Note that while most hotels and inns offer free local calls, international calls from your room phone will become prohibitively expensive quite quickly without a prepaid phone card. International calling codes are available at Ⓦ countrycallingcodes.com.

Post

It takes up to a week for **postal mail** to arrive at international destinations from California; the current international postcard rate is $1.15. To read a list of local post offices, head to Ⓦ usps.com.

Smoking

San Francisco was one of the first US cities to ban **smoking** inside restaurants and, later, enclosed bars. Today, smoking is also not allowed in taxis, parks and within 15 feet of building entrances, windows and vents.

Tax

San Francisco imposes a **sales tax** of 8.5 percent – seldom included in any quoted price – on almost all purchased goods other than groceries and prescription drugs; tax rates in surrounding counties vary slightly (Oakland and Berkeley charge 9.25 percent). San Francisco's **hotel occupancy tax** is 14 percent, while rental cars are subject to numerous local surcharges.

Time

California is on **Pacific Standard Time**, always three hours behind Eastern Standard Time, and typically eight hours behind Greenwich Mean Time and eighteen hours behind Australian Eastern Standard Time. In observation of Daylight Saving Time, clocks move forward one hour on the second Sunday in March and back one hour on the first Sunday in November.

Tipping

The practice of **tipping** for service is customary in San Francisco, as waiting staff, bartenders and taxi drivers depend on the extra income to supplement low hourly wages. A gratuity of 20 percent on the

Emergency numbers

In any medical, personal security or fire emergency, dial ☎ **911**.

pre-tax total of a restaurant bill is appropriate (less if you feel the service was substandard); in bars, leave $1 per drink. Taxi drivers hope for at least a 15 percent tip, while hotel porters get $1 per bag, chambermaids $1–2 per day and valet parking attendants $1–2.

Tourist information

San Francisco Travel Association operates its sizeable **Visitor Information Center** just outside Powell BART and Muni station, 900 Market St at Halladie Plaza (Mon–Fri 9am–5pm, Sat & Sun 9am–3pm, closed Sun Nov–April; ☏ 415 391 2000, ⓦ sftravel.com); drop in for maps and information on attractions and accommodation. They also sell the **CityPass** ($89; ⓦ citypass.com/san-francisco), which gets you into several top local destinations – California Academy of Sciences and the Exploratorium, among others – and acts as a seven-day Muni pass, including cable-car fares.

Helpful local **websites** include: SF Station (ⓦ sfstation.com), for reliable listings of what's on; populist news and culture site SFist (ⓦ sfist.com); San Francisco Arts (ⓦ sfarts.org), for comprehensive arts listings; Tablehopper (ⓦ tablehopper.com), the top place for opinionated takes on the Bay Area's roaring restaurant and bar scene; Burritoeater (ⓦ burritoeater.com), home to an entertaining archive of reviews devoted exclusively to the city's favourite budget food; the Virtual Museum of the City of San Francisco (ⓦ sfmuseum.org), a repository of historical information on the city; and community site craigslist (ⓦ sfbay.craigslist.org), which started up in San Francisco in the nascent days of the web.

The "Media" section of Essentials has details on local newspapers, radio and television (see page 154).

Travellers with disabilities

All public buildings in San Francisco, as well as hotels and restaurants, are required to have **wheelchair--accessible** entrances and bathrooms (though not all restaurants do), while both Muni and BART are impressively wheelchair-friendly transport systems – to say nothing of a Muni bus' ability to conquer steep slopes that may be too much to face in a wheelchair. Visit **Access Northern California** (ⓦ accessnca.org) for accessibility information on many Bay Area attractions and accommodation options, as well as for a link to a PDF of the San Francisco Travel Association's excellent, though slightly dated, San Francisco Access Guide, also available as a booklet at SFTA's Visitor Information Center.

Travelling with children

Though often characterized as an adult playground, the Bay Area features plenty of attractions to keep **children** happy and engaged. Both the Exploratorium (see page 46) and California Academy of Sciences (see page 116) are top youth destinations, while Oakland's Chabot Space & Science Center (see page 125) and the San Francisco Zoo (see page 121) are also popular with kids. The region's myriad forests, beaches and urban parks also hold great appeal for youngsters – the playground at San Francisco's Dolores Park (see page 87), for example, is a wonder unto itself. There are also several amusement parks in the region, albeit a bit further afield, with Santa Cruz Beach Boardwalk (75 miles south; ⓦ beachboardwalk.com), Vallejo's Six Flags Discovery Kingdom (35 miles north; ⓦ sixflags.com/discoverykingdom) and California's Great America theme park in Santa Clara (45 miles south; ⓦ cagreatamerica.com) among the most notable.

Festivals and events

Chinese New Year Festival & Parade

Late Jan or early/mid-Feb

Ⓦ chineseparade.com.
The largest celebration of Asian culture outside Asia, this week-long event culminates with a serpentine parade.

Valentine's Day Pillow Fight

Feb 14

Bring your own cushy weapon and join one of the world's largest pillow fights at 6pm on Valentine's Day, when locals let loose in Justin Herman Plaza.

Sisters of Perpetual Indulgence Easter Celebration

Easter Sun Ⓦ thesisters.org.

With a "Hunky Jesus" contest plus kids' activities such as egg-hunting, this free celebration at Dolores Park is orchestrated by a legendary order of cheeky, cross-dressing "nuns".

San Francisco International Film Festival

Late April to early May Ⓦ sffs.org.

Based at the Castro Theatre and Victoria Theatre (2961 16th St), this is the city's largest film festival ($15 and upwards).

Bay to Breakers

Third Sun in May

Ⓦ baytobreakers.com.
Few races are as camp as this seven-mile cross-town stumble – a moveable, loony feast for the senses ($75 and up to enter, free to watch).

North Beach Festival

Mid-June Ⓦ sresproductions.com/events/north-beach-festival.

The longest-running street fair in San Francisco, this free weekend-long festival features pizza-tossing contests, chalk street art and the always-popular "Blessing of the Animals" event.

San Francisco Pride

Late June Ⓦ sfpride.org.

The city explodes in rainbow colours for one of the largest street parties in the country, including a parade down Market Street that draws huge crowds ($5 suggested donation).

Folsom Street Fair

Last Sun in Sept

Ⓦ folsomstreetfair.com.
Voyeurs and fetishists convene at this popular South of Market leather festival ($10 donation), but a surprisingly fun atmosphere dominates the event.

Public holidays

January 1: New Year's Day
Third Monday in January: Martin Luther King Jr's Birthday
Third Monday in February: Presidents' Day
Last Monday in May: Memorial Day
July 4: Independence Day
First Monday in September: Labor Day
Second Monday in October: Columbus Day
November 11: Veterans Day
Last Thursday in November: Thanksgiving Day
December 25: Christmas Day.

Hardly Strictly Bluegrass

Early Oct
ⓦ hardlystrictlybluegrass.com.
Big names such as Robert Plant and
Emmylou Harris invariably headline
this massive three-day festival in
Golden Gate Park. Admission is free.

Treasure Island Music Festival

Mid-Oct ⓦ treasureislandfestival.com.
This electronic and indie rock music
fête (from $170) is tough to top,
though in 2018 it was forced to
relocate from Treasure Island itself –
check the website for the latest.

Chronology

Circa 4000 BC Native Americans
establish villages near the present-day
East Bay cities of Emeryville and Newark.

1579 Sir Francis Drake claims "Nova
Albion" for England upon landing near
Point Reyes in the *Golden Hind*.

1603 Sebastian Vizcaino charts the
California coast, but misses San
Francisco Bay.

1769 Travelling overland, Spanish
explorer Gaspàr de Portola is the
first recorded European to sight San
Francisco Bay.

1776 The Spanish military establishes
the Presidio of San Francisco as a
fort overlooking the Golden Gate.
Mission San Francisco de Asís (Mission
Dolores) is established later the same
year.

1822 Englishman William Richardson
is the first European to receive a land
grant in the nascent city, then known
as Yerba Buena.

1846 Early in the Mexican–American
War, the US Navy seizes the Presidio.

1847 Tycoon Sam Brannan begins
publishing the *California Star*, the West
Coast's first local newspaper.

1848 Gold is discovered in the
foothills of California's Sierra Nevada
mountains. Brannan's spirited

publicizing of the event leads directly
to the following year's Gold Rush.

1849 San Francisco's population
balloons to 25,000, up from 1000 the
previous year.

1856 Comprised of 6000 men, the
San Francisco Committee of Vigilance
effectively assumes control of the city
in an effort to quell increasing anarchy.

1865 The Confederate ship
Shenandoah is poised to attack San
Francisco, but is negated by the US
Civil War's truce.

1869 Largely through the labour of
Chinese immigrants, the transcontinental railroad is completed.

1873 Scottish immigrant Andrew
Hallidie invents the cable car to scale
San Francisco's steep hills.

1873 The University of California's
flagship campus opens in Berkeley.

1887 William Randolph Hearst
becomes owner of the *San Francisco
Examiner* newspaper.

1892 The Sierra Club is founded in
San Francisco; famed conservation
writer John Muir is the environmental
organisation's first president.

1906 A 7.8-magnitude earthquake
strikes San Francisco and is followed

by three days of raging fires; 3000 are killed, up to 300,000 are left homeless and over three-quarters of the city is levelled.

1910 Angel Island, the West Coast's version of New York's Ellis Island, is opened to process (mostly Asian) immigrants.

1915 The lavish Panama-Pacific International Exhibition along San Francisco's northern waterfront marks the San Francisco's recovery from the 1906 calamities.

1934 Alcatraz Island becomes a federal prison.

1934 "Bloody Thursday" sees the fatal shooting of two union picketers by police along the city's waterfront; a four-day general strike ensues.

1936 The dual double-deck spans of the San Francisco–Oakland Bay Bridge open.

1937 The elegant Golden Gate Bridge debuts.

1941-45 Numerous wartime shipbuilding yards operate in and around the city during World War II.

1945 The Charter of the United Nations is signed at the War Memorial Opera House.

1953 Beat poet Lawrence Ferlinghetti opens City Lights bookshop in North Beach.

1964 San Francisco's cable cars are declared the US's sole moving National Historic Landmark.

1964 The Republican National Convention takes place at the Cow Palace in Daly City, just south of San Francisco.

1964 The Free Speech Movement takes root on the University of California campus in Berkeley.

1966 Huey Newton and Bobby Seale form the militant Black Panther group in Oakland.

1967 The "Human Be-in" in Golden Gate Park heralds the hippies' "Summer of Love".

1969 Originally slated for Golden Gate Park, the Rolling Stones' free concert at nearby Altamont Speedway is sullied by murder and chaos.

1972 The Transamerica Pyramid, San Francisco's signature skyscraper, opens to business tenants.

1972 Golden Gate National Recreation Area, one of the largest urban parks in the world, is created.

1978 Over 900 members of Jim Jones' Peoples Temple cult, having departed San Francisco the year before, commit mass suicide in Jonestown, Guyana.

1978 Mayor George Moscone and Supervisor Harvey Milk – the highest-profile gay public official in the US – are slain in City Hall by former Supervisor Dan White.

1978 Board of Supervisors president Dianne Feinstein succeeds Moscone, becoming San Francisco's sole female mayor to date.

1984 The Democratic National Convention takes place at Moscone Center in South of Market.

1989 The 6.9-magnitude Loma Prieta earthquake strikes, killing over 60 and collapsing the I-880 freeway in Oakland and a section of the Bay Bridge's upper deck.

1994 The US Army turns the Presidio over to the National Park Service to become part of Golden Gate National Recreation Area.

2001 The dotcom bust leads to a major Bay Area-wide recession.

2011 Ed Lee becomes first elected Asian-American mayor of San Francisco.

2014 San Francisco Giants win the World Series for the third time.

2016 Fire in the Oakland warehouse known as the "Ghost Ship" claims 36 lives during a dance party.

2018 London Breed is elected mayor of San Francisco, the first African-American woman to hold this office.

Publishing information

Third Edition 2019

Distribution

UK, Ireland and Europe
Apa Publications (UK) Ltd; sales@roughguides.com
United States and Canada
Ingram Publisher Services; ips@ingramcontent.com
Australia and New Zealand
Woodslane; info@woodslane.com.au
Southeast Asia
Apa Publications (SN) Pte; sales@roughguides.com
Worldwide
Apa Publications (UK) Ltd; sales@roughguides.com

Special sales, content licensing and copublishing

Rough Guides can be purchased in bulk quantities at discounted prices. We can create special editions, personalised jackets and corporate imprints tailored to your needs. sales@roughguides.com.

roughguides.com

Printed in China by RR Donnelley Asia Printing Solutions Limited

A catalogue record for this book is available from the British Library

The publishers and authors have done their best to ensure the accuracy and currency of all the information in **Pocket Rough Guide San Francisco**, however, they can accept no responsibility for any loss, injury, or inconvenience sustained by any traveller as a result of information or advice contained in the guide.

Rough Guide credits

Editor: Joanna Reeves
Cartography: Katie Bennett
Managing editor: Rachel Lawrence
Picture editor: Michelle Bhatia
Cover photo research: Sarah Stewart-Richardson

Original design: Richard Czapnik
Senior DTP coordinator: Dan May
Head of DTP and Pre-Press:
Rebeka Davies

Author: Currently based in New York, **Stephen Keeling** has been travelling to San Francisco since his first trip via Greyhound bus in 1991, and has been covering California for Rough Guides since 2013.

Acknowledgements

The **author** would like to thank Brian, Sunshine, Chloe and Adele Fisher in San Francisco; Keith Drew and Joanna Reeves in the UK for all their hard work and editing; and, lastly, Tiffany Wu, the world's greatest travel companion.

Photo credits

(Key: T-top; C-centre; B-bottom; L-left; R-right)

Alamy 2T, 2CR, 4, 6, 13, 17T, 20T, 22/23, 28, 51, 54, 73, 80, 85, 106, 110, 130, 136, 139
Artem Kevorkov 122/123
BAMPFA 127
Domini Dragoone/Elbo Room 97
Dreamstime.com 86, 99, 148/149
Dylan + Jeni 20B
Ed Anderson/Roam Artisan Burgers 65
Ed Anderson/Hog Island Oyster Co
Getty Images 14B, 47, 76, 104, 105
Greta Miersma 94
iStock 1, 79
Jenny Pfeiffer/PfeifferFoto 31
Jonathan Costello/Scoma's 66
Kevin Berne/American Conservatory Theater 35
Matt Morris 43
MKawanophotography/Schein & Schein 50
Miette 112
Museum of the African Diaspora 69

Nader Khouri/La Mar 33
Nick Simonite 140-141
Nik Pledger 67
Paul Dyer/Hog Island Oyster Co 32
Paulette Knight / The Ribbonerie 63
Rough Guides 10, 12B, 18C, 19C, 19B, 25, 38, 39, 42, 52, 55, 56, 60, 62, 77, 81, 82, 83, 84, 87, 90, 91, 93, 96, 102, 103, 107, 111, 114, 117, 120, 121, 122, 128/129, 131, 135
Sarah Deragon/El Rio 95
SFJAZZ 115
Shutterstock 2BL, 5, 11T, 11B, 12T, 12/13T, 12/13B, 14T, 15B, 15T, 16T, 16B, 17B, 18C, 18B, 19T, 21T, 21C, 21B, 26, 29, 34, 36, 37, 41, 45, 48, 49, 57, 58, 61, 68, 70, 72, 78, 101, 124, 125, 133, 137
SoMa StrEat Food Park 20C, 75

Cover: Golden Gate Bridge **Anna Serrano/4Corners**

Index